WHAT RELIGION IS

in the words of
Swami Vivekananda

WITH A BIOGRAPHICAL INTRODUCTION BY
CHRISTOPHER ISHERWOOD

Edited by
SWAMI VIDYATMANANDA

𝒜dvaita 𝒜shrama
(Publication Department)
5 Dehi Entally Road
Kolkata 700 014

Published by
Swami Bodhasarananda
President, Advaita Ashrama
Mayavati, Champawat, Uttaranchal
from its Publication Department, Kolkata
Email: *mail@advaitaashrama.org*
Website: *www.advaitaashrama.org*

First Edition, September 1972
Twenty-second Impression, May 2006
5M3C

ISBN 81-85301-45-X

Printed in India at
Trio Process
Kolkata 700 014

PREFACE TO THE
FIRST INDIAN EDITION

What Religion is in the Words of Swami Vivekananda was first produced by Phoenix House, Ltd., London, (copyright: Advaita Ashrama, Mayavati) in 1963 as a Birth Centenary tribute to the great teacher. It was designed by its compiler, John Yale, who is Swami Vidyatmananda of the Ramakrishna Order, to present Vivekananda's thoughts and words on religion (spread over nearly 4200 pages of the eight volumes of his Complete Works) to the Western reader in as systematic and concise a manner as possible. He has succeeded in collecting such essential thoughts in a volume not exceeding 100,000 words, which has served a generally-helpful purpose for readers both in the West and the East. This explains our publishing a moderately priced Indian edition of the book.

In this book we have all that is authentic and abiding, challenging and refreshing in Religion, and stated in a language that is perfectly understandable to modern mind. Hence we think that the book will be welcomed as a publication of absorbing interest everywhere in the world.

THE PUBLISHER

Advaita Ashrama
Mayavati, Pithoragarh
Himalayas
17 September 1972

EDITOR'S PREFACE

ALTHOUGH his public life covered only nine years, Swami Vivekananda's literary output was very large. He gave lectures by the hundred, wrote articles and poems, and carried on a correspondence with people all over the world. By 1907, five years after the Swami's death, the first collection of his works had been prepared for publication. This was printed on a hand press at a Himalayan monastery called the Advaita Ashrama, which Vivekananda himself had established a few years before. This initial compilation consisted of four volumes of about 250 pages each. At the time of their publication it was thought possible that enough additional lectures and writings might be collected to fill one further volume. What happened, however, was that material kept coming to light in such quantity that several more books were required; so that at the present time Vivekananda's Complete Works comprise eight volumes of about 525 pages each, containing well over a million words. And even today previously unpublished lectures taken down by listeners two generations ago, letters from the Swami's hand, and other literary relics associated with him continue to appear. As volumes of the Complete Works are reprinted, such additional selections must needs be added, further swelling their size.

Nevertheless, people in western nations wishing to

acquaint themselves with the Swami's thought would not have an easy time doing so. The eight-volume set is published in India, and although distributed in America and Europe, is too extensive to appeal to the average reader and too 'special' to be stocked in most book shops. A one-volume compilation of the Swami's most important work—1,000 pages in length and containing 600,000 words—was brought out a few years ago by Swami Nikhilananda of the Ramakrishna-Vivekananda Center of New York. It is entitled *The Yogas and Other Works*. But again, the size and cost of this volume preclude popular circulation. Small booklets containing particular lectures or other self-contained writings by the Swami have been printed both in India and in western countries (some in several languages besides English); but unless taken together, these do not give a rounded presentation of his message.

What has been needed is a book of agreeable size and modest price, representative of the Swami's teachings, published in the West for western people. And if possible the material should be arranged so that a reader, devoid of previous knowledge of the subject, may follow the thread of Vivekananda's thought in a systematic way. The present volume has been designed to meet these objectives.

It was felt that, ideally, the compact Vivekananda should be no more than 100,000 words long—in size roughly that of the average serious work of non-fiction. Obviously this book would need to be a compendium made of portions selected from the vast array of the Swami's works, and these condensed. How to reduce to the desired dimension a quantity of material of more than ten times that size, and achieve a result both representative and balanced, required much study. Since the book was to be primarily for western audiences, however, the Swami's many utterances about reforms in India could be omitted at the outset. It was also decided that for lack of space the poems and letters must be left out, although the latter especially are highly interesting.

What was done was to bring together those broadly applicable lectures and writings conceded to be the most important. These were arranged in an order which would assist the new reader to move into and through the Swami's thought. An indication of the ideas covered and the order in which material dealing with them has been arranged is given in the following outline:

Today, as always, man seeks God—and often without knowing he is doing so. All human activity—good, bad, or indifferent—is actually the misapplied search for God.

The fact is that man in his true nature is already divine; but this divinity is covered. Life's one purpose is the realization of divinity.

Realization of divinity is religion. At base, all religions teach this same truth although accretions often obscure it. Vedanta emphasizes the one objective of realization but accepts diverse methods of reaching it.

Realization may be gained by the practice of the yoga of knowledge, or of control of mind, or of selfless work, or of love of God—or by a combination of yogas.

The great prophets of the world afford living examples of the realization of divinity. As models they inspire man, and as dispensers of grace they assist him towards realization.

From the works selected, overlappings, repetitions, and other material which could be sacrificed were cut out. Modern paragraphing, spelling, and punctuation were introduced. Except for a few explanations or definitions of Sanskrit terms and Editor's additions inserted in square brackets, there is not a single word in the body of the text or the introductions to chapters and sections which is not Vivekananda's own. The Editor's principal task consisted of: 1. arrangement; and 2. subtraction. The final text comes close to meeting the objective of being no more than 100,000 words in length.

Many reading this compact Vivekananda will want to acquaint themselves with the Swami's life and words more fully. To this end, several recommendations can be made. *The Yogas and Other Works* furnishes the full text of many of the selections included here in abbreviated form, together with a 200-page biography. The Complete Works, of course, are recommended. There are at least two full-length biographies of Vivekananda available, one the official *Life*, published by the Advaita Ashrama; and the other a life by the celebrated French writer Romain Rolland, which is available in English. A list of these works, as well as of source books on Vedanta generally, can be had by writing to the Vedanta Society of Southern California, 1946 Vedanta Place, Hollywood 28, California, and asking for the Vivekananda Reading List.

CONTENTS

CONTENTS

INTRODUCTION

By Christopher Isherwood

ONE MORNING early in September 1893, a lady named Mrs George W. Hale looked out through a window of her handsome home on Chicago's Dearborn Avenue and saw, seated on the opposite side of the street, a young man of oriental appearance who was dressed in a turban and the ochre robe of a Hindu monk.

Mrs Hale was, fortunately, not a conventional woman. She did not call the police to tell the stranger to move on; she did not even ring for the servants to go and ask him what he wanted. She noticed that he was unshaven and that his clothes were crumpled and dirty, but she was aware, also, that there was a kind of royal air about him. There he sat, perfectly composed, meditative, serene. He did not look as if he had lost his way. (And, indeed, he was quite the opposite of lost, for he had just resigned himself to the will of God.) Mrs Hale suddenly made a most intelligent guess; coming out of her house and crossing the street, she asked him politely, 'Sir, are you a delegate to the Parliament of Religions?'

She was answered with equal politeness, in fluent educated English. The stranger introduced himself as Swami Vivekananda and told her that he had indeed come to Chicago to attend the meetings of the Parliament, although he was not officially a delegate. As a matter of fact, he had first arrived in Chicago from India in the middle of July, only to find that the Parliament's opening had been postponed till September. His money was running short and someone had advised him that he would be able to live more cheaply in Boston, so he had taken the train there. On the train, he had met a lady who had invited him to stay at her home, which was called 'Breezy Meadows'. Since then, he had given talks to various church and social groups, been asked a lot of silly questions about his country, been laughed at by children because of his funny clothes. The day before yesterday, Professor J. H. Wright, who taught Greek at Harvard University, had bought him a ticket back to Chicago, assuring him that he would be welcome at the Parliament, even though he had no invitation: 'To ask you, Swami, for credentials is like asking the sun if it has permission to shine.' The Professor had also given him the address of the committee which was in charge of the delegates to the Parliament, but this address Vivekananda somehow lost on his way to Chicago. He tried to get information from passers-by on the street but, as ill luck would have it, the station was situated in the midst of a district where German was chiefly spoken, and the Swami could not make himself understood. Meanwhile, night was coming on. The Swami did not know how to obtain or use a city directory and so was at a loss how to find a suitable hotel. It seemed to him simpler to sleep in a big empty boxcar in the freight yards of the railroad. Next morning, hungry and rumpled, he woke, as he put it, 'smelling fresh water', and had begun to walk in a direction which brought him, sure enough, to the edge of Lake Michigan. But the wealthy homes of Lake Shore Drive proved inhospitable; he had knocked at the doors of several and had been rudely turned away. At length, after further wanderings, he had found himself here, and had decided to go no farther but to sit down and await whatever event God might send. And now, Vivekananda concluded, 'What a romantic deliverance! How strange are the ways of the Lord!'

Mrs Hale must have laughed as she listened to this; for Vivekananda always related his adventures and misadventures with humour, and his own deep chuckles were most infectious. They went back together into the house, where the Swami was invited to wash and shave and eat breakfast. Mrs Hale then accompanied him to the headquarters of the committee, which arranged for his accommodation with the other oriental delegates to the Parliament.

The idea of holding a Parliament of Religions in Chicago had been conceived at least five years before this, in relation to the main project of the World's Columbian Exposition, which was to be held to commemorate the four-hundredth anniversary of the discovery of America by Columbus. The Exposition was designed to demonstrate Western Man's material progress, especially in science and technology. It was agreed, however, that all forms of progress must be represented, and there were congresses devoted to such varied themes as woman's progress, the public press, medicine and surgery, temperance, commerce and finance, music, government and legal reform, economic science, and—strange as it may sound to us nowadays—Sunday rest. And since, to quote the official language of the committee, 'faith in a Divine Power has been, like the sun, a light-giving and fructifying potency in Man's intellectual and moral development', there had also to be a Parliament of Religions.

One may smile at all the pomposity, but it must be agreed that the calling of such a parliament was an historic act of liberalism. This was probably the first time in the history of the world that representatives of all the major religions had been brought together in one place, with freedom to express their beliefs. Paradoxically, the most genuinely liberal of the Parliament's organizers were the agnostics; for they were interested solely in promoting inter-religious tolerance. The zealous Christians took a less impartial view, as was only to be expected. In the words of a Catholic priest: 'It is not true that all religions are equally good; but neither is it true that all religions except one are no good at all. The Christianity of the future, more just than that of the past, will assign to each its place in that work of evangelical preparation which the elder doctors of the Church discern in heathenism itself, and which is not yet completed.' In other words, heathenism has its uses as a preparation for Christianity.

But what really mattered was the acceptance of an invitation to preside at the Parliament by Cardinal Gibbons, leader of the American Catholics. This was all the more valuable because the Archbishop of Canterbury had refused to attend, objecting that the very meeting of such a parliament implied the equality of all religions. In addition to the Christians, the Buddhists, the Hindus, the Moslems, the Jews, the Confucianists, the Shintoists, the Zoroastrians, and a number of smaller sects and groups were represented. Vivekananda could, of course, be counted as a recruit to the Hindu delegation; but in fact, as we shall see, he was standing for something larger than any one sect; the ancient Indian doctrine of the universality of spiritual truth.

When the Parliament opened, on the morning of 11th September, Vivekananda immediately attracted notice as one of the most striking figures seated on the platform, with his splendid robe, yellow turban, and handsome bronze face. In his photographs, one is struck by the largeness of his features—they have something of the lion about them—the broad strong nose, the full expressive lips, the great dark burning eyes. Eyewitnesses were also impressed by the majesty of his presence. Though powerfully built, Vivekananda was not above medium height, but he seems always to have created the effect of bigness. It was said of him that, despite his size, he moved with a natural masculine grace; 'like a great cat', as one lady expressed it. In America, he was frequently taken for an Indian prince or aristocrat, because of his quiet but assured air of command.

Others commented on his look of being 'inly-pleased'; he seemed able to draw upon inner reserves of strength at all times, and there was a humorous, watchful gleam in his eyes which suggested calm, amused detachment of spirit. Everyone responded to the extraordinarily deep, bell-like beauty of his voice; certain of its vibrations caused a mysterious psychic excitement among his hearers. And no doubt this had something to do with the astonishing reaction of the audience to Vivekananda's first speech.

During that first morning's session, Vivekananda's turn came to speak; but he excused himself and asked for more time. Later, in a letter to friends in India, he confessed that he had been suffering from stage fright. All the other delegates had prepared addresses; he had none. However, this hesitation only increased the general interest in him.

At length, during the afternoon, Vivekananda rose to his feet. In his deep voice, he began, 'Sisters and Brothers of America'—and the entire audience, many hundred people, clapped and cheered wildly for two whole minutes. Hitherto, the audience had certainly been well-disposed; some of the speakers had been greeted enthusiastically and all of them with sufficient politeness. But nothing like this demonstration had taken place. No doubt the vast majority of those present hardly knew why they had been so powerfully moved. The appearance, even the voice, of Vivekananda cannot fully explain it. A large gathering has its own strange kind of subconscious telepathy, and this one must have been somehow aware that it was in the presence of that most unusual of all beings, a man whose words express exactly what he is. When Vivekananda said, 'Sisters and Brothers', he actually meant that he regarded the American women and men before him as his sisters and brothers: the well-worn oratorical phrase became simple truth.

As soon as they would let him, the Swami continued his speech. It was quite a short one, pleading for universal tolerance and stressing the common basis of all religions. When it was over, there was more, thunderous applause. A lady who was present recalled later, 'I saw scores of women walking over to the benches to get near him, and I said to myself, "Well, my lad, if you can resist that onslaught you are indeed a God!"' Such onslaughts were to become a part of the daily discipline of Vivekananda's life in America.

He made several more speeches during the days that followed, including an important statement of the nature.

and ideals of Hinduism. By the time the Parliament had come to an end, he was, beyond comparison, its most popular speaker. He had his pick of social invitations. A lecture bureau offered to organize a tour for him; and he accepted.

In those days, when the Frontier was still a living memory, one did not have to go far from the great cities to find oneself in the pioneer world of the tent-show. Politicians, philosophers, writers, the great Sarah Bernhardt herself—all were treated more or less as circus attractions. Even today, the name 'Swami' is associated with theatrical trickery, and most Americans are quite unaware that those who have the right to call themselves by it have taken formal monastic vows; that it is, in fact, a title just as worthy of respect as that of 'Father' in the Catholic Church. Vivekananda called himself Swami, and therefore, in the eyes of the public, he was regarded as some kind of an entertainer; he might hope for applause but he could expect no consideration for his privacy. He had to face the crudest publicity, the most brutal curiosity, hospitality which was lavish but ruthless and utterly exhausting. It exhausted him and eventually wrecked his health but, for the time being, he was equal to it and even seemed to enjoy it. He was outspoken to the point of bluntness, never at a loss for repartee, never thrown off balance even when he roared with momentary indignation because of some idiotic question about his 'heathen' countrymen. No one could laugh at him as he laughed at himself; for no one else could appreciate the rich and subtle joke of his very presence in these surroundings—a monk preaching in a circus!

Vivekananda had come to America to speak for his native land. He wanted to tell Americans about India's poverty and appeal for their help. But he also had a message to the West. He asked his hearers to forsake their materialism and learn from the ancient spirituality of the Hindus. What he was working for was an exchange of values. He recognized great virtues in the West—energy and initiative and courage—which he found lacking among Indians; and he had not come to America in a spirit of negative criticism. It is significant that when, during the earliest days of his visit, he was taken to see a prison near Boston, his reaction was as follows:

How benevolently the inmates are treated, how they are reformed and sent back as useful members of society—how grand, how beautiful, you must see to believe! And oh, how my heart ached to think of what we think of the poor, the low, in India. They have no chance, no escape, no way to climb up. They sink lower and lower every day.

Yet he offended many by his outspokenness. 'In New York', he used to say smilingly, 'I have emptied entire halls.' And no wonder! To the ears of rigid fundamentalists, his teaching of Man's essential divinity must have sounded utterly blasphemous, especially as it was presented in his picturesque, serio-comic phrases: 'Look at the ocean and not at the wave; see no difference between ant and angel. Every worm is the brother of the Nazarene.... Obey the Scriptures until you are strong enough to do without them.... Every man in Christian countries has a huge cathedral on his head, and on top of that a book.... The range of idols is from wood and stone to Jesus and Buddha....'

Vivekananda taught that God is within each one of us, and that each one of us was born to rediscover his own God-nature. His favourite story was of a lion who imagined himself to be a sheep, until another lion showed him his reflection in a pool. 'And you are lions,' he would tell his hearers, 'you are pure, infinite and perfect souls. ... He, for whom you have been weeping and praying in churches and temples ... is your own Self.' He was the prophet of self-reliance, of individual search and effort.

He spoke little about the cults of Hinduism—the particular devotion to Rama, Kali, Vishnu, or Krishna which is practised by the devotees of the various sects. It was only occasionally that Vivekananda referred to his own personal cult and revealed that he, too, had a Master whom he regarded as a divine incarnation—a Master named Ramakrishna, who had died less than ten years previously, and whom he himself had intimately known. (See the very last section of this book.)

Vivekananda was a very great devotee; but he did not proclaim his devotion to all comers. His refusal to do so was a considered decision. Speaking of his work in America after returning to India, he said: 'If I had preached the personality of Ramakrishna, I might have converted half the world; but that kind of conversion is short-lived. So instead I preached Ramakrishna's principles. If people accept the principles, they will eventually accept the personality.'

At the time of the Parliament of Religions, Vivekananda was only thirty years old; he had been born in Calcutta on 12th January 1863. The name of his family was Datta, and his parents gave him the name Narendranath; Naren for short. As a monk, he had wandered about India under various names; he assumed the name of Vivekananda only just before embarking for the United States, at the suggestion of the Maharaja of Khetri, who, with the Maharaja of Mysore, paid the expenses of his journey.

Viveka is a Sanskrit word meaning discrimination, more particularly in the philosophic sense of discrimination between the real (God) and the unreal (the phenomena recognized by our sense-perceptions). *Ananda* means divine bliss, or the peace which is obtained through enlightenment; it is a frequently used suffix to any name which is assumed by a monk.

When Naren was in his middle teens, he started going to college in Calcutta. He was a good-looking, athletic youth and extremely intelligent. He was also a fine singer and could play several musical instruments. Already, he showed a great power for leadership among the boys of his own age. His teachers felt sure that he was destined to make a mark in life.

At that period, Calcutta was the chief port of entry for European ideas and cultural influences; and no young Indian student could remain unaffected by them. To meet the challenge of missionary Christianity, a movement had been formed to modernize Hinduism—to do away with ancient ritual and priestcraft, to emancipate women, and to abolish child marriage. This movement was called the Brahmo Samaj. Naren joined it, but soon found its aims superficial; they did not satisfy his own spiritual needs. He read Hume, Herbert Spencer, and John Stuart Mill, and began to call himself an agnostic. His parents urged him to marry, but he refused, feeling that he must remain chaste and unattached so as to be ready to devote himself body and soul to a great cause. What cause? He did not yet exactly know. He was still looking for someone and something in which he could whole-heartedly believe. Meanwhile, his restless and fearless spirit was on fire for action.

It so happened that a relative of Naren's was a devotee

of Ramakrishna, and that one of Naren's teachers, Professor Hastie, was among the few Englishmen who had ever met him. What these two had to say about Ramakrishna excited Naren's curiosity. Then, in November 1881, he was invited to sing at a house where Ramakrishna was a guest. They had a brief conversation and Ramakrishna invited the young man to come and visit him at the Dakshineswar Temple, on the Ganges a few miles outside Calcutta, where he lived.

From the first, Naren was intrigued and puzzled by Ramakrishna's personality. He had never met anyone quite like this slender, bearded man in his middle forties who had the innocent directness of a child. He had about him an air of intense delight, and he was perpetually crying aloud or bursting into song to express his joy, his joy in God the Mother Kali, who evidently existed for him as a live presence. Ramakrishna's talk was a blend of philosophical subtlety and homely parable. He spoke with a slight stammer, in the dialect of his native Bengal village, and sometimes used coarse farmyard words with the simple frankness of a peasant. By this time, his fame had spread, and many distinguished Bengalis were his constant visitors, including Keshab Sen, the leader of the Brahmo Samaj. Keshab loved and admired Ramakrishna in spite of his own reformist principles; for Ramakrishna was a ritualist and an orthodox Hindu, and Keshab's social concern seemed to him merely an amusing and necessarily fruitless game. The world, according to a Hindu saying, is like the curly tail of a dog—how can you ever straighten it out?

So Naren went to Dakshineswar with a divided mind —half of him eager for self-dedication and devotion; the other, western-educated half, sceptical, impatient of superstition. When Naren and a few of his friends came into Ramakrishna's room, Ramakrishna asked him to sing. Naren did so. The extraordinary scene which followed can best be described in his words:

Well, I sang that song, and then, soon after, he suddenly rose, took me by the hand and led me out on to the porch north of his room, shutting the door behind him. It was locked from the outside, so we were alone. I thought he was going to give me some advice in private. But, to my utter amazement, he began shedding tears of joy—floods of them—as he held my hand, and talking to me tenderly, as if to an old friend. 'Ah!' he said, 'you've come so late! How could you be so unkind—keeping me waiting so long? My ears are almost burnt off, listening to the talk of worldly people. Oh, how I've longed to unburden my heart to someone who can understand everything—my innermost experience!' He went on like this, amidst his sobbing. And then he folded his palms and addressed me solemnly, 'Lord I know you!' You are Nara, the ancient sage, the incarnation of Narayana. You have come to earth to take away the sorrows of mankind...' And so forth.

I was absolutely dumbfounded by his behaviour. 'Who is this man I've come to see?' I said to myself. 'He must be raving mad! Why, I'm nobody—the son of Vishwanath Datta—and he dares to call me Nara!' But I kept quiet and let him go on. Presently he went back into his room and brought me out some sweets—sugar candy and butter; and he fed me with his own hands. I kept telling him, 'Please give them to me—I want to share them with my friends', but it was no good. He wouldn't stop until I'd eaten all of them. Then he seized me by the hand and said, 'Promise me you'll come back here alone, soon!' He was so pressing that I had to say yes. Then I went back with him to join my friends.

This was certainly a searching psychological test for an eighteen-year-old college intellectual! But Naren's intuition went much deeper than his sophistication. He was unable to dismiss Ramakrishna from his mind as a mere eccentric. If this man was mad, then even his madness was somehow holy; Naren felt that he had been in the presence of a great saint, and already he began to love him.

At their second meeting, Ramakrishna revealed himself in a quite different aspect, as a being endowed with supernatural and terrifying power. This time, Naren found him alone in his room. He greeted Naren affectionately and asked him to sit down beside him. Then, as Naren described it later:

muttering something to himself, with his eyes fixed on me, he slowly drew near me ... in the twinkling of an eye, he placed his right foot on my body. At his touch, I had an entirely new experience. With my eyes wide open, I saw that the walls and everything else in the room were whirling around, vanishing into nothingness; the whole universe, together with my own individuality, was about to be lost in an all-encompassing, mysterious Void! I was terribly frightened and thought I must be facing death—for the loss of my individuality meant nothing less than that to me. I couldn't control myself: I cried out, 'What are you doing to me! I have my parents at home!' At this, he laughed aloud. Stroking my chest, he said, 'All right, that's enough for now. Everything will come in time.' The wonderful thing was, as soon as he'd said that, the whole experience came to an end. I was myself again. And everything inside and outside the room was just as it had been before.

Ramakrishna had, by his touch, taken Naren to the very brink of that superconscious experience which the Hindus call *samadhi*. In samadhi, all sense of personal identity vanishes and the real Self, the indwelling Godhead, is known. The Godhead, being a unity, is experienced as a sort of Void, in contrast to the multiplicity of objects which make up our ordinary sense-consciousness. Within that Void, personal identity is lost—and loss of identity must necessarily seem, to those who are not prepared for it, like death.

For Ramakrishna, in his almost unimaginably high state of spiritual consciousness, samadhi was a daily experience, and the awareness of God's presence never left him. Vivekananda recalls that, 'I crept near him and asked him the question I had been asking others all my life: "Do you believe in God, sir?" "Yes", he replied. "Can you prove it, sir?" "Yes." "How?" "Because I see Him just as I see you here, only much more intensely." That impressed me at once. For the first time, I found a man who dared to say that he saw God, that religion was a reality—to be felt, to be sensed in an infinitely more intense way than we can sense the world.'

After this, Naren became a frequent visitor to Dakshineswar. He found himself gradually drawn into the circle of youthful disciples—most of them about his own age—whom Ramakrishna was training to follow the monastic life. But Naren did not yield to this influence easily. He kept asking himself if Ramakrishna's power could not be explained away as hypnotism. He refused, at first, to have anything to do with the worship of Kali, saying that this was mere superstition. And Ramakrishna seemed pleased at his scruples. He used to say: 'Test me as the money-changers test their coins. You mustn't believe me till you've tested me thoroughly.' And, in his turn, he tested Naren, ignoring him for weeks on end to find if this would stop him from coming to Dakshineswar. When it did not, Ramakrishna was delighted and congratulated him on his inner strength. 'Anyone else', he said, 'would have left me long ago.'

Indeed, Naren's temperamental doubt is one of his most inspiring qualities. Doubt is something we have all experienced, and it should reassure us greatly that this keen observer took nothing for granted. It may even seem to us, as we read the life of Ramakrishna and see how often he granted Naren the deepest revelations, that Naren doubted too long and too much. But we must remember that Naren's faith was no facile thing. He doubted greatly because he was capable of believing greatly. For most of us, the consequences of conversion to a belief are not very far-reaching. For Naren, to believe meant absolute self-dedication to the object of his belief. No wonder he hesitated! No wonder his inner struggles were so severe!

In 1885 Ramakrishna developed cancer of the throat. As it became increasingly evident that their Master would not be with them much longer, the young disciples drew more and more closely together. Naren was their leader, together with the boy named Rakhal who later became Swami Brahmananda. One day, when Ramakrishna lay in the last stages of his illness, Naren was meditating in a room downstairs. Suddenly, he lost outward consciousness and went into samadhi. For a moment, he was terrified and cried out, 'Where is my body?' Another of the disciples thought he must be dying and ran upstairs to tell their Master. 'Let him stay that way for a while,' said Ramakrishna with a smile, 'he has been teasing me to give him this experience long enough.' Much later, Naren came into Ramakrishna's room, full of joy and peace. 'Now Mother has shown you everything', Ramakrishna told him. 'But I shall keep the key. When you have done Mother's work, you will find the treasure again.' This was only one of several occasions on which Ramakrishna made it clear that he had destined Naren for a mission of teaching in the world.

On 16th August 1886, Ramakrishna uttered the name of Kali in a clear ringing voice and passed into the final samadhi. At noon next day, the doctor pronounced him dead.

The boys felt that they must hold together, and a devotee found them a house at Baranagore, about half-way between Calcutta and Dakshineswar, which they could use for their monastery. It was a dilapidated old place, with cobras under the floor, which could be rented cheaply because it was supposed to be haunted. Here they installed the ashes of Ramakrishna within a shrine, which they worshipped daily. Encouraged by Naren, they resolved to renounce the world; later they took the monastic vow in the prescribed fashion.

There were only fifteen of them. They had almost no money and few friends. Sometimes they were altogether without food, at others they lived only on boiled rice, salt, and bitter herbs. Each had two pieces of loincloth, nothing more. They owned a set of clothes in common, however, to be worn by anyone who had to go out into the city. They slept on straw mats on the floor. Yet they joked and laughed continually, sang hymns and engaged in eager philosophic discussions; they were silent only when they meditated. At all times they felt Ramakrishna's presence in their midst. Far from regarding him with awe and sadness, they could even make fun of him. A visitor to the house describes how Naren mimicked Ramakrishna going into ecstasy, while the others roared with laughter.

But gradually the boys became restless for the life of the wandering monk. With staff and begging bowl, they wandered all over India, visiting shrines and places of pilgrimage, preaching, begging, passing months of meditation in lonely huts. Sometimes they were entertained by Rajas or wealthy devotees; much more often, they shared the food of the very poor.

Such experiences were particularly valuable to Naren. During the years 1890-93 he acquired the first-hand knowledge of India's hunger, misery, nobility, and spiritual wisdom which he was to carry with him on his journey to the West. After travelling the whole length of the country he reached Cape Comorin, and here he had a vision. He saw that India had a mission in the modern world as a force for spiritual regeneration, but he also saw that this force could not become effective until India's social conditions had been radically improved. Funds must be raised for schools and hospitals; thousands of teachers and workers must be recruited and organized. It was then that he formed his decision to go to the United States in search of help. And this decision was later confirmed when the Raja of Ramnad suggested he should attend the then newly announced Chicago Parliament of Religions. Thus the specific opportunity was related to Naren's general intention. At the end of May 1893 he sailed from Bombay, via Hong Kong and Japan, to Vancouver; from there he went on by train to Chicago.

After the closing of the Parliament of Religions, Vivekananda spent nearly two whole years lecturing in various parts of the eastern and central United States, appearing chiefly in Chicago, Detroit, Boston, and New York. By the spring of 1895 he was desperately weary and in poor health; but, characteristically, he made light of it. 'Are you never serious, Swamiji?' someone once asked him, perhaps with a hint of reproach. 'Oh yes,' he replied, 'when I have the belly-ache.' He could even see the funny side of the many cranks and healers who unmercifully pestered him, hoping to steal a reflection of his glory. In his letters he refers jokingly to 'the sect of Mrs Whirlpool' and to a certain mental healer 'of metaphysico-chemico-physico-religioso, what-not'.

At the same time he met and made an impression on people of a more serious kind—Robert Ingersoll the agnostic, Nikola Tesla the inventor, Madame Calvé the singer. And, most important of all, he attracted a few students whose interest and enthusiasm were not temporary; who were prepared to dedicate the rest of their lives to the practice of his teaching. In June 1895 he was invited to bring a dozen of these to a house in Thousand Island Park on the St Lawrence River. Here, for nearly two months, he taught them informally, as Ramakrishna had taught him and his brother disciples. Nobody who was present ever forgot this period, and it must certainly have been much the happiest part of Vivekananda's first visit to America.

In August he sailed for France and England, returning to New York in December. It was then that, at the urgent request of his devotees, he founded the first of the Vedanta Societies in America: the Vedanta Society of New York. (Vedanta means the non-dualistic philosophy which is expounded in the Vedas, the most ancient of Hindu Scriptures; and it is, of course, in line with Vivekananda's general beliefs—referred to above—that he did not call his foundation 'The Ramakrishna Society'.) It was then, also, that he received two academic offers, the chair of Eastern Philosophy at Harvard and a similar position at Columbia. He declined both, saying that, as a wandering monk, he could not settle down to work of this kind. In any case, he was longing to return to India. In April he sailed for England, which was to be the first stage of his journey home.

From England he took with him two of his most faithful and energetic disciples, Captain and Mrs Sevier —also J. J. Goodwin, an Englishman whom he had first met in America and who had become the recorder of his lectures and teachings. Later, he was followed to India by Margaret Noble, the Irishwoman who became Sister Nivedita and devoted the rest of her life to the education of Indian women and the cause of India's independence. All of these eventually died in India.

Vivekananda landed in Ceylon in the middle of January 1897. From there on, his journey to Calcutta was a triumphal progress. His countrymen had followed the accounts of his American lectures in the newspapers. Perhaps Vivekananda's success had sometimes been exaggerated. But they quite rightly regarded his visit to the West as a symbolic victory far exceeding in its proportions the mere amount of money he had collected for his cause or the number of disciples he had made. Indeed, one may claim that no Indian before Vivekananda had ever made Americans and Englishmen accept him on such terms—not as a subservient ally, not as an avowed opponent, but as a sincere well-wisher and friend, equally ready to teach and to learn, to ask for and to offer help. Who else had stood, as he stood, impartially between East and West, prizing the virtues and condemning the defects of both cultures? Who else could represent in his own person Young India of the Nineties in synthesis with Ancient India of the Vedas? Who else could stand forth as India's champion against poverty and oppression and yet sincerely praise American idealism and British singleness of purpose? Such was Vivekananda's greatness.

In the midst of all this adulation, Vivekananda never forgot who he was: the disciple of Ramakrishna and the equal brother of his fellow monks. On 1st May 1897 he called a meeting of the monastic and householder disciples of Ramakrishna in order to establish their work on an organized basis. What Vivekananda proposed was an integration of educational, philanthropic, and religious activities; and it was thus that the Ramakrishna Mission and the Ramakrishna Math, or monastery, came into existence. The Mission went to work immediately, taking part in famine and plague relief and founding its first hospitals and schools. Brahmananda was elected as its president, and to him Vivekananda handed over all the money he had collected in America and Europe. Having done this, he was obliged to ask for a few pennies in order to take the ferryboat across the Ganges. Henceforward, he insisted on sharing the poverty of his brother monks.

The Math was consecrated some time later, at Belur, a short distance downriver from Dakshineswar Temple, on the opposite bank of the Ganges. This Belur Math is still the chief monastery of the Ramakrishna Order, which now has nearly a hundred centres in different parts of India and neighbouring Asian lands, devoted either to the contemplative life or to social service, or to a combination of both. The Ramakrishna Mission has its own hospitals and dispensaries, its own colleges and high schools, industrial and agricultural schools, libraries and publishing houses, with monks of the Order in charge of them.

In June 1899 Vivekananda sailed for a second visit to the Western world, taking with him Nivedita and Swami Turiyananda, one of his brother monks. This time, he went by way of Europe and England, but he spent most of the next year in America. He went to California, and left Turiyananda to teach in San Francisco. It was Vivekananda's wish to found a number of Vedanta centres in the West. At the present day, there are ten centres in the United States, one in the Argentine, one in England and one in France.

By the time he returned to India, Vivekananda was a very sick man; he had said himself that he did not expect to live much longer. Yet he was happy and calm—glad, it seemed, to feel a release from the anxious energy which had driven him throughout his earlier years. Now he longed only for the peace of contemplation. Just before leaving America, he wrote a beautiful and remarkably self-revealing letter to a friend:

I am glad I was born, glad I suffered so, glad I did make big blunders, glad to enter peace. Whether this body will fall and release me or I enter into freedom in the body, the old man is gone, gone for ever, never to come back again! Behind my work was ambition, behind my love was personality, behind my purity was fear. Now they are vanishing and I drift.

Some say that Vivekananda's departure from this life, on 4th July 1902, at the Belur Math, had the appearance of a premeditated act. For several months previously, he had been releasing himself from his various responsibilities, and training successors. His health was better. He ate his midday meal with relish, talked philosophy and went for a two-mile walk. In the evening, he passed into deep meditation, and the heart stopped beating. For hours they tried to rouse him. But his work, it seemed, was done and Ramakrishna had given him back the key to the treasure.

The best introduction to Vivekananda is not, however, to read about him but to read him. The Swami's personality, with all its charm and force, its courageousness, its spiritual authority, its fury and its fun, comes through to you very strongly in his writings and recorded words.

In reading him, it is always well to remember that 'a foolish consistency is the hobgoblin of little minds'. When Emerson wrote these words in his essay on Self-Reliance, he was contrasting the 'little minds' with the great minds of Jesus, Socrates, and others. No doubt Emerson would have added Vivekananda to his list if they could have met and come to know each other. But he died in 1882.

Vivekananda was the last person in the world to worry about formal consistency. He almost always spoke extempore, fired by the circumstances of the moment, addressing himself to the condition of a particular group of hearers, reacting to the intent of a certain question. That was his nature—and he was supremely indifferent if his words of today seemed to contradict those of yesterday. As a man of enlightenment, he knew that the truth is never contained in arrangements of sentences. It is within the speaker himself. If what he is, is true, then words are unimportant. In this sense, Vivekananda is incapable of self-contradiction.

Vivekananda was not only a great teacher with an international message; he was also a very great Indian, a patriot and an inspirer of his countrymen down to the present generation. But it is a mistake to think of him as a political figure, even in the best meaning of the word.

First and last, he was the boy who dedicated his life to Ramakrishna. His mission was spiritual, not political or even social, in the last analysis.

The policy of the Ramakrishna Order has always been faithful to Vivekananda's intention. In the early twenties, when India's struggle with England had become intense and bitter, the Order was harshly criticized for refusing to allow its members to take part in Gandhi's Non-Co-operation Movement. But Gandhi himself never joined in this criticism. He understood perfectly that a religious body which supports a political cause—no matter how noble and just—can only compromise itself spiritually and thereby lose that very authority which is its justification for existence within human society. In 1921 Gandhi came to the Belur Math on the anniversary of Vivek-ananda's birthday and paid a moving tribute to him. The Swami's writings, Gandhi said, had taught him to love India even more. He reverently visited the room over-looking the Ganges in which Vivekananda spent the last months of his life.

You can visit that room today; it is still kept exactly as Vivekananda left it. But it does not seem museum-like or even unoccupied. Right next to it is the room which is used by the President of the Ramakrishna Order. There they are, dwelling side by side, the visible human authority and the invisible inspiring presence. In the life of the Belur Math, Vivekananda still lives and is as much a participant in its daily activities as any of its monks.

June 1960

1

THE IDEAL OF A
UNIVERSAL RELIGION

Each soul is potentially divine.

The goal is to manifest this divinity within by controlling nature, external and internal.

Do this either by work or worship or psychic control or philosophy—by one or more or all of these—and be free.

This is the whole of religion. Doctrines or dogmas or rituals or books or temples or forms are but secondary details.

Section 1

We see that the apparent contradictions and perplexities in every religion mark but different stages of growth. The end of all religions is the realizing of God in the soul. That is the one universal religion.

THROUGH THE VISTAS of the past the voice of the centuries is coming down to us: the voice of the sages of the Himalayas and the recluses of the forest; the voice that came to the Semitic races; the voice that spoke through Buddha and other spiritual giants. This voice is like the little rivulets that come from the mountains. Now they disappear, and now they appear again in stronger flow till finally they unite in one mighty majestic flood. The messages that are coming down to us from the prophets and holy men and women of all sects and nations are joining their forces and speaking to us with the trumpet voice of the past. And the first message it brings us is: 'Peace be unto you and to all religions.' It is not a message of antagonism, but of one united religion.

At the beginning of this century [the nineteenth century] it was almost feared that religion was at an end. Under the tremendous sledge-hammer blows of scientific research old superstitions were crumbling away like masses of porcelain. Those to whom religion meant only a bundle of creeds and meaningless ceremonials were at their wits' end. For a time it seemed inevitable that the surging tide of agnosticism and materialism would sweep all before it. Many thought the case hopeless and the cause of religion lost once and for ever.

But the tide has turned and to the rescue has come—what? The study of comparative religions. By the study of different religions we find that in essence they are one.

The proof of one religion depends on the proof of all the rest. For instance, if I have six fingers, and no one else has, you may well say that it is abnormal. The same reasoning may be applied to the argument that only one religion is true and all others false. One religion only, like one set of six fingers in the world, would be unnatural. We see, therefore, that if one religion is true, all others must be true. There are differences in nonessentials, but in essentials they are all one. If my five fingers are true, they prove that your five fingers are true too.

I find in the study of the various religions of the world that there are three different stages of ideas with regard to the soul and God. In the first place, all religions admit that, apart from the body which perishes, there is a certain part or something which does not change like the body, a part that is immutable, eternal, and never dies. We—the essential part of us—never had a beginning and will never have an end. And above us all, above this eternal nature, there is another eternal Being without end—God. People talk about the beginning of the world, the beginning of man. The word 'beginning' simply means the beginning of the cycle. That which has a beginning must have an end. Wherever the beginning of creation is mentioned, it means the beginning of a cycle. Your body will meet with death, but your soul, never.

Along with this idea of the soul we find another group of ideas in regard to perfection. The soul in itself is perfect. The New Testament admits man perfect at the beginning. Man made himself impure by his own actions. But he is to regain his old nature, his pure nature. Some speak of these things in allegories, fables, and symbols. But when we begin to analyse these statements we find that they all teach that the human soul is in its very nature perfect, and that man is to regain that original purity. How? By knowing God.

We find that all religions teach the eternity of the soul, as well as that its lustre has been dimmed, but that its primitive purity is to be regained by the knowledge of God. What is the idea of God in these different religions? The primary idea of God was very vague. The most ancient nations had different deities—sun, earth, fire, water. Among the ancient Jews we find numbers of these gods ferociously fighting with each other. Then we find Elohim whom the Jews and the Babylonians worshipped. We next find one God standing supreme. But the idea differed according to different tribes. They each asserted that their God was the greatest. And they tried to prove it by fighting. The one that could do the best fighting proved thereby that its God was the greatest. Those races were more or less savage. But gradually better and better ideas took the place of the old ones. All those old ideas are gone or going into the lumber room. All those religions were the outgrowth of centuries; not one fell from the skies. Each had to be worked out bit by bit.

Next came the monotheistic ideas: belief in one God who is omnipotent and omniscient, the one God of the universe. This one God is extra-cosmic; he lives in the heavens. He is invested with the gross conceptions of his originators: he had a right side and a left side, and a bird in his hand, and so on and so forth. But one thing we find, that the tribal gods have disappeared for ever and the one God of the universe has taken their place—the God of gods. Still he is only an extra-cosmic God. He is unapproachable; nothing can come near him. In the New Testament it is taught, 'Our Father who art in heaven'—God in the heavens separated from men. We are living on earth and he is living in heaven.

Farther on we find the teaching that he is a God immanent in nature; he is not only God in heaven, but on earth, too. He is the God in us.

In the Hindu philosophy we find a stage of the same proximity of God to us. But we do not stop there. There is the non-dualistic stage, in which man realizes that the God he has been worshipping is not only the Father in heaven and on earth but that 'I and my Father are one.' He realizes in his soul that he is God himself, only a lower expression of him. All that is real in me is he; all that is real in him is I. The gulf between God and man is thus bridged. Thus we find how, by knowing God, we find the kingdom of heaven within us.

In the first, or dualistic, stage, man knows he is a little personal soul—John, James, or Tom—and he says, 'I will be John, James, or Tom to all eternity, and never anything else.' As well might the murderer come along and say, 'I will remain a murderer for ever.' But as time goes on Tom vanishes and goes back to the original pure Adam.

'Blessed are the pure in heart for they shall see God.' Can we see God [with physical eyes]? Of course not. Can we know God [in normal consciousness]? Of course not. If God can be known he will be God no longer. Knowledge is limitation. But I and my Father are one:

I find the reality in my soul. These ideas are expressed in some religions, and in others only hinted. In some they were expatriated. Christ's teachings are now very little understood in this country. If you will excuse me, I will say that they have never been very well understood.

The different stages of growth are absolutely necessary to the attainment of purity and perfection. The varying systems of religion are at bottom founded on the same ideas. Jesus says the kingdom of heaven is within you. Again he says, 'Our Father who art in heaven.' How do you reconcile the two sayings? In this way. He was talking to the uneducated masses when he said the latter, the masses who were uneducated in religion. It was necesary to speak to them in their own language. The masses want concrete ideas, something the senses can grasp. A man may be the greatest philosopher in the world but a child in religion. When a man has developed a high state of spirituality he can understand that the kingdom of heaven is within him.

Thus we see that the apparent contradictions and perplexities in every religion mark but different stages of growth. And as such we have no right to blame anyone for his religion. There are stages of growth in which forms and symbols are necessary; they are the language that the souls in that stage can understand.

The next idea that I want to bring to you is that religion does not consist in doctrines or dogmas. It is not what you read or what dogmas you believe that is of importance, but what you realize. 'Blessed are the pure in spirit, for they shall see God', yea, in this life. And that is salvation. There are those who teach that this can be gained by the mumbling of words. But no great Master ever taught that external forms were necessary for salvation. The power of attaining it is within ourselves. We live and move in God. Creeds and sects have their parts to play, but they are for children; they last but temporarily. Books never make religions, but religions make books. We must not forget that. No book ever created a soul. We must never forget that. The end of all religions is the realizing of God in the soul. That is the one universal religion.

If there is one universal truth in all religions, I place it here, in realizing God. Ideals and methods may differ, but that is the central point. There may be a thousand different radii, but they all converge to the one centre, and that is the realization of God: something behind this world of sense, this world of eternal eating and drinking and talking nonsense, this world of false shadows and selfishness. There is that beyond all books, beyond all creeds, beyond the vanities of this world, and it is the realization of God within yourself. A man may believe in all the churches in the world, he may carry in his head all the sacred books ever written, he may baptize himself in all the rivers of the earth; still, if he has no perception of God, I would class him with the rankest atheist.

And a man may have never entered a church or a mosque, nor performed any ceremony, but if he feels God within himself and is thereby lifted above the vanities of the world, that man is a holy man, a saint, call him what you will.

As soon as a man stands up and says he is right or his church is right, and all others are wrong, he is himself all wrong. He does not know that upon the proof of all the others depends the proof of his own.

So far as they are not exclusive, I see that the sects and creeds are all mine; they are all grand. They are all helping man towards the one real religion. I will add, it is good to be born in a church, but it is bad to die there. It is good to be born a child, but bad to remain a child. Churches, ceremonies, and symbols are good for children, but when the child is grown, he must burst the church or himself. We must not remain children for ever. It is like trying to fit one coat to all sizes and growths. I do not deprecate the existence of sects in the world. Would to God there were twenty millions more, for the more there are, the greater field there will be for selection. What I do object to is trying to fit one religion to every case. Though all religions are essentially the same, they must have the varieties of form produced by dissimilar circumstances among different nations. We must each have our own individual religion—individual as far as the externals go.

I will tell you a story. A lioness in search of prey came upon a flock of sheep, and as she jumped at one of them she gave birth to a cub and died on the spot. The young lion was brought up in the flock, ate grass, and bleated like a sheep. It never knew that it was a lion. One day a lion came across this flock and was astonished to see in it a huge lion eating grass and bleating like a sheep. At his sight the flock fled and the lion-sheep with them.

But the lion watched his opportunity and one day found the lion-sheep asleep. He woke him up and said, 'You are a lion.'

The other said, 'No', and began to bleat like a sheep. But the stranger lion took him to a lake and asked him to look in the water at his own image and see if he did not resemble him, the stranger lion. He looked and acknowledged that he did. Then the stranger lion began to roar and asked him to do the same. The lion-sheep tried his voice and was soon roaring as grandly as the other. And he was a sheep no longer.

My friends, I would like to tell you that you are mighty as lions.

If the room is dark, do you go about beating your chest and crying, 'It is dark, dark, dark'? No, the only way to get the light is to strike a light, and then the darkness goes. The only way to realize the light above you is to strike the spiritual light within you, and the darkness of sin and impurity will flee away. Think of your higher Self, not of your lower.

Section 2

Religion is to be realized now. And for you to become religious means that you will work your way up, and realize things, see things for yourself.

There were times in olden days when prophets were many in every society. The time is to come when prophets will walk through every street in every city in the world. We shall come to understand that the secret of religion is being able not only to think and say all these thoughts, but to realize them, to realize newer and higher ones than have ever been realized, to discover them, to bring them to society; and the study of religion should be the training to make prophets. The schools and colleges should be the training grounds for prophets.

Until a man becomes a prophet, religion is a mockery. We must see religion, feel it, realize it, in a thousand times more intense sense than that in which we see the wall.

But there is one principle which underlies all these various manifestations of religion and which has been already mapped out for us. Every science must end where it finds a unity, because we cannot go any farther; when a perfect unity is reached, that science has nothing more of principles to tell us. Take any science—chemistry, for example. Suppose we can find one element out of which we can manufacture all other elements. Then chemistry, as a science, will have become perfect. What will remain for us is to discover every day new combinations of that one material, and the application of those combinations for all the purposes of life. So with religion. The gigantic principles, the scope, the plan, of religion were already discovered ages ago, when men found the last words, as they are called, in the Vedas, 'I am He'— the truth that there is that One in whom this whole universe of matter and mind finds its unity, whom they call God or Brahman or Allah or Jehovah, or any other name. We cannot go beyond that. The grand principle has been already mapped out for us. Our work lies in filling it in, working it out, applying it to every part of our lives. We have to work now so that everyone will become a prophet.

This, the training of prophets, is the great work that lies before us, and consciously or unconsciously, all the great systems of religion are working towards this one great goal, only with this difference, that in many religions you will find they declare that this direct perception of spirituality is not to be had in this life, that man must die, and after his death there will come a time in another world when he will have visions of spirituality, when he will realize things which now he must believe. But Vedanta will ask all people who make such assertions: 'Then how do you know that spirituality exists?' And they will have to answer that there must have been always certain particular people who, even in this life, got a glimpse of things which are unknown and unknowable.

Even this makes a difficulty. If they were peculiar people, having this power simply by chance, we have no right to believe in them. It would be a sin to believe in anything that is by chance, because we cannot know it. What is meant by knowledge? Destruction of peculiarity. Suppose a boy goes into a street or a menagerie and sees a peculiarly shaped animal. He does not know what it is. Then he goes to a country where there are hundreds like that one, and he is satisfied; he knows what the species is. Our knowledge is knowing the principle. Our non-knowledge is finding the particular without reference to principle. When we find one case or a few cases separate from the principle, without any reference to the principle, we are in darkness and do not know. Now, if these prophets, as they say, were peculiar persons who alone had the right to catch a glimpse of that which is beyond, and no one else has the right, we should not believe in these prophets, because they are peculiar cases without any reference to a principle. We can believe in them only if we ourselves become prophets.

Religion is to be realized now. And for you to become

religious means that you will start without any religion, work your way up, and realize things, see things for yourself. When you have done that, then, and then alone, you have religion. Before that you are no better than atheists, or worse, because the atheist is sincere; he stands up and says, 'I do not know about these things', while those others do not know but go about the world saying, 'We are very religious people.' What religion they have no one knows; they have swallowed some grandmother's story, and priests have asked them to believe these things.

Realization of religion is the only way. Each one of us will have to discover it for himself. Of what use, then, are these books, these Bibles of the world? They are of great use; they are like maps of a country. I had seen maps of England all my life before I went there, and they were great helps to me in forming some sort of conception of England. Yet when I arrived in this country, what a difference between the maps and the country itself! So is the difference between realization and scriptures.

This is the first principle, that realization is religion, and he who realizes is the religious man. You will find many persons in this world who will say, 'I wanted to become religious, I wanted to realize these things, but I have not been able, so I do not believe in anything.' Even among the educated you will find these. Large numbers of people will tell you, 'I have tried to be religious all my life, but there is nothing in it.'

Suppose a man is a chemist, a great scientific man. You say to him, 'I do not believe anything about chemistry, because I have all my life tried to become a chemist and have not succeeded.'

He will ask, 'When did you try?'

'When I went to bed I repeated, "O chemistry, come to me", and it never came.'

The chemist will laugh at you and say, 'Oh, that is not the way. Why did you not go to the laboratory and get all the acids and alkalis and burn your hands from time to time?'

Do you take the same trouble with religion? Every science has its own method of learning, and religion is to be learned the same way.

Section 3

My idea, therefore, is that all these religions are different forces in the economy of God, working for the good of mankind. I believe that they are not contradictory; they are supplementary. That universal religion about which philosophers have dreamed is already here.

No search has been dearer to the human heart than that which brings us light from God. No study has taken so much of human energy, whether in times past or present, as the study of the soul, of God, and of human destiny. Thus it has been throughout the ages in all countries. Man has wanted to look beyond, wanted to expand himself; and all that we call progress, evolution, has always been measured by that one search—the search for human destiny, the search for God.

As our social struggles are represented, among different nations, by different social organizations, so is man's spiritual struggle represented by various religions;

and as different social organizations are constantly quarrelling, so these spiritual organizations have been constantly at war with one another. Men belonging to a particular social organization claim that the right to live belongs only to them, and so long as they can, they want to exercise that right at the cost of the weak. Similarly, each religious sect has claimed the exclusive right to live. And thus we find that there is nothing that has brought to man more blessings than religion, yet at the same time there is nothing that has brought more horror than religion.

We know that there has always been an opposing under-current of thought; there have been always parties of men, philosophers, students of comparative religion, who have tried and still are trying to bring about harmony in the midst of all these jarring and discordant sects. As regards certain countries, these attempts have succeeded, but as regards the whole world, they have failed.

Now, taking a common-sense view of the thing, we find at the start that there is a tremendous life power in all the great religions of the world. Some may say that they are ignorant of this; but ignorance is no excuse. If a man says, 'I do not know what is going on in the external world, therefore things that are said to be going on in the external world do not exist', that man is inexcusable. Those of you who watch the movement of religious thought all over the world are perfectly aware that not one of the great religions of the world has died; not only so, each one of them is progressing. Christians are multiplying, Mohammedans are multiplying, the Hindus are gaining ground, and the Jews also are increasing, and by their spreading all over the world and increasing rapidly, the fold of Judaism is constantly expanding. The Buddhists are spreading over Central Asia all the time.

This, then, is a fact in the present history of the human race, that all these great religions exist and are spreading and multiplying. Now there is a meaning, certainly, to this; and had it been the will of an all-wise and all-merciful Creator that one of these religions should alone exist and the rest should die, it would have become a fact long, long ago. If it were a fact that only one of these religions were true and all the rest false, by this time it would have covered the whole world. But this is not so; not one has gained all the ground. All religions sometimes advance, sometimes decline.

Sects are multiplying all the time. If the claims of a religion, that it has all the truth, and that God has given it all this truth in a certain book, were true, why are there so many sects? Fifty years do not pass before there are twenty sects founded upon the same book. Take the Bible, for instance, and all the sects that exist among Christians; each one puts its own interpretation upon the same text, and each says that it alone understands that text and all the rest are wrong. So with every religion. There are many sects among the Mohammedans and among the Buddhists, and hundreds among the Hindus.

Now, I place these facts before you in order to show you that any attempt to bring all humanity to one method of thinking in spiritual things has been a failure and always will be a failure. Every man that starts a theory, even at the present day, finds that if he goes twenty miles away from his followers they will make twenty sects. You see that happening all the time. You cannot make all conform to the same idea; that is a fact, and I thank God that it is so. I am not against any sect. I am glad that sects exist, and I only wish they may go on multiplying more and more. Why? Simply because of this: if you and I were to think exactly the same thoughts, there would be no thoughts for us to think. We know that two or more forces must come into collision in order to produce motion. It is the clash of thought, the differentiation of thought, that awakes thought. Now if we all thought alike, we would be like Egyptian mummies in a museum, looking vacantly at one another's faces—no more than that! Whirls and eddies occur only in a rushing, living stream. There are no whirlpools in stagnant, dead water. When religions are dead, there will be no more sects; it will be the perfect peace and harmony of the grave. But so long as mankind thinks, there will be sects. Variation is the sign of life.

Then arises the question: how can all this variety be true? If one thing is true, its negation is false. How can contradictory opinions be true at the same time? This is the question which I intend to answer. But I shall first ask you: are all the religions of the world really contradictory? I do not mean the external forms in which great thoughts are clad. I do not mean the different buildings, languages, rituals, books, and so forth, employed in various religions; but I mean the internal soul of every religion. Every religion has a soul behind it, and that soul may differ from the soul of another religion; but are they contradictory? Do they contradict or supplement each other—that is the question.

I believe that they are not contradictory; they are supplementary. Each religion, as it were, takes up one part of the great universal truth and spends its whole force in embodying and typifying that part of the great truth. It is therefore addition, not exclusion. That is the idea. System after system arises, each one embodying a great idea, and ideals must be added to ideals. And this is the march of humanity. Man never progresses from error to truth, but from truth to truth, from lesser truth to higher truth—but it is never from error to truth.

Then again, we know that there may be almost contradictory points of view, but they will all indicate the same thing. Suppose a man is journeying towards the sun and as he advances he takes a photograph of the sun at every stage. When he comes back he has many photographs of the sun, which he places before us. We see that no two are alike, and yet who will deny that all these are photographs of the same sun, from different standpoints? In the same way, we are all looking at truth from different standpoints, which vary according to our birth, education, surroundings, and so on. We are viewing truth, getting as much of it as these circumstances will permit, colouring the truth with our own feelings, understanding it with our own intellect, and grasping it with our own mind. We can only know as much of truth as is related to us, as much of it as we are able to receive. This makes the difference between man and man and occasions, sometimes, even contradictory ideas; yet we all belong to the same great universal truth.

My idea, therefore, is that all these religions are different forces in the economy of God, working for the good of mankind; and that not one can become dead, not one can be killed.

And that universal religion about which philosophers and others have dreamed in every country already exists. It is here. If the priests and other people who have taken upon themselves the task of preaching different religions simply cease preaching for a few moments, we shall see it is there. They are disturbing it all the time, because it is to their interest.

You see that priests in every country are very conservative. Why is it so? There are very few priests who lead the people; most of them are led by the people and are their slaves and servants. If you say something is dry, they say it is so; if you say it is black, they say it is black. If the people advance, the priests advance. They cannot lag behind. So before blaming the priests—it is the fashion to blame the priest—you ought to blame yourselves. You get only what you deserve.

There are various grades and types of human minds, and what a task religions take upon themselves! A man brings forth two or three doctrines and claims that his religion ought to satisfy all humanity. He goes out into the world, God's menagerie, with a little cage in hand, and says: 'God and the elephant and everybody have to go into this. Even if we have to cut the elephant into pieces, he must go in.'

Think of little sects, born out of fallible human brains, making this arrogant claim of knowing the whole of God's infinite truth! Think of the arrogance of it! If it shows anything, it shows how vain human beings are. And it is no wonder that such claims have always failed, and by the mercy of the Lord are always destined to fail. In this line the Mohammedans were the best off. Every step forward was made with the sword—the Koran in one hand and the sword in the other. 'Take

the Koran, or you must die; there is no alternative!'
You know from history how phenomenal was their
success; for six hundred years nothing could resist them.
And then there came a time when they had to cry halt.
So will it be with other religions if they follow the same
methods.

We are such babes! We always forget human nature.
When we begin life we think that our fate will be something extraordinary, and nothing can make us disbelieve
that. But when we grow old we think differently. So
with religions. In their early stages, when they spread
a little, they get the idea that they can change the minds
of the whole human race in a few years, and go on
killing and massacring to make converts by force. Then
they fail and begin to understand better. We see that
these sects did not succeed in what they started out to
do, which was a great blessing. Just think if one of
those fanatical sects had succeeded all over the world,
where should man be today? Now the Lord be blessed
that they did not succeed! Yet each one represents a
great truth; each religion represents a particular excellence—something which is its soul.

There is an old story which comes to my mind. There
were some ogresses who used to kill people and do all
sorts of mischief; but they themselves could not be
killed, until someone found out that their souls were
in certain birds, and so long as the birds were safe,
nothing could destroy the ogresses. So each one of us
has, as it were, such a bird, where his soul is—has an
ideal, a mission to perform in life. Every human being
is an embodiment of such an ideal, such a mission. Whatever else you may lose, so long as that ideal is not lost

and that mission is not hurt, nothing can kill you. Wealth may come and go, misfortunes may pile mountain high, but if you have kept the ideal entire, nothing can kill you. You may have grown old, even a hundred years old, but if that mission is fresh and young in your heart, what can kill you? But when that ideal is lost and that mission is hurt, nothing can save you. All the wealth, all the power of the world, will not save you.

And what are nations but multiplied individuals? So each nation has a mission of its own to perform in this harmony of races, and so long as that nation keeps to that ideal, that nation nothing can kill; but if that nation gives up its mission and goes after something else, its life becomes short and it vanishes.

And so with religions. The fact that all these old religions are living today proves that they must have kept that mission intact. In spite of all their mistakes, in spite of all difficulties, in spite of all quarrels, in spite of all the incrustations of forms, the heart of every one of them is sound—is a throbbing, beating, living heart. They have not lost, any one of them, the great mission they came for. And it is splendid to study that mission. Take Mohammedanism for instance. Christian people hate no religion in the world so much as Mohammedanism. They think it is the very worst form of religion that ever existed. But as soon as a man becomes a Mohammedan the whole of Islam receives him as a brother with open arms, without making any distinction, which no other religion does. If one of your American Indians becomes a Mohammedan, the Sultan of Turkey would have no objection to dining with him. If he has brains, no position is barred to him. In many places in the Koran you will find very sensual

ideas of life. Never mind. What Mohammedanism comes
to preach to the world is this practical brotherhood of
all belonging to their faith. That is the essential part of
the Mohammedan religion; and all the other ideas about
heaven and life and so forth are not Mohammedanism.
They are accretions.

With the Hindus you will find one national idea—
spirituality. In no other religion, in no other sacred
books of the world, will you find so much energy spent
in defining the idea of God. They tried to define the
idea of soul so that no earthly touch might mar it. Spirit
must be seen as divine and must not be identified with
the physical man. This same idea of unity, of the realization of God, the omnipresent, is preached throughout.
They think it is all nonsense to say that God lives in
heaven, and all that. It is a mere human, anthropomor-
phic idea. All the heaven that ever existed is now and
here. One moment in infinite time is quite as good as
any other moment. If you believe in a God, you can
see him even now. We think religion begins when you
have realized something. It is not believing in doctrines
or giving intellectual assent or making declarations. If
there is a God, have you seen him? If you say no, then
what right have you to believe in him? If you are in
doubt whether there is a God, why do you not struggle
to see him? Why do you not renounce the world and
spend the whole of your life for this one object?
Renunciation and spirituality are the two great ideas of
India, and it is because India clings to these ideas that
all her mistakes count for so little.

With the Christians, the central idea that has been
preached by them is: Watch and pray, for the kingdom
of heaven is at hand—which means: Purify your minds

and be ready. And that spirit never dies. You recollect that the Christians, even in the darkest days, even in the most superstitious Christian countries, have always tried to prepare themselves for the coming of the Lord by trying to help others, building hospitals, and so on. So long as the Christians keep to that ideal, their religion lives.

Now an ideal presents itself to my mind. It may be only a dream. I do not know whether it will ever be realized in this world; but sometimes it is better to dream a dream than die on hard facts. Great truths, even in a dream, are good, better than bad facts. So let us dream a dream.

You know that there are various grades of mind. You may be a matter-of-fact, common-sense rationalist; you do not care for forms and ceremonies; you want intellectual, hard, ringing facts, and they alone will satisfy you. Then there are the Puritans and the Mohammedans, who will not allow a picture or a statue in their place of worship. Very well. But there is another man who is more artistic. He wants a great deal of art —beauty of lines and curves, colours, flowers, forms; he wants candles, lights, and all the insignia and paraphernalia of ritual, that he may see God. His mind grasps God in those forms, as yours grasps him through the intellect. Then there is the devotional man, whose soul is crying for God; he has no other idea but to worship God and to praise him. Then again, there is the philosopher, standing outside all these, mocking at them. He thinks: 'What nonsense they are! What ideas about God!'

They may laugh at one another, but each one has a

place in this world. All these various minds, all these various types, are necessary. If there is ever going to be an ideal religion, it must be broad and large enough to supply food for all these minds. It must supply the strength of philosophy to the philosopher, the devotee's heart to the worshipper; to the ritualist it must give all that the most marvellous symbolism can convey; to the poet, it must give as much of heart as he can take in, and other things besides. To make such a broad religion, we shall have to go back to the beginnings of the religions and take them all in.

Our watchword, then, will be acceptance and not exclusion. Not only toleration, for so-called toleration is often blasphemy, and I do not believe in it. I believe in acceptance. Why should I tolerate? Toleration means that I think that you are wrong and I am just allowing you to live. Is it not a blasphemy to think that you and I are allowing others to live? I accept all religions that were in the past and worship with them all. I worship God with every one of them, in whatever form they worship him. I shall go to the mosque of the Mohammedan; I shall enter the Christian's church and kneel before the crucifix; I shall enter the Buddhist temple, where I shall take refuge in Buddha and in his Law. I shall go into the forest and sit down in meditation with the Hindu who is trying to see the Light which enlightens the heart of everyone.

Not only shall I do all this, but I shall keep my heart open for all that may come in the future. Is God's book finished? Or is it still a continuous revelation, going on? It is a marvellous book—those spiritual revelations of the world. The Bible, the Vedas, the Koran, and all other sacred books are but so many pages, and an infinite number of pages remain yet to be unfolded. I would leave it open for all of them. We stand in the present, but open ourselves to the infinite future. We take in all that has been in the past, enjoy the light of the present, and open every window of the heart for all that will come in the future. Salutation to all the prophets of the past, to all the great ones of the present, and to all that are to come in the future!

Section 4

Unity in variety is the plan of the universe. If it be true that God is the centre of all religions, and that each of us is moving towards him along one of these radii, then it is certain that all of us *must* reach that centre. And at the centre, where all the radii meet, all our differences will cease.

In every religion there are three parts. First there is the philosophy, which presents the whole scope of that religion, setting forth its basic principles, the goal, and the means for reaching it. The second part is mythology, which is philosophy made concrete. It consists of legends relating to the lives of men or of supernatural beings, and so forth. It is the abstractions of philosophy concretized in the more or less imaginary lives of men and supernatural beings. The third part is ritual. This is still more concrete and is made up of forms and ceremonies, various physical attitudes, flowers and incense, and many other things that appeal to the senses.

You will find that all recognized religions have these

three elements. Some lay more stress on one, some on another.

Let us now take into consideration the first part, philosophy. Is there one universal philosophy? Not yet. Each religion brings out its own doctrines and insists upon them as being the only true ones. And not only does it do that, but it thinks that he who does not believe in them must go to some horrible place. Some will even draw the sword to compel others to believe as they do. This is not through wickedness, but through a particular disease of the human brain called fanaticism. They are very sincere, these fanatics, the most sincere of human beings; but they are quite as irresponsible as other lunatics in the world. This disease of fanaticism is one of the most dangerous of all diseases. All the wickedness of human nature is roused by it. Anger is stirred up, nerves are strung high, and human beings become like tigers.

Is there any mythological similarity, is there any mythological harmony, any universal mythology accepted by all religions? Certainly not. All religions have their own mythology; only each one of them says, 'My stories are not mere myths.' Let us try to understand the question by illustration. (I simply mean to illustrate, I do not mean criticism of any religion.) The Christian believes that God took the shape of a dove and came down to earth; to him this is history, and not mythology. The Hindu believes that God is manifested in the cow. Christians say that to believe so is mere mythology, and not history, that it is superstition. The Jews think that if an image is made in the form of a box or a chest, with an angel on either side, then it may be placed in the holy of holies; it is sacred to Jehovah. But if the image is made in the form of a beautiful man or woman, they say, 'This is a horrible idol; break it down!'

This is our unity in mythology! If a man stands up and says, 'My prophet did such and such a wonderful thing', others will say, 'That is only superstition.' But at the same time they say that their own prophet did still more wonderful things, which they hold to be historical. Nobody in the world, as far as I have seen, is able to make out the fine distinction between history and mythology, as it exists in the brains of these persons. All such stories, to whatever religion they may belong, are really mythological, mixed up occasionally, it may be, with a little history.

Next come the rituals. One sect has one particular form of ritual, and thinks that that is holy, while the rituals of another sect are simply arrant superstition. If one sect worships a peculiar sort of symbol, another sect says, 'Oh, it is horrible.' Take for instance a general form of symbol. The phallus symbol is certainly a sexual symbol, but gradually that aspect of it has been forgotten, and it stands now as a symbol of the Creator. Those nations which have this as their symbol never think of it as the phallus; it is just a symbol, and there it ends. But a man from another race or creed sees in it nothing but the phallus and begins to condemn it; yet at the same time he may be doing something which to the so-called phallus worshippers appears most horrible. Let me take two points for illustration, the phallus symbol and the sacrament of the Christians. To the Christians the phallus is horrible, and to the Hindus the Christian sacrament is horrible. They say that the Christian sacrament, the killing of a man and the eating of his flesh

and the drinking of his blood to get the good qualities
of that man, is cannibalism. This is what some of the
savage tribes do; if a man is brave they kill him and eat
his heart, because they think that it will give them
qualities of courage and bravery possessed by that man.
The Christians, of course, do not admit this view of its
origin; and what it may imply never comes to their
minds. It stands for a holy thing, and that is all they
want to know. So even in rituals there is no universal
symbol, which can command general recognition and
acceptance.

Where, then, is any universality? How is it possible,
then, to have a universal form of religion? That, however, already exists. And let us see what it is.

We all hear about universal brotherhood, and how
societies stand up especially to preach this. I remember
an old story. In India taking wine is considered very
bad. There were two brothers who wished, one night, to
drink wine secretly; and their uncle, who was a very
orthodox man, was sleeping in a room quite close to
theirs. So before they began to drink they said to each
other, 'We must be very silent, or Uncle will wake up.'
When they were drinking they continued repeating to
each other, 'Silence! Uncle will wake up', each trying
to shout the other down. And as the shouting increased
the uncle woke up, came into the room, and discovered
the whole thing.

Now we all shout like these drunken men, 'Universal
brotherhood! We are all equal, therefore let us make a
sect.' As soon as you make a sect you protest against
equality, and equality is no more. Mohammedans talk of
universal brotherhood, but what comes out of that talk

in reality? Why, that anybody who is not a Mohammedan will not be admitted into the brotherhood; he will more likely have his throat cut. Christians talk of universal brotherhood; but anyone who is not a Christian must go to that place where he will be eternally barbecued.

So far we see that it is hard to find any universal features in regard to religion; and yet we know that they exist. We are all human beings, but are we all equal? Certainly not. Who says we are equal? Only the lunatic. Are we all equal in our brains, in our powers, in our bodies? One man is stronger than another; one man has more brain-power than another. If we are all equal, why is there this inequality? Who made it? We. Because we have more or less powers, more or less brains, more or less physical strength, these must make a difference between us.

Yet we know that the doctrine of equality makes an appeal to our heart. We are all human beings; but some are men, and some are women. Here is a black man, there is a white man; but all are men, all belong to one humanity. Various are our faces; I see no two alike; yet we are all human beings. Where is this one humanity? I find a man or a woman, either dark or fair; and among all these faces, I know that there is an abstract humanity which is common to all. I may not find it when I try to grasp it, to sense it, and to actualize it, yet I know for certain that it is there. If I am sure of anything, it is of this humanity which is common to us all. It is through this generalized entity that I see you as a man or a woman.

So it is with this universal religion, which runs through all the various religions of the world in the form of God;

it must and does exist through eternity. 'I am the thread that runs through all these pearls', and each pearl is a religion or even a sect thereof. Such are the different pearls, and the Lord is the thread that runs through all of them; only the majority of mankind are entirely unconscious of it.

Unity in variety is the plan of the universe. As a man you are separate from an animal, but as living beings man, woman, animal, and plant are all one; and as existence you are one with the whole universe. That universal existence is God, the ultimate Unity in the universe. In him we are all one. At the same time, in manifestation these differences must always remain.

What makes us formed beings? Differentiation. Perfect balance would be our destruction. Suppose the amount of heat in this room, the tendency of which is towards equal and perfect diffusion, gets that kind of diffusion; then for all practical purposes that heat will cease to be. What makes motion possible in this universe? Lost balance. The unity of sameness can come only when this universe is destroyed; otherwise such a thing is impossible. Not only so; it would be dangerous to have it. We must not wish that all of us should think alike. There would then be no thought to think. It is this difference, this differentiation, this losing of the balance between us, which is the very soul of our progress, the soul of our thought. This must always be.

What, then, do I mean by the ideal of a universal religion? I do not mean any one universal philosophy, or any one universal mythology, or any one universal ritual, held alike by all; for I know that this world must go on working, wheel within wheel, this intricate mass of machinery, most complex, most wonderful. What can *we* do then? We can make it run smoothly, we can lessen the friction, we can grease the wheels, as it were. How? By recognizing the natural necessity of variation. Just as we have recognized unity by our very nature, so we must also recognize variation. We must learn that truth may be expressed in a hundred thousand ways, and that each of these ways is true as far as it goes. We must learn that the same thing can be viewed from a hundred different standpoints and yet be the same thing.

Suppose we all go with vessels in our hands to fetch water from a lake. One has a cup, another a jar, another a bucket, and so forth; and we all fill our vessels. The water in each case naturally takes the form of the vessel carried by each of us. He who brought the cup has the water in the form of a cup; he who brought the jar has water in the shape of a jar. But in every case water, and nothing but water, is in the vessel.

So it is in the case of religion. Our minds are like these vessels, and each one of us is trying to arrive at the realization of God. God is like that water filling these different vessels, and in each vessel the vision of God comes in the form of the vessel. Yet he is one. He is God in every case.

So far it is all right theoretically, but is there any way of practically working out this harmony of religions? We find that this recognition that all the various views of religion are true is very, very old. Hundreds of attempts have been made in India, in Alexandria, in Europe, in China, in Japan, in Tibet, and lastly in America, to formulate a harmonious religious creed, to make all religions come together in love. They have all failed, because they did not adopt any practical plan. That plan alone is practical which does not destroy the individuality of any man in religion, and at the same time shows him a point of union with all others. But so far all the plans of religious harmony that have been tried, while proposing to take in all the various views of religion have, in practice, tried to bind them all down to a few doctrines, and so have produced more new sects, fighting, struggling, and pushing against each other.

I also have my little plan. I do not know whether it will work or not; and I want to present it to you for discussion. What is my plan? In the first place, I would ask mankind to recognize this maxim: 'Do not destroy.' Iconoclastic reformers do no good to the world. Break not, pull not anything down, but build. Help, if you can; if you cannot, fold your hands and stand by and see things go on. Do not injure if you cannot render help. Say not a word against any man's convictions so far as they are sincere. Secondly, take man where he stands, and from there give him a lift. If it be true that God is the centre of all religions, and that each of us is moving towards him along one of these radii, then it is certain that all of us must reach that centre. And at the centre, where all the radii meet, all our differences will cease.

In society we see so many different natures. There are thousands and thousands of varieties of minds and inclinations. A thorough generalization of them is impossible, but for our practical purpose it is sufficient to have them characterized into four classes. First, there is the active man, the worker; he wants to work, and there is tremendous energy in his muscles and nerves. His aim is to work—to build hospitals, do charitable deeds, make streets, plan, and to organize. Then there is the emotional man, who loves the sublime and the beautiful to an excessive degree. He loves to think of the beautiful, to enjoy the aesthetic side of nature, and to adore love and the God of love. He loves with his whole heart the great souls of all times, the prophets of religions. Then there is the mystic, whose mind wants to analyse its own self, to understand the workings of the human mind, what the forces are that are working inside, and how to know, manipulate, and obtain control over them. This is the mystical mind. Then there is the philosopher who wants to weigh everything and use his intellect even beyond the possibilities of all human philosophy.

Now, a religion, to satisfy the largest portion of mankind, must be able to supply food for all these various types of minds; and where this capability is wanting, the existing sects all become one-sided. Suppose you go to a sect which preaches love and emotion. They sing and weep and preach love. But as soon as you say, 'My friend, that is all right, but I want something stronger than this; a little reason and philosophy; I want to understand things step by step and more rationally', 'Get out', they say. The result is that that sect can only help people of an emotional turn of mind. They not only do not help others, but try to destroy them. And the most wicked part of the whole thing is that they will not only *not* help others, but do not believe in their sincerity.

Again, there are philosophers who talk of the wisdom of India and the East and use big psychological terms, fifty syllables long; but if an ordinary man like me goes to them and says, 'Can you tell me anything to make me spiritual?' the first thing they will do will be to smile and say, 'Oh, you are too far below us in your reason. What can you understand about spirituality?' These are high-up philosophers. They simply show you the door.

Then there are the mystical sects who speak all sorts of things about different planes of existence, different states of mind, and what the power of the mind can do, and so on. If you are an ordinary man and say, 'Show me something good that I can do; I am not much given to speculation; can you give me anything that will suit me?' they will smile, and say, 'Listen to that fool; he knows nothing, his existence is for nothing.'

And this is going on everywhere in the world.

What I want to propagate is a religion that will be equally acceptable to all minds; it must be equally philosophic, equally emotional, equally mystic, and equally conducive to action. And this combination will be the ideal, the nearest approach to a universal religion. Would to God that all men were so constituted that in their minds *all* these elements were equally present in full! That is the ideal, my ideal of a perfect man. Everyone who has only one or two of these elements of character I consider one-sided; and this world is almost full of such one-sided men with knowledge of that one road only in which they move; and everything else is dangerous and horrible to them. To become harmoniously balanced in all these four directions, is *my* ideal of religion.

And this religion is attained by what we in India call yoga—union. To the worker it is union between men and the whole of humanity; to the mystic, between his lower and higher Self; to the lover, union between himself and the God of love; and to the philosopher, it is the union of all existence. This is what is meant by yoga. This is a Sanskrit term, and these four divisions of yoga have, in Sanskrit, different names. The man who seeks after this kind of union is called a yogi. The worker is called a *karma* yogi. He who seeks the union through love is called the *bhakti* yogi. He who seeks it through mysticism is called the *raja yogi*. And he who seeks it through philosophy is called the *jnana* yogi. So this word yogi comprises them all.

In this country you associate all sorts of hobgoblins with the word yoga. I am afraid, therefore, I must start by telling you that it has nothing to do with such things. No one of these yogas gives up reason; no one of them asks you to be hoodwinked or to deliver your reason into the hands of priests of any type whatsoever. Not one of them asks that you should give your allegiance to any superhuman messenger. Each one of them tells you to *cling* to your reason, to hold fast to it.

We find in all beings three sorts of instruments of knowledge. The first is instinct which you find most highly developed in animals; this is the lowest instrument of knowledge. What is the second instrument of knowledge? Reasoning. You find that most highly developed in man. Now in the first place, instinct is an inadequate instrument; to animals the sphere of action is very limited, and within that limit instinct acts. When you come to man, you see it is largely developed into reason. The sphere of action also has here become enlarged. Yet even reason is still insufficient. Reason can go only a little way and then it stops, it cannot go any farther; and if you try to push it, the result is helpless confusion; reason itself becomes unreasonable. Logic becomes argument in a circle. Take for instance the very basis of our perception—matter and force. What is matter? That which is acted upon by force. And force? That which acts upon matter. You see the complication, what the logicians call a seesaw, one idea depending on the other, and this again depending on that. You find a mighty barrier before reason, beyond which reasoning cannot go. Yet it always feels impatient to get into the region of the Infinite beyond. This world, this universe which our senses feel or our mind thinks, is but one atom, so to say, of the Infinite, projected on to the plane of consciousness. Within that narrow limit defined by the network of consciousness works our reason, and not beyond. Therefore there must be some other instrument to take us beyond, and that instrument is called inspiration.

So instinct, reason, and inspiration are the three instruments of knowledge. Instinct belongs to animals, reason to man, and inspiration to God-men. But in all human beings are to be found in more or less developed condition the germs of all these three instruments of knowledge. To have these mental instruments evolved, the germs must be there. And this must also be remembered, that one instrument is a development of another and therefore does not contradict it. It is reason that develops into inspiration, and therefore inspiration does not contradict reason, but fulfils it. Things which reason cannot get at are brought to light by inspiration, and they do not contradict reason. The old man does not contradict the child, but fulfils the child.

Therefore you must always bear in mind that the great danger lies in mistaking the lower form of instrument to be the higher. Many times instinct is presented before the world as inspiration, and then come all the spurious claims to the gift of prophecy. A fool or a semi-lunatic thinks that the confusion going on in his brain is inspiration, and he wants men to follow him. The most contradictory, irrational nonsense that has been preached in the world is simply the instinctive jargon of confused lunatic brains trying to pass for the language of inspiration.

The first test of true teaching must be that the teaching should *not contradict reason*. And you may see that such is the basis of all these yogas. We take the raja yoga, the psychological yoga, the psychological way to union. It is a vast subject, and I can only point out to you now the central idea of this yoga. We have but one method of acquiring knowledge. From the lowest man to the highest yogi, all have to use the same method; and that method is what is called concentration. The chemist who works in his laboratory concentrates all the powers of his mind, brings them into one focus, and throws them on the elements; and the elements stand analysed, and thus his knowledge comes. The astronomer also concentrates the powers of his mind, and brings them into one focus; and he throws them on to objects through his telescope; and stars and systems roll forward and give up their secrets to him. So it is in every case—with the professor in his chair, the student with his book, with every man who is working to know. Even the lowest shoeblack, if he gives more concentration, will black shoes better; the cook with concentration will cook a meal all the better. In making money or in worshipping God or in doing anything, the stronger the power of concentration, the better will that thing be done. This is the one call, the one knock, which opens the gates of nature and lets out floods of light. This, the power of concentration, is the only key to the treasure house of knowledge.

The system of raja yoga deals almost exclusively with concentration. In the present state of our body we are so much distracted, and the mind is frittering away its energies upon a hundred sorts of things. As soon as I try to calm my thoughts and concentrate my mind upon any one object of knowledge, thousands of undesired impulses rush into the brain, thousands of thoughts rush into the mind and disturb it. How to check them and bring the mind under control is the whole subject of study in raja yoga.

Now take karma yoga, the attainment of God through work. It is evident that in society there are many persons who seem to be born for some sort of activity or other, whose minds cannot be concentrated on the plane of thought alone, and who can function best through work, visible and tangible. There must be a science for this kind of life too. Each one of us is engaged in some work, but the majority of us fritter away the greater portion of our energies because we do not know the secret of work. Karma yoga explains this secret and teaches where and how to work, how to employ to the greatest advantage the largest part of our energies in the work that is before us.

But with this secret we must take into consideration the great objection against work—namely, that it causes pain. All misery and pain come from attachment. I want to do work, I want to do good to a human being; and it is ninety to one that that human being whom I have helped will prove ungrateful and go against me. And the result to me is pain. Such things deter mankind from working; and it spoils a good portion of the work and energy of mankind, this fear or pain and misery. Karma yoga teaches us how to work for work's sake, unattached, without caring who is helped and what for. The karma yogi works because it is his nature, because he *feels* that it is good for him to do so; and he has no object beyond that. His position in this world is that of a giver, and he never cares to receive anything. He knows that he is giving, and does not ask for anything in return and therefore he eludes the grasp of misery. Pain, whenever it comes, is the result of attachment.

Then there is bhakti yoga for the man of emotional nature, the lover. He wants to love God; he relies upon and uses all sorts of rituals, flowers, incense, beautiful buildings, forms, and all such things. Do you mean to say ey are wrong? One fact I must tell you. It is good for you to remember, in this country especially, that the world's great spiritual giants have all been produced only by those religious sects which have been in possession of very rich mythology and ritual. All sects that have attempted to worship God without any form or ceremony have crushed without mercy everything that is beautiful and sublime in religion. Their religion is a fanaticism—at best a dry thing. The history of the world is a standing witness to this fact. Therefore, do not decry these rituals and mythologies. Let people have them; let those who so desire have them. Do not exhibit that unworthy derisive smile and say, 'They are fools; let them have it.' Not so. The greatest men I have seen in my life, the most wonderfully developed in spirituality, have all come through the discipline of these rituals. Bhakti yoga teaches them how to love without any ulterior motives, loving God and loving the good because it is good to do so, not for going to heaven, or to get children, wealth, or anything else. It teaches them that love itself is the highest recompense of love —that God himself is love. It teaches them to pay all kinds of tribute to God as the Creator, the omnipresent, omniscient, almighty Ruler, the Father and the Mother.

We lastly come to the jnana yogi, the philosopher, the thinker, he who wants to go beyond the visible. He is the man who is not satisfied with the little things of this world. His idea is to go beyond the daily routine of eating, drinking, and so on. Not even the teachings of thousands of books will satisfy him. Not even all the sciences will satisfy him; at best they only bring this little world before him. What else will give him satisfaction? Not even myriads of systems of worlds will satisfy him; they are to him but a drop in the ocean of existence. His soul wants to go beyond all that into the very heart of Being, by seeing Reality as it is—by realizing it, by being it, by becoming one with that universal Being. That is the philosopher. To say that God is the Father or the Mother, the Creator of this universe, its protector and guide, is to him quite inadequate to express him. To him, God is the life of his life, the soul of his soul. God is his own Self. Nothing else remains which is other than God. All the mortal parts of him become pounded by the weighty strokes of philosophy and are brushed away. What at last truly remains is God himself.

Upon the same tree there are two birds, one on the top, the other below. The one on the top is calm, silent, and majestic, immersed in his own glory; the one on the lower branches, eating sweet and bitter fruits by turns, hopping from branch to branch, becomes happy and miserable by turns. After a time the lower bird eats an exceptionally bitter fruit and gets disgusted. He looks up and sees the other bird, that wondrous one of golden plumage, who eats neither sweet nor bitter fruit, who is neither happy nor miserable, but is calm, Self-centred, and sees nothing beyond the Self. The lower bird longs for this condition, but soon forgets it and again begins to eat the fruit. In a little while he eats another exceptionally bitter fruit, which makes him feel miserable, and he again looks up and tries to get nearer to the upper bird. Once more he forgets, and after a time he looks up and so on he goes again and again, until he comes very near to the beautiful bird and sees the reflection of light from his plumage playing around his own body, and he feels a change and seems to melt away. Still nearer he comes, and everything about him melts away, and at last he understands this wonderful change. The lower bird was, as it were, only the substantial-looking shadow, the reflection of the higher; he himself was in essence the upper bird all the time.

It is imperative that all these various yogas should be carried out in practice. Mere theories about them will not do any good. First we have to hear about them; then we have to think about them. We have to reason the thoughts out, impress them on our minds, and meditate on them, realize them, until at last they become our whole life. No longer will religion remain a bundle of ideas or theories, or an intellectual assent; it will enter into our very self. By means of intellectual assent we may today subscribe to many foolish things, and change our minds altogether tomorrow. But true religion never changes. Religion is realization; not talk, nor doctrine, nor theories, however beautiful they may be. It is being and becoming, not hearing or acknowledging. It is the whole soul's becoming changed into what it believes. That is religion.

2

PRINCIPLES AND
PRACTICES OF VEDANTA

Now all these various manifestations of religion, in whatever shape and form they come to mankind, have this one common central basis. It is the preaching of freedom, the way out of this world. They never came to reconcile the world and religion, but to cut the Gordian knot, to establish religion in its own ideal, and not to compromise with the world. That is what every religion preaches, and the duty of Vedanta is to harmonize all these aspirations, to make manifest the common ground between all the religions of the world.

Section 1

When a man has reached the universal brotherhood,
that man alone is a Vedantist.

I REPRESENT a philosophy of India, which is called
the Vedanta philosophy. This philosophy is very, very
ancient; it is the outcome of that mass of ancient Aryan
literature known by the name of the Vedas. It is, as it
were, the very flower of all the speculations and experiences and analyses embodied in that mass of literature,
collected and culled through centuries.

This Vedanta philosophy has certain peculiarities. In
the first place, it is perfectly impersonal; it does not
owe its origin to any person or prophet; it does not build
itself around one man as a centre. Yet it has nothing to
say against philosophies which do build themselves around
certain persons. In later days in India other philosophies
and systems arose, built around certain persons—such as
Buddhism or many of our present sects. They each have
a certain leader to whom they owe allegiance, just as the
Christians and Mohammedans have. But the Vedanta
Philosophy stands as the background of all these sects,
and there is no fight and no antagonism between Vedanta
and any other system in the world.

One principle it lays down—and that, Vedanta claims,
is to be found in every religion of the world—that man
is divine, that all this which we see around us is the
outcome of that consciousness of the divine. Everything
that is strong and good and powerful in human nature
is the outcome of that divinity, and though potential in
many, there is no difference between man and man

essentially, all being alike divine. There is, as it were, an infinite ocean behind, and you and I are so many waves coming out of that infinite ocean; and each one of us is trying our best to manifest that infinite outside. So potentially each of us has that infinite ocean of Existence, Knowledge, and Bliss as our birthright, our real nature; and the difference between us is caused by the greater or lesser power to manifest that Divine.

It also teaches that all the vast mass of energy that we see displayed in society and in every plane of action is really from inside out; and therefore what is called 'inspiration' by other sects, the Vedantist begs the liberty to call the 'expiration' of man! At the same time, it does not quarrel with other sects; Vedanta has no quarrel with those who do not understand this divinity of man. Consciously or unconsciously, every man is trying to unfold that divinity.

Man is like an infinite spring, coiled up in a small box, and that spring is trying to unfold itself; and all the social phenomena that we see are the result of this trying to unfold. All the competitions and struggles and evils that we see around us are neither the causes of these unfoldments nor the effects. As one of our great philosophers says, in the case of the irrigation of a field the pond is somewhere up on a higher level, and the water is trying to rush into the field and is barred by a gate. But as soon as the gate is opened the water rushes in by its own nature; and if there are dust and dirt in the way, the water rolls over them. But dust and dirt are neither the result nor the cause of this unfolding of the divine nature of man. They are co-existent circumstances, and therefore can be remedied.

Now this idea, claims Vedanta, is to be found in all

religions, whether in India or outside of it; only in some of them the idea is expressed through mythology, and in others, through symbology. Vedanta claims that there has not been one religious inspiration, one manifestation, of the divine man, however great, but it has been the expression of the infinite oneness in human nature; and that all we call ethics and morality and doing good to others is also but the manifestation of this oneness. There are moments when every man feels that he is one with the universe, and he rushes forth to express it, whether he knows it or not. This expression of oneness is what we call love and sympathy, and it is the basis of all our ethics and morality. This is summed up in the Vedanta philosophy by the celebrated aphorism, *Tat Tvam Asi*, 'Thou art That.'

To every man this is taught: Thou art one with this universal Being and, as such, every soul that exists is your soul; and every body that exists is your body; and in hurting anyone you hurt yourself; in loving anyone you love yourself. As soon as a current of hatred is thrown outside, whomsoever else it hurts, it also hurts you; and if love comes out from you, it is bound to come back to you. For I am the universe—this universe is my body. I am the Infinite, only I am not conscious of it now; but I am struggling to get this consciousness of the Infinite, and perfection will be reached when full consciousness of this Infinite comes.

Another peculiar idea of Vedanta is that we must allow this infinite variation in religious thought and not try to bring everybody to the same opinion, because the goal is the same. As the Vedantist says in his poetical language: 'As so many rivers, having their source in different mountains, roll down, crooked or straight and at last come into the ocean, so all these various creeds and religions, taking their start from various standpoints and running through crooked or straight courses, at last come unto Thee.'

As a manifestation of that, we find that this most ancient philosophy has, through its influence, directly inspired Buddhism, the first missionary religion of the world, and indirectly it has also influenced Christianity, through the Alexandrians, the Gnostics, and the European philosophers of the Middle Ages. And later, influencing German thought, it has produced almost a revolution in the regions of philosophy and psychology.

Yet all this mass of influence has been given to the world almost unperceived. As the gentle falling of the dews at night brings support to all vegetable life, so, slowly and imperceptibly, this divine philosophy has been spread through the world for the good of mankind. No march of armies has been used to preach this religion. In Buddhism, one of the most missionary religions of the world, we find inscriptions remaining of the great Emperor Asoka, recording how missionaries were sent to Alexandria, to Antioch, to Persia, to China, and to various other countries of the then civilized world. Three hundred years before Christ, instructions were given them not to revile other religions: 'The basis of all religions is the same, wherever they are; try to help them all you can, teach them all you can, but do not try to injure them.'

Thus in India there never was any religious persecution by the Hindus, but only that wonderful reverence which they have for all the religions of the world. They sheltered a portion of the Hebrews, when they were driven out of their own country, and the Malabar Jews remain as a result. They received at another time the remnant of the Persians when they were almost annihilated; and they remain to this day, as a part of us and loved by us, as the modern Parsis of Bombay. There were Christians who claimed to have come with St Thomas, the disciple of Jesus Christ; and they were allowed to settle in India and hold their own opinions; and a colony of them is even now in existence in India. And this spirit of toleration has not died out. It will not and cannot die there.

This is one of the great lessons that Vedanta has to teach. Knowing that, consciously or unconsciously, we are struggling to reach the same goal, why should we be impatient? If one man is slower than another, we need not be impatient, we need not curse him or revile him. When our eyes are opened and the heart is purified, the work of the same divine influence, the unfolding of the same divinity in every human heart, will become manifest and then alone we shall be in a position to claim the brotherhood of man.

When a man has reached the highest, when he sees neither man nor woman, neither sex, nor creed, nor colour, nor birth, nor any of these differentiations, but goes beyond and finds that divinity which is the real man behind every human being, then alone he has reached the universal brotherhood, and that man alone is a Vedantist.

Section 2

This maya is everywhere. It is terrible. Yet we have to work through it. The way is not with maya, but against it.

Almost all of you have heard of the word *maya*. Generally it is used, though incorrectly, to denote illusion or delusion or some such thing. But the theory of maya forms one of the pillars upon which Vedanta rests; it is therefore necessary that it should be properly understood.

We find that our whole life is a contradiction, a mixture of existence and non-existence. There is this contradiction in knowledge. It seems that man can know everything if he only wants to know; but before he has gone a few steps he finds an adamantine wall which he cannot pass. All his work is in a circle and he cannot go beyond that circle. The problems which are nearest and dearest to him are impelling him on and calling, day and night, for a solution; but he cannot solve them, because he cannot go beyond his intellect. And yet that desire is implanted strongly in him.

Every child is a born optimist; he dreams golden dreams. In youth he becomes still more optimistic. It is hard for a young man to believe that there is such a thing as death, such a thing as defeat or degradation. Old age comes, and life is a mass of ruins. Dreams have vanished into the air, and the man becomes a pessimist. Thus we go from one extreme to another, buffeted by nature, without knowing where we are going.

Then there is the tremendous fact of death. The whole world is going towards death. Everything dies. All our progress, our vanities, our reforms, our luxuries, our wealth, our knowledge, have that one end—death. That is all that is certain. Cities come and go, empires rise and fall, planets break into pieces and crumble into dust, to be blown about by the atmospheres of other planets. Thus it has been going on from time without beginning. Death is the end of everything. Death is the end of life, of beauty, of wealth, of power, of virtue, too. Saints die and sinners die, kings die and beggars die. They are all going to death. And yet this tremendous clinging to life exists. Somehow, we do not know why, we cling to life; we cannot give it up. And this is maya.

The mother is nursing a child with great care; all her soul, her life, is in that child. The child grows, becomes a man, and perchance becomes a blackguard and a brute, kicks her and beats her every day; and yet the mother clings to the child, and when her reason awakes, she covers it up with the idea of love. She little thinks that it is not love, that it is something which has got hold of her nerves, which she cannot shake off. However, she may try, she cannot shake off the bondage she is in. And this is maya.

We are all after the Golden Fleece. Every one of us thinks that this will be his. Every reasonable man sees that his chance is perhaps one in twenty millions, yet everyone struggles for it. And this is maya.

Death is stalking day and night over this earth of ours; but at the same time we think we shall live eternally. A question was once asked of King Yudhisthira, 'What is the most wonderful thing on earth?' And the king replied, 'Every day people are dying around us, and yet men think they will never die.' And this is maya.

These tremendous contradictions in our intellect, in our knowledge, yea, in all the facts of our life, face us on all sides. A reformer arises and wants to remedy the evils existing in a certain nation; and before they have been remedied, a thousand other evils arise in another place. It is like an old house that is falling; you patch it up in one place and the ruin extends to another. It is like chronic rheumatism: you drive it from the head and it goes to the body; you drive it from there and it goes to the feet. Reformers arise and preach that learning, wealth, and culture should not be in the hands of a select few; and they do their best to make them accessible to all. These may bring more happiness to some, but perhaps, as culture comes, physical happiness lessens. The knowledge of happiness brings the knowledge of unhappiness. Which way, then, shall we go? The least amount of material prosperity that we enjoy is elsewhere causing the same amount of misery. This is the law. And this is maya.

Maya is a statement of the fact of this universe, of how it is going on. People generally get frightened when these things are told to them. But bold we must be. Hiding facts is not the way to find a remedy. As you know, a hare hunted by dogs puts its head down and thinks itself safe. When we take refuge in optimism we do just like the hare. But that is no remedy. There are objections against this, but you may remark that they are generally from people who possess many of the good things of life.

In this country it is very difficult to become a pessimist. Everyone tells me how wonderfully the world is going on, how progressively. But what he himself is, is his own world. Old questions arise; Christianity must be the only true religion of the world because Christian nations are prosperous! But that assertion contradicts itself, because the prosperity of the Christiain nations depends on the misfortune of non-Christian nations. There must be some to prey on. Suppose the whole world were to become Christian; then the Christian nations would become poor, because there would be no non-Christian nations for them to prey upon. Thus the argument kills itself. Animals are living upon plants, men upon animals, and worst of all, upon one another, the strong upon the weak. This is going on everywhere. And this is maya.

What solution do you find for this? We hear every day many explanations and are told that in the long run all will be good. Taking it for granted that this is possible, why should there be this diabolical way of doing good? Why cannot good be done through good, instead of through these diabolical methods? The descendants of the human beings of today will be happy; but why must there be all this suffering now? There is no solution. This is maya.

Again, we often hear that it is one of the features of evolution that it eliminates evil, and this evil being continually eliminated from the world, at last only good will remain. That is very nice to hear, and it panders to the vanity of those who have enough of this world's goods, who have no hard struggle to face every day and are not being crushed under the wheel of this so-called evolution. It is very good and comforting indeed to such fortunate ones. The common herd may suffer, but they do not care; let them die, they are of no consequence.

Very good. Yet this argument is fallacious from beginning to end. It takes for granted, in the first place, that manifested good and evil in this world are two absolute realities. In the second place, it makes a still worse assumption, that the amount of good is an increasing quantity, and the amount of evil is a decreasing quantity.

So if evil is being eliminated in this way, by what they call evolution, there will come a time when all this evil will be eliminated and what remains will be all good. Very easy to say, but can it be proved that evil is a lessening quantity?

Take, for instance, the man who lives in a forest, who does not know how to cultivate the mind, cannot read a book, has not heard of such a thing as writing. If he is severely wounded, he is soon all right again; while we die if we get a scratch. Machines are making things cheap, making for progress and evolution, but millions are crushed that one may become rich. While one becomes rich, thousands at the same time become poorer and poorer, and whole masses of human beings are made slaves. That way it is going on.

The animal man lives in the senses. If he does not get enough to eat, he is miserable, or if something happens to his body, he is miserable. In the senses both his misery and his happiness begin and end. As soon as this man progresses, as soon as his happiness increases, his horizon of unhappiness increases proportionately. The man in the forest does not know what it is to be jealous, to be in the law courts, to pay taxes, to be blamed by society.

Thus it is that, as we emerge out of the senses, we develop higher powers of enjoyment, and at the same time we have to develop higher powers of suffering too. The nerves become finer and capable of more suffering. In every society we often find that the ignorant common man, when abused, does not feel much, but he feels a good thrashing. But the gentleman cannot bear a single word of abuse; he has become so finely nerved; misery has increased with his susceptibility to happiness. This does not go far to prove the evolutionist's case. As we increase our power to be happy, we also increase our power to suffer, and sometimes I am inclined to think that if we increase our power to become happy in arithmetical progression, we shall increase, on the other hand, our power to become miserable in geometrical progression. We who are progressing know that the more we progress, the more avenues are opened to pain as well as to pleasure. And this is maya.

Thus we find that maya is not a theory for the explanation of the world; it is simply a statement of facts as they exist—that the very basis of our being is contradiction, that everywhere we have to move through this tremendous contradiction, that wherever there is good, there must also be evil, and wherever there is evil, there must also be some good; wherever there is life, death must follow as its shadow, and everyone who smiles will have to weep, and vice versa.

Thus the Vedanta philosophy is neither optimistic nor pessimistic. It voices both these views and takes things as they are. It admits that this world is a mixture of good and evil, happiness and misery, and that to increase the one must of necessity increase the other. There will never be a perfectly good or bad world, because the very idea is a contradiction in terms.

The great secret revealed by this analysis is that good and bad are not two cut-and-dried, separate existences. There is not one thing in this world of ours which you can label as good, and good alone; and there is not one thing in the universe which you can label as bad, and bad alone. The very same phenomenon which is appearing to be good now may appear to be bad tomorrow. The same thing which is producing misery in one may produce happiness in another. The fire that burns the child may cook a good meal for a starving man. The same nerves that carry the sensations of misery carry also the sensations of happiness.

The only way to stop evil, therefore, is to stop good also; there is no other way. To stop death we shall have to stop life also. Life without death and happiness without misery are contradictions, and neither can be found alone, because each of them is but a different manifestation of the same thing.

What I thought to be good yesterday, I do not think to be good now. When I look back upon my life and see what were my ideals at different times, I find this to be so. At one time my ideal was to drive a strong pair of horses; at another time I thought if I could make a certain kind of sweetmeat, I should be perfectly happy; later I imagined that I should be entirely satisfied if I had a wife and children and plenty of money. To-day I laugh at all these ideals as mere childish nonsense. Vedanta says there must come a time when we shall look back and laugh at the ideals which make us afraid of giving up our individuality. Each one of us wants to keep this body for an indefinite time, thinking we shall be very happy, but there will come a time when we shall laugh at this idea.

Now, if such be the truth, we are in a state of hopeless contradiction—neither existence nor non-existence, neither misery nor happiness, but a mixture of them. What, then, is the use of Vedanta and all other philosophies and religions? And above all, what is the use of doing good work? This is a question that comes to the mind. The answer is, in the first place, that we must work for lessening misery, for that is the only way to make ourselves happy. Every one of us finds it out sooner or later in our lives. The bright ones find it out a little earlier, and the dull ones a little later. The dull ones pay very dearly for the discovery, and the bright ones less dearly. In the second place, we must do our part, because that is the only way of getting out of this life of contradiction. Both the forces of good and evil will keep the universe alive for us until we awake from our dreams and give up this building of mud pies. That lesson we shall have to learn, and it will take a long, long time to learn it.

Vedanta says that it is true that the Absolute or the Infinite is trying to express itself in the finite, but there will come a time when it will find that it is impossible, and it will then have to beat a retreat; and this beating a retreat means renunciation, which is the real beginning of religion. Nowadays it is very hard even to talk of renunciation. Yet it is true that that is the only path of religion. Renounce and give up. What did Christ say? 'He that loseth his life for my sake shall find it.' Again and again did he preach renunciation as the only way to perfection.

There comes a time when the mind awakes from this long and dreary dream. The child gives up its play and wants to go back to its mother. It finds the truth of the statement, 'Desire is never satisfied by the enjoyment of desire; it only increases the more, as fire, when butter is poured upon it.'

This maya is everywhere. It is terrible. Yet we have to work through it. The man who says that he will work when the world has become all good and then he will enjoy bliss is as likely to succeed as the man who sits beside the Ganges and says, 'I will ford the river when all the water has run into the ocean.'

The way is not with maya, but against it. This is another fact to learn. We are not born as helpers of nature but competitors with nature. We are its bond-masters, but we bind ourselves down. Why is this house here? Nature did not build it. Nature says, 'Go and live in the forest.' Man says, 'I will build a house and fight with nature.' And he does so. The whole history of humanity is a continuous fight against the so-called laws of nature. And man gains in the end. Coming to the internal world, there too the same fight is going on, this fight between the animal man and the spiritual man, between light and darkness. And here too man becomes victorious. He, as it were, cuts his way out of nature to freedom.

We see, then, that beyond this maya the Vedantic philosophers find something which is not bound by maya; and if we can get there, we shall not be bound by maya. This idea is in some form or other the common property of all religions. But with Vedanta it is only the beginning of religion and not the end. The idea of a personal God, the Ruler and Creator of this universe, as he has been styled—the ruler of maya or nature—is not the end of these Vedantic ideas; it is only the beginning. The idea grows and grows until the Vedantist finds that he who, he thought, was standing outside, is he himself and is in reality within. He is the one who is free, but who through limitation thought he was bound.

Section 3

At every step we are knocked down by maya and shown that we are bound; and yet at the same moment, together with this blow, comes the other feeling that we are free. The same world that was the ghastly battlefield of maya is now changed into something good and beautiful.

A legend tells how once Narada said to Krishna, 'Lord, show me maya.'

A few days passed, and Krishna asked Narada to make a trip with him towards a desert. After walking for several miles, Krishna said, 'Narada, I am thirsty; can you fetch some water for me?'

'I will go at once, sir, and get you water.'

So Narada went. At a little distance there was a village. He entered the village in search of water and knocked at a door, which was opened by a most beautiful young girl. At the sight of her he immediately forgot that his master was waiting for water, perhaps dying for the want of it. He forgot everything and began to talk with the girl. All that day he did not return to his master. The next day he was again at the house talking to the girl. The talk ripened into love. He asked the father for the daughter, and they were married and lived there and had children.

Thus twelve years passed. His father-in-law died; he inherited his property. He lived, as he seemed to think, a very happy life with his wife and children, his fields and his cattle, and so forth.

Then came a flood. One night the river rose until it overflowed its banks and flooded the whole village.

Houses fell, men and animals were swept away and drowned, and everything was floating in the rush of the stream. Narada had to escape. With one hand he held his wife, and with the other, two of his children; another child was on his shoulders, and he was trying to ford this tremendous flood. After a few steps he found the current was too strong, and the child on his shoulders fell and was borne away. A cry of despair came from Narada. In trying to save that child, he lost his grasp on the others, and they also were lost. At last his wife, whom he clasped with all his might, was torn away by the current, and he was thrown on the bank, weeping and wailing in bitter lamentation.

Behind him there came a gentle voice, 'My child, where is the water? You went to fetch a pitcher of water, and I am waiting for you. You have been gone for quite half an hour.'

'Half an hour!' Narada exclaimed. Twelve whole years had passed through his mind, and all these scenes had happened in half an hour!

And this is maya. In one form or another we are all in it. It is a most difficult and intricate state of things to understand. It has been preached in every country, taught everywhere, but only believed in by a few, because until we get the experiences ourselves we cannot believe in it.

Time, the avenger of everything, comes, and nothing is left. He swallows up the saint and the sinner, the king and the peasant, the beautiful and the ugly; he leaves nothing. Everything is rushing towards that one goal, destruction. Our knowledge, our arts, our sciences— everything is rushing towards it. None can stem the tide, none can hold it back for a minute. We may try to forget it, in the same way that persons in a plague-stricken city try to create oblivion by drinking, dancing, and other vain attempts, and so becoming paralysed. So we are trying to forget, trying to create oblivion by all sorts of sense pleasures. And this is maya.

Two ways have been proposed. One method, which everyone knows, is very common, and that is: 'It may be very true, but do not think of it. "Make hay while the sun shines", as the proverb says. It is all true, it is a fact, but do not mind it. Seize the few pleasures you can, do what little you can, do not look at the dark side of the picture, but always towards the hopeful, the positive side.' There is some truth in this, but there is also a danger. The truth is that it is a good motive power; hope and a positive ideal are very good motive powers in our lives. But there is a certain danger in them. The danger lies in our giving up the struggle in despair. Such is the case with those who preach: 'Take the world as it is; sit down as calmly and comfortably as you can, and be contented with all these miseries. When you receive blows, say they are not blows but flowers; and when you are driven about like slaves, say that you are free. Day and night tell lies to others and to your own souls, because that is the only way to live happily.'

That is what is called practical wisdom, and never was it more prevalent in the world than in this century, because never were harder blows hit than at the present time, never was competition keener, never were men so cruel to their fellow men as now; and therefore this consolation must be offered. It is put forward in the strongest way at the present time; but it fails, as it always must fail.

Is there no hope, then? True it is that we are all slaves of maya, born in maya, and live in maya. Is there then no way out, no hope? That we are all miserable, that this world is really a prison, and that even our intellects and minds are prison houses, has been known for ages upon ages. There has never been a man, there has never been a human soul, who has not felt this some time or other, however he may talk. And the old people feel it most, because in them is the accumulated experience of a whole life, because they cannot be easily cheated by lies of nature.

Is there no way out? We find that with all this, with this terrible fact before us, in the midst of sorrow and suffering, even in this world where life and death are synonymous, even here there is a still small voice that is ringing through all ages, in every country, and in every heart: 'This my maya is divine, made up of qualities, and very difficult to cross. Yet those that come unto me cross the river of life.' 'Come unto me, all ye that labour and are heavy laden, and I will give you rest.' This is the voice that is leading us forward. Man has heard it —and is hearing it—all through the ages. This voice comes to man when everything seems to be lost and hope had fled, when man's dependence on his own strength has been crushed down, and everything seems to melt away between his fingers, and life is a hopeless ruin. Then he hears it. This is called religion.

On the one side, therefore, is the bold assertion that this is all nonsense, that this is maya; but along with it there is the most hopeful assertion that beyond maya there is a way out. On the other hand, practical men tell us: 'Don't bother your heads about such nonsense as religion and metaphysics. Live here; this is a very bad world, indeed, but make the best of it.' Which, put in plain language, means: Live a hypocritical, lying life, a life of continuous fraud, covering all sores in the best way you can; go on putting patch over patch, until everything is lost and you are a mass of patchwork. This is what is called practical life. Those that are satisfied with this patchwork will never come to religion.

Religion begins with a tremendous dissatisfaction with the present state of things, with our lives, and a hatred, an intense hatred, for this patching up of life, an unbounded disgust for fraud and lies. He alone can be religious who dares say, as the mighty Buddha once said under the Bo Tree, when this idea of practicality appeared before him and he saw that it was nonsense, and yet could not find a way out. When the temptation came to him to give up his search after truth, to go back to the world and live the old life of fraud, calling things by wrong names, telling lies to oneself and to everybody, he, the giant, conquered it and said, 'Death is better than a vegetating ignorant life; it is better to die on the battlefield than to live a life of defeat.' This is the basis of religion.

When a man takes this stand he is on the way to find the truth, he is on the way to God. That determination must be the first impulse towards becoming religious. I will hew out a way for myself. I will know the truth or give up my life in the attempt. For on this side is nothing, it is gone, it is vanishing every day. That is one side. On the other, there are the great charms of conquest, victories over all the ills of life, victories over life itself, the conquest of the universe. On that side men can stand. Those who dare, therefore, to struggle for victory, for truth, for religion, are in the right way, and that is what the Vedas preach: 'Be not in despair; the way is very difficult, like walking on the blade of a razor. Yet despair not; arise, awake, and find the ideal, the goal.'

One curious fact present in the midst of all our joys and sorrows, difficulties, and struggles is that we are surely journeying towards freedom. The question was practically this: 'What is this universe? From what does it arise? Into what does it go?' And the answer was, 'In freedom it rises, in freedom it rests, and into freedom it melts away.' This idea of freedom you cannot relinquish; your actions, your very lives, will be lost without it. Every moment nature is proving us to be slaves and not free. Yet simultaneously rises the other idea, that still we are free. At every step we are knocked down, as it were, by maya, and shown that we are bound; and yet at the same moment, together with this blow, together with this feeling that we are bound, comes the other feeling that we are free. Some inner voice tells us that we are free. But if we attempt to realize that freedom, to make it manifest, we find the difficulties almost insuperable. Yet, in spite of that, it insists on asserting itself inwardly: 'I am free, I am free.' And if you study all the various religions of the world you will find this idea expressed.

Not only religion—you must not take this word in its narrow sense—but the whole life of society is the assertion of that one principle of freedom. All movements are the assertion of that one freedom. That voice has been heard by everyone, whether he knows it or not, that voice which declares, 'Come unto me, all ye that labour and are heavy laden.' We are all rushing towards freedom, we are all following that voice, whether we know it or not; as the children of the village were attracted by the music of the flute player, so we are all following the music of the voice without knowing it.

We are ethical when we follow that voice. Not only the human soul, but all creatures from the lowest to the highest have heard the voice and are rushing towards it, and in the struggle are either combining with each other or pushing each other out of the way. Thus come competition, joys, struggles, life, pleasure, and death; and the whole universe is nothing but the result of this mad struggle to reach the voice. This is the manifestation of nature.

What happens then? The scene begins to shift. As soon as you know the voice and understand what it is, the whole scene changes. The same world which was the ghastly battlefield of maya is now changed into something good and beautiful. We no longer curse nature or say that the world is horrible and that it is all vain; we need no longer weep and wail. As soon as we understand the voice, we see the reason why this struggle should be here—this fight, this competition, this difficulty, this cruelty, these little pleasures and joys; we see that they are in the nature of things, because without them there would be no going towards the voice, to attain which we are destined, whether we know it or not.

All human life, all nature, therefore, is struggling to attain to freedom. The sun is moving towards the goal; so is the earth in circling around the sun; so is the moon in circling round the earth. To that goal the planet is moving and the air is blowing. Everything is struggling towards that. The saint is going towards that voice, he cannot help it, it is no glory to him. So is the sinner. The charitable man is going straight towards that voice, and cannot be hindered. The miser is also going towards the same destination. The greatest worker of good hears the same voice within and he cannot resist it, he must go towards the voice. So with the most arrant idler. One stumbles more than another; he who stumbles more we call bad, he who stumbles less we call good. Good and bad are never two different things; they are one and the same; the difference is not one of kind, but of degree.

Now, if the manifestation of this power of freedom is really governing the whole universe, applying that to religion, our special study, we find this idea has been the one assertion throughout. Take the lowest form of religion, where there is the worship of departed ancestors or certain powerful and cruel gods. What is the prominent idea about the gods or departed ancestors? That they are superior to nature, not bound by its restrictions. The worshipper has, no doubt, very limited powers over nature. He himself cannot pass through a wall, or fly up into the skies, but the gods whom he worships can do these things. What is meant by that, philosophically? That the assertion of freedom is there, that the gods whom he worships are superior to nature as he knows it. So with those who worship still higher beings. As the idea of nature expands, the idea of the soul which is superior to nature also expands, until we come to what we call monotheism, which holds that there is maya and that there is some being who is the Ruler of this maya.

Here Vedanta begins, where these monotheistic ideas first appear. But the Vedanta philosophy wants further explanation. This explanation—that there is a Being beyond all these manifestations of maya, who is superior to and independent of maya, and who is attracting us towards himself, and that we are all going towards him —is very good, says Vedanta; but yet the perception is not clear, the vision is dim and hazy, although it does not directly contradict reason. Just as in your hymn it is said, 'Nearer, my God, to Thee', the same hymn would be very good to the Vedantist, only he would change a word and make it 'Nearer, my God, to Me'. The idea that the goal is far off, far beyond nature, attracting us all towards it, has to be brought nearer and nearer, without degrading or degenerating it. The God of heaven becomes the God in nature, and the God in nature becomes the God who is nature, and the God who is nature becomes the God within this temple of the body, and the God dwelling in the temple of the body at last becomes the temple itself, becomes the soul and man—and there Vedanta reaches the last words it can teach.

He whom the sages have been seeking in all these places is in our own hearts; the voice that you heard was right, says Vedanta, but the direction you gave it was wrong. That ideal of freedom that you perceived was correct, but you projected it outside yourself, and that was your mistake. Bring it nearer and nearer, until you find that it was all the time within you, it was the Self of your own self. That freedom was your own nature, and this maya never bound you. Nature never had power over you. Like a frightened child you were dreaming that it was throttling you. The release from this fear is the goal; not only to see it intellectually, but to perceive it, actualize it, much more definitely than we perceive this world.

Then we shall know that we are free. Then, and then alone, will all difficulties vanish, then will all the perplexities of the heart be smoothed away, all crookedness made straight; then will vanish the delusion of manifoldness and nature. Maya, instead of being a horrible, hopeless dream as it is now, will become beautiful; and this earth, instead of being a prison house, will become our playground; and even dangers and difficulties, even all sufferings, will become deified and show us their real nature, will show us that behind everything, as the substance of everything, he is standing, and that he is the one real Self.

Section 4

This is the gist of Vedantic morality, this sameness for all.

The idea of privilege is the bane of human life. Two forces, as it were, are constantly at work, one making caste, and the other breaking caste; in other words, the one making for privilege, the other breaking down privilege. And whenever privilege is broken down, more and more light and progress come to a race. This struggle we see all around us.

Of course there is first the brutal idea of privilege, that of the strong over the weak. There is the privilege of wealth. If a man has more money than another, he wants a little privilege over those who have less. These is the still more subtle and more powerful privilege of intellect; because one man knows more than others he claims more privilege. And the last of all, and the worst, because the most tyrannical, is the privilege of spirituality. If some persons think they know more of spirituality, of God, they claim a superior privilege over everyone else. They say, 'Come and worship us, ye common herd; we are the messengers of God, and you have to worship us.'

None can be Vedantists and at the same time admit of privilege to anyone, either mental, physical, or spiritual—absolutely no privilege for anyone. The same power is in every man, the one manifesting more, the other less; the same potentiality is in everyone. Where is the claim to privilege? All knowledge is in every soul, even in the most ignorant; he has not manifested it, but perhaps he has not had the opportunity, the environments were not, perhaps, suitable to him. When he gets the opportunity he will manifest it. The idea that one man is born superior to another has no meaning in Vedanta; that between two nations one is superior and the other inferior has no meaning whatsoever. Put them in the same circumstance and see whether the same intelligence comes out or not. Before that you have no right to say that one nation is superior to another.

The work of the Advaita, therefore, is to break down all these privileges. It is the hardest work of all, and curious to say, it has been less active in India, the land of its birth, than anywhere else. If there is any land of privilege, it is the land which gave birth to this philosophy—privilege for the spiritual man as well as for the man of birth. There money does not confer much privilege—that is one of the benefits, I think—but the privilege of birth and spirituality is everywhere.

Once a gigantic attempt was made to preach Vedantic ethics, which succeeded to a certain extent for several hundred years; and we know historically that those years were the best times of that nation. I mean the Buddhist attempt to break down privilege. Some of the most beautiful epithets addressed to Buddha that I remember are, 'Thou breaker of castes, destroyer of privileges, preacher of equality to all beings.' So he preached this one idea of equality. Its power has been misunderstood to a certain extent in the brotherhood of Sramanas, where we find that hundreds of attempts have been made to make them into a church, with superiors and inferiors. You cannot make much of a church when you tell people they are all gods. One of the good effects of Vedanta has been freedom of religious thought, which India enjoyed throughout all times of its history. It is something to glory in, that it is the land where there was never a religious persecution, where people were allowed perfect freedom in religion.

The practical side of Vedantic morality is necessary as much today as it ever was—more necessary, perhaps, than it ever was; for all this privilege-claiming has become tremendously intensified with the extension of knowledge. The idea of God and the Devil has a good deal of poetry in it. The difference between God and the Devil is in nothing except in unselfishness and selfishness. The Devil knows as much as God, is as powerful as God; only he has no holiness: that makes him a Devil. Apply the same idea to the modern world; excess of knowledge and power, without holiness, makes human beings devils.

Tremendous power is being acquired through machines and other appliances, and privilege is claimed today as it never has been claimed in the history of the world. That is why Vedanta wants to preach against it, to break down this tyrannizing over the souls of man.

Those of you who have studied the Bhagavad-Gita will remember the memorable passages: 'He who looks upon the learned brahmin, upon the cow, the elephant, the dog, or the outcast with the same eye—he indeed is the sage and the wise man.' 'Even in this life he has conquered relative existence whose mind is firmly fixed on this sameness, for the Lord is one and the same to all, and the Lord is pure. Therefore those who feel this sameness for all and are pure are said to be living in God.'

This is the gist of Vedantic morality, this sameness for all. We have seen that it is the subjective world that rules the objective. Change the subject, and the object is bound to change; purify yourself, and the world is bound to be purified. This one thing requires to be taught now more than ever before. We are becoming more and more busy about our neighbours, and less and less about ourselves. The world will change if we change; if we are pure the world will become pure. The question is, Why should I see evil in others? I cannot see evil unless I be evil. I cannot be miserable unless I am weak. Things that used to make me miserable when I was a child do not do so now. The subject has changed, so the object was bound to change. So says the Vedantist. All these things which we call causes of misery and evil, we shall laugh at when we arrive at that wonderful state of equality, that sameness. This is what is called in Vedanta 'attaining to freedom'. The sign of approaching that freedom is more and more of this sameness and equality.

You ask one of your great men, of great birth and wealth, if he believes as a Christian in the brotherhood of mankind, since all came from God. He answers in the affirmative; but in five minutes he shouts something uncomplimentary about the common herd. Thus it has been a theory only for several thousand years and has never come into practice. All understand it, declare it as the truth, but when you ask them to practise it, they say it will take millions of years.

There was a certain king who had a huge number of courtiers; and each one of these courtiers declared he was ready to sacrifice his life for his master and that he was the most sincere being ever born. In course of time a monk came to the king. The king said to him that there never was a king who had so many sincere courtiers as he had. The monk smiled and said he did not believe it. The king said the monk could test it if he liked. So the monk declared that he would make a great sacrifice by which the king's reign would be extended for a long time; part of the sacrifice was that each of the courtiers should pour a pitcher of milk into a small pond at midnight. The king smiled and said, 'Is this the test?' And he asked his courtiers to come to him, and told them what was to be done. They all expressed their joyful assent to the proposal and returned. In the dead of night they came and emptied their pitchers into the pond. But in the morning it was found full of water only. The courtiers were assembled and questioned about the matter. Each one of them had thought there would be so many pitchers of milk that his water would not be detected.

Unfortunately most of us have the same idea, and we do our share of work as did the courtiers in the story.

Do you believe what Christ says, 'Go and sell that thou hast and give to the poor?' Practical equality there —no trying to torture the texts, but taking the truth as it is. Do not try to torture texts. I have heard it said that that was preached only to a handful of Jews who listened to Jesus. The same argument will apply to other things also. Do not torture texts; dare to face truth as it is. Even if we cannot reach it, let us confess our weakness, but let us not destroy the ideal. Let us hope that we shall attain to it sometime, and strive for it. There it is: 'Sell that thou hast, and give to the poor, and follow me.'

Thus trampling on every privilege and everything in us that works for privilege, let us work for that knowledge which will bring the feeling of sameness towards all mankind. You think that because you talk a little more polished language you are superior to the man in the street. Remember that when you are thinking this, you are not going towards freedom, but are forging a fresh chain for your feet. And above all, if the pride of spirituality enters into you, woe unto you. It is the most awful bondage that ever existed. Neither can wealth nor any other bondage of the human heart bind the soul so much as this. 'I am purer than others' is the most awful idea that can enter into the human heart. In what sense are you pure? The God in you is the God in all. If you have not known this, you have known nothing. How can there be difference? It is all one. Every being is the temple of the Most High; if you can see that, good; if not, spirituality has not yet come to you.

Section 5

The alpha and omega of Vedanta philosophy is to 'give up the world', giving up the unreal and taking the real.

According to the Advaita philosophy, there is only one thing real in the universe, which it calls Brahman. Everything else is unreal, manifested and manufactured out of Brahman by the power of maya. To reach back to that Brahman is our goal, We are, each of us, that Brahman, that Reality, plus this maya. If we get rid of this maya, or ignorance, then we become what we really are.

According to this philosophy, each man consists of three parts: the body, the internal organ or mind, and behind that, what is called the Atman, the Self. The body is the external coating, and the mind is the internal coating, of the Atman, who is the real perceiver, the real enjoyer, the being in the body who is working the body by means of the internal organ or mind.

The Atman is the only existence in the human body which is immaterial. Because it is immaterial, it cannot be a compound, and because it is not a compound, it does not obey the law of cause and effect; and so it is immortal. That which is immortal can have no beginning, because everything with a beginning must have an end. It also follows that it must be formless; there cannot be any form without matter. Everything that has form must have a beginning and an end. We have none of us seen a form which had not a beginning and will not have an end.

A form comes out of a combination of force and matter. This chair has a peculiar form; that is to say, a certain quantity of matter is acted upon by a certain amount of force and made to assume a particular shape. The shape is the result of a combination of matter and force. The combination cannot be eternal; there must come to every combination a time when it will dissolve. So all forms have a beginning and an end. We know our body will perish; it had a beginning and it will have an end. But the Self, having no form, cannot be bound by the law of beginning and end. It is existing from infinite time; just as time is eternal, so is the Self of man eternal.

Secondly, it must be all-pervading. It is only form that is conditioned and limited by space; that which is formless cannot be confined in space. So, according to advaita Vedanta, the Self, the Atman, in you, in me, in everyone, is omnipresent. You are as much in the sun now as on this earth, as much in England as in America. But the Self acts through the mind and the body, and where they are, its action is visible.

Each work we do, each thought we think, produces an impression, called in Sanskrit *samskara*, upon the mind; and the sum total of these impressions becomes the tremendous force which is called character. The character of a man is what he has created for himself; it is the result of the mental and physical actions that he has done in his life. The sum total of the samskaras is the force which gives a man the next direction after death. A man dies; the body falls away and goes back to the elements; but the samskaras remain, adhering to the mind which, being made of fine material, does not dissolve, because the finer the material, the more persistent it is. But the mind also dissolves in the long run, and that is what we are struggling for.

In this connection, the best illustration that comes to my mind is of the whirlwind. Different currents of air coming from different directions meet, and at the meeting point become united and go on rotating. As they rotate they form a column, drawing in dust, bits of paper, straw, and so forth, at one place, only to drop them and go on to another, and so go on rotating, raising and forming bodies out of the materials which are before them. Even so the forces called *prana* in Sanskrit come together and form the body and the mind out of matter, and move on until the body falls down, when they raise other materials to make another body; and when this falls, another rises; and thus the process goes on.

Force cannot travel without matter. So when the body falls down, the mind-stuff remains, prana in the form of samskaras acting on it, and then it goes on to another point, raises up another whirl from fresh materials, and begins another motion; and so it travels from place to place until the force is all spent, and then it falls down, ended. So when the mind will end, be broken to pieces entirely, without leaving any samskara, we shall be entirely free, and until that time we are in bondage; until then the Atman is covered by the whirl of the mind, and imagines it is being taken from place to place. When the whirl falls down, the Atman finds that it is all-pervading. It can go where it likes, is entirely free, and is able to manufacture any number of minds or bodies it likes. But until then it can go only with the whirl. This freedom is the goal towards which we are all moving.

Suppose there is a ball in this room, and we each have a mallet in our hands and begin to strike the ball, giving it hundreds of blows, driving it from point to point, until at last it flies out of the room. With what force and in what direction it will go out will be determined by the forces that have been acting upon it all through the room. All the different blows that have been given will have their effects. Each one of our actions, mental and physical, is such a blow. The human mind is a ball which is being hit. We are being hit about this room of the world all the time, and our passage out of it is determined by the force of all these blows. In each case the speed and direction of the ball are determined by the hits it has received. So all our actions in this world will determine our future birth.

Similarly we are in this world by our own actions. Just as we go out with the sum total of our present actions upon us, so we see that we come into it with the sum total of our past actions upon us; that which takes us out is the very same thing that brings us in. What brings us in? Our past deeds. What takes us out? Our own deeds *here*. And so on and on we go. Like the caterpillar, that takes the thread from its own mouth and builds its cocoon, and at last finds itself caught inside the cocoon, we have bound ourselves by our own actions, we have thrown the network of our actions around ourselves. We have set the law of causation in motion and we find it hard to get ourselves out of it. We have set the wheel in motion and we are being crushed under it. So this philosophy teaches us that we are uniformly being bound by our own actions, good and bad.

The Atman never comes nor goes, is never born nor dies. It is nature moving before the Atman; and the reflection of this motion is on the Atman and the Atman ignorantly thinks it is moving, and not nature. When the Atman thinks that, it is in bondage, but when it comes to find that it never moves, that it is omnipresent, then freedom comes. The Atman in bondage is called *jiva*. Thus you see that when it is said that the Atman comes and goes; it is said only for facility in understanding, just as for convenience in studying astronomy you are asked to suppose that the sun moves around the earth, though such is not the case. So the jiva, the bound soul, comes to higher and lower states. This is the well-known law of reincarnation, and this law binds all creation.

People in this country think it too horrible that man should come up from an animal. Why? What will be the end of these millions of animals? Are they nothing? If we have a soul, so have they, and if they have none, neither have we. It is absurd to say that man alone has a soul, and the animals none. I have seen men worse than animals.

The human soul has sojourned in lower and higher forms, migrating from one to another according to its samskaras or impressions; but it is only in the highest form, as man, that it attains to freedom. The man form is higher than even the angel form; of all forms it is the highest. Man is the highest being in creation, because he attains to freedom.

All this universe was in Brahman, and it was, as it were, projected out of him and has been moving on, to go back to the source from which it was projected, like the electricity which comes out of the dynamo, completes the circuit, and returns to it. The same is the case with the soul. Projected from Brahman, it passed through all sorts of vegetable and animal forms, and at last it is in man, and man is the nearest approach to Brahman.

To go back to Brahman, from which we have been projected, is the great struggle of life. Whether people know it or not does not matter. In the universe, whatever we see of motion, of struggles in minerals or plants or animals, is the effort to come back to the centre and be at rest. There was an equilibrium, and that has been destroyed, and all parts—atoms and molecules—are struggling to find their lost equilibrium again. In this struggle they are combining and re-forming, giving rise to all the wonderful phenomena of nature. All struggles and competitions in animal life, plant life, and in everything else, all social struggles and wars, are but expressions of that eternal struggle to get back to that equilibrium.

The going from birth to death, this travelling, is what is called *samsara* in Sanskrit, literally, the round of birth and death. All creation, passing through this round, will sooner or later become free. The question may be raised: If we all shall come to freedom, why should we *struggle* to attain it? If everyone is going to be free, we will sit down and wait. It is true that every being will become free, sooner or later; no one can be lost. Nothing can come to destruction; everything must come up. If that is so, what is the use of our struggling?

In the first place, the struggle is the only means that will bring us to the centre; and in the second place, we do not know why we struggle. We have to. 'Of thousands of men, some are awakened to the idea that they will

become free.' The vast masses of mankind are content
with material things, but there are some who awake and
want to get back, who have had enough of this playing
down here. These struggle consciously, while the rest
do it unconsciously.

The alpha and omega of Vedanta philosophy is to 'give
up the world', giving up the unreal and taking the real.
Those who are enamoured of the world may ask, 'Why
should we attempt to get out of it, to go back to the
centre? Suppose we have all come from God; but we
find the world is pleasurable and nice. Then why should
we not rather try to get more and more of the world?
Why should we try to get out of it? They say, 'Look
at the wonderful improvements going on in the world
every day—how much luxury is being manufactured for
it. This is very enjoyable. Why should we go away and
strive for something which is not this?'

The answer is that the world is certain to die, to be
broken into pieces, and that many times we have had
the same enjoyments. All the forms which we are seeing
now have been manufactured again and again, and the
world in which we live has been here many times before.
I have been here and talked to you many times before.
You will know that it must be so; and the very words
that you are listening to now, you have heard many
times before. And many times more it will be the same.
Souls were never different; the bodies have been constantly dissolving and recurring. Secondly, these things
periodically occur. Suppose here are three or four dice,
and when we throw them, one comes up five, another four,
another three, and another two. If you keep on throwing,
there must come times when those very same numbers will

recur. Go on throwing, and no matter how long may be the interval, those numbers must come again. It cannot be asserted in how many throws they will come again; this is the law of chance. So with souls and their associations. However distant may be the periods, the same combinations and dissolutions will happen again and again. The same birth, eating and drinking, and then death, come round again and again. Some never find anything higher than the enjoyments of the world, but those who want to soar higher find that these enjoyments are never final, are only by the way.

Every form, let us say, beginning from the little worm and ending in man, is like one of the cars of the Ferris wheel, which is in motion all the time, but the occupants change. A man goes into a car, moves with the wheel, and comes out. The wheel goes on and on. A soul enters one form, resides in it for a time, then leaves it and goes into another, and quits that again for a third. Thus the round goes on, till it comes out of the wheel and becomes free.

So long as there is desire or want, it is a sure sign that there is imperfection. A perfect, free being cannot have any desire. God cannot want anything. If he desires, he cannot be God. He will be imperfect. So all the talk about God desiring this and that, of becoming angry and pleased by turns, is babies' talk; it means nothing. Therefore it has been taught by all teachers, 'Desire nothing; give up all desires and be perfectly satisfied.'

A child comes into the world crawling and without teeth, and the old man goes out without teeth and crawling. The extremes are alike, but the one has no experience of the life before him, while the other has gone through it all. When the vibrations of ether are very low, we do not see light; it is darkness. When very high, the result is also darkness. The extremes generally appear to be the same, though one is as distant from the other as the poles. The wall has no desires, and neither has the perfect man. But the wall is not sentient enough to desire, while for the perfect man there is nothing to desire. There are idiots who have no desires in this world because their brains are imperfect. At the same time, the highest state is reached when we have no desires. But the two are opposite poles of the same existence. One is near the animal, and the other near to God.

Section 6

Each thought and deed lays up a store for you; as bad thoughts and bad works are ready to spring upon you like tigers, so also there is the inspiring hope that good thoughts and good deeds are ready with the power of a hundred thousand angels to defend you.

No question is so near and dear to man's heart as that of the internal man. How many millions of times, in how many countries, has this question been asked! Is there nothing permanent in this evanescent human life? Is there nothing which does not die away when the body dies? And if so, what is its destiny? Where does it go? Whence did it come? These questions have been asked again and again, and so long as this creation lasts, so long as there are human brains to think, this question will have to be asked.

I am looking at you. How many things are necessary

for this vision? First, the eyes. For if I am perfect in every other way, and yet have no eyes, I shall not be able to see you. Secondly, the real organ of vision. For the eyes are not the organs; they are but the instruments of vision, and behind them is the real organ, the nerve centre in the brain. If that centre be injured, a man may have the clearest pair of eyes, yet he will not be able to see anything. So it is necessary that this centre, or the real organ, be there. Thus with all our senses. The external ear is but the instrument for carrying the vibration of sound inward to that centre. Yet that is not sufficient. Suppose in your library you are intently reading a book, and the clock strikes; yet you do not hear it. The sound is there, the pulsations in the air are there, the ear and the centre are also there, and these vibrations have been carried through the ear to the centre, and yet you do not hear it. What is wanting? The mind is not there.

Thus we see that the third thing necessary is that the mind must be there. First the external instruments, then the organ to which this external instrument will carry the sensation, and lastly the organ itself must be joined to the mind. When the mind is not joined to the organ, the organ and the ear may take the impression and yet we shall not be conscious of it.

The mind, too, is only the carrier; it has to carry the sensation still forward, and present it to the intellect. The intellect is the determining faculty and decides upon what is brought to it. Still this is not sufficient. The intellect must carry it forward and present the whole thing before the ruler of the body, the human soul, the king on the throne. Before him this is presented, and then from him comes the order as to what to do or what not to do; and the order goes down, in the same sequence, to the intellect, to the mind, to the organs; and the organs convey it to the instruments, and perception is complete.

The instruments are in the external body, the gross body, of man; but the mind and the intellect are not. They are in what is called in Hindu philosophy the finer body, and what in Christian theology you read of as the spiritual body of man—finer, very much finer than the body, and yet not the soul. This soul is beyond them all. The external body perishes in a few years; any simple cause may disturb and destroy it. The finer body is not as easily perishable; yet it sometimes degenerates and at other times becomes strong. We see how, in the old man, the mind loses its strength, how, when the body is vigorous, the mind becomes vigorous, how various medicines and drugs affect it, how everything external acts on it, and how it reacts on the external world. Just as the body has its progress and decadence, so also has the mind, and therefore the mind is not the soul, because the soul can neither decay nor degenerate.

How can we know that? How can we know that there is something behind the mind? Because knowledge, which is self-illuminating and the basis of intelligence, cannot belong to dull, dead matter. Never was seen any gross matter which had intelligence as its own essence. No dull or dead matter can illumine itself. It is intelligence that illumines all matter. The body is not self-luminous; if it were, it would be so in a dead man also. Neither can the mind, nor the spiritual body, be self-luminous. They are not of the essence of intelligence. That which is self-luminous cannot decay. The luminosity of that which shines through a borrowed light comes and goes; but that which is light itself—what can make that come and go, flourish and decay? We see that the moon waxes and wanes because it shines through the borrowed light of the sun. If a lump of iron is put into the fire and made red-hot, it glows and shines; but its light will vanish because it is borrowed. So decadence is possible only of that light which is borrowed and is not light in its own essence.

Now we see that the body, the external shape, has no light as its own essence, is not self-luminous, and cannot know itself; neither can the mind. Why not? Because the mind waxes and wanes, because it is vigorous at one time and weak at another, because it can be acted upon by anything and everything. Therefore the light which shines through the mind is not its own. Whose is it, then? It must belong to That which has it as its own essence, and as such, can never decay or die, never become stronger or weaker; it is self-luminous; it is luminosity itself. It cannot be that the Soul knows; but it *is* knowledge. It cannot be that the Soul has existence, but it *is* existence. It cannot be that the Soul is happy; it *is* happiness itself. That which is happy has borrowed its happiness; that which has knowledge has received its knowledge; and that which has relative existence has only a reflected existence. Wherever there are qualities, these qualities have been reflected upon the substance. But the Soul has not knowledge, existence, and blessedness as its qualities; they are the essence of the Soul.

Again, it may be asked, why should we take this for granted? Why should we admit that the Soul has knowledge, blessedness, and existence as its essence, and has not borrowed them? It may be argued: Why not say that the Soul's luminosity, the Soul's blessedness, the Soul's knowledge are borrowed in the same way as the luminosity of the body is borrowed from the mind? The fallacy of arguing in this way will be that there will be no limit. From whom were these borrowed? If we say from some other source, the same question will be asked again. So at last we shall have to come to one who is self-luminous. To make matters short then, the logical way is to stop where we get self-luminosity, and proceed no farther.

We see, then, that this human being is composed first of this external covering, the body; secondly, of the finer body, consisting of mind, intellect, and ego. Behind them is the real Self of man. We have seen that all the powers of the gross body are borrowed from the mind, and the mind, the finer body, borrows its powers and luminosity from the Soul, standing behind.

A great many questions now arise about the nature of the Soul. If the existence of the Soul is drawn from the argument that it is self-luminous, that knowledge, existence, blessedness are its essence, it naturally follows that the Soul cannot have been created. A self-luminous existence, independent of any other existence, could never have been the outcome of anything. It always existed; there was never a time when it did not exist, because if the Soul did not exist, where was time? Time is in the Soul; it is when the Soul reflects its powers on the mind and the mind thinks, that time comes. When there was no Soul, certainly there was no thought, and without thought there was no time. How can the Soul, therefore, be said to be existing in time, when time itself exists in the Soul? It has neither birth nor death, but it is passing through all these various stages. It is manifesting slowly and gradually from lower to higher. It is expressing its own grandeur, working through the mind on the body, and through the body it is grasping the external world and understanding it. It takes up a body and uses it, and when that body has failed and is used up, it takes another body, and so on it goes.

Here comes a very interesting question, that question which is generally known as the reincarnation of the soul. Sometimes people get frightened at the idea; and superstition is so strong that even thinking men believe that they are the outcome of nothing, and then, with the grandest logic, try to deduce the theory that although they have come out of zero, they will be eternal ever afterwards. Those that come out of zero will certainly have to go back to zero. Neither you nor I nor anyone has come out of zero, nor will go back to zero. We have been existing eternally, and will exist, and there is no power under the sun, or above the sun, which can undo your or my existence or send us back to zero. Now, this idea of reincarnation is not only not a frightening idea, but is most essential for the moral well-being of the human race. It is the only logical conclusion that thoughtful men can arrive at. If you are going to exist in eternity hereafter, it must be that you have existed through eternity in the past; it cannot be otherwise.

The objection is, Why do we not remember our past? Do we remember all our past in this life? How many of you remember what you did when you were babies? None of you remember your early childhood; and if upon memory depends your existence, then this argument proves that you did not exist as babies, because you do not remember your babyhood. It is simply unmitigated nonsense to say that our existence depends on our remembering it. Why should we remember the past? The brain is gone, broken into pieces, and a new brain has been manufactured. What has come to this brain is the resultant, the sum total, of the impressions acquired in our past, with which the mind has come to inhabit the new body. I, as I stand here, am the effect, the result, of all the infinite past which is tacked on to me.

And why is it necessary for me to remember all the past? When a great ancient sage, a seer or a prophet of old who came face to face with the truth, says something, these modern men stand up and say, 'Oh, he was a fool!' But just use another name, 'Huxley says it, or Tyndall', then it must be true, and they take it for granted. In place of ancient superstitions they have erected modern superstitions; in place of the old popes of religion, they have installed modern popes of science.

So we see that this objection as to memory is not valid, and that is about the only serious objection that is raised against this theory.

Although we have seen that it is not necessary for the acceptance of this theory that there shall be the memory of past lives, yet at the same time we are in a position to assert that there are instances which show that this memory does come, and that each one of us will get back this memory in that life in which he will become free. Then alone you will find that this world is but a dream; then alone you will realize in the soul of your soul that you are but actors and the world is a stage; then alone will the idea of non-attachment come to you with the power of thunder; then all this thirst for enjoyment, this clinging on to life and this world, will vanish for ever; then the mind will see clearly as

daylight how many times all these existed for you—
how many millions of times you had fathers and mothers,
sons and daughters, husbands and wives, relatives and
friends, wealth and power. They came and went. How
many times you were on the topmost crest of the wave,
and how many times you were down at the bottom of
despair! When memory will bring all these to you, then
alone will you stand as a hero and smile when the world
frowns upon you. Then alone will you stand up and say,
'I care not for thee even, O Death! What terrors hast
thou for me?' This will come to all.

Are there any arguments, any rational proofs, for this
reincarnation of the soul? So far we have been giving
the negative side, showing that the opposite argument
to disprove it is not valid. Are there any positive proofs?
There are—and most valid ones, too. No other theory
except that of reincarnation accounts for the wide
divergence that we find between man and man in their
powers to acquire knowledge.

First, let us consider the process by means of which
knowledge is acquired. Suppose I go into the street and
see a dog. How do I know that it is a dog? I refer it
to my mind, and in my mind are groups of all my past
experiences, arranged and pigeonholed, as it were. As
soon as a new impression comes, I take it up and refer
it to some of the old pigeonholes, and as soon as I find a
group of the same impressions already existing, I place
it in that group and I am satisfied I know it is a dog
because it coincides with impressions already there. When
I do not find the cognate of this new experience inside,
I become dissatisfied; this state of the mind is called
ignorance. But when, finding the cognates of an impres-

sion already existing, we become satisfied, this is called knowledge. When one apple fell men became dissatisfied. Then gradually they found out the group. What was the group they found? That all apples fell, so they called it gravitation.

Now, we see that without a fund of already existing experience any new experience would be impossible, for there would be nothing to which to refer the new impression. So if, as some European philosophers think, a child came into the world with what they call a *tabula rasa*, such a child would never attain to any degree of intellectual power, because he would have nothing to which to refer his new experiences. We see that the power of acquiring knowledge varies in each individual, and this shows that each one of us has come with his own fund of knowledge. Knowledge can only be got in one way, the way of experience; there is no other way to know. If we have not experienced it in this life, we must have experienced it in other lives.

How is it that the fear of death is everywhere? A little chicken is just out of an egg and an eagle comes, and the chicken flies in fear to its mother. There is an old explanation (I should hardly dignify it with such a name). It is called instinct. What makes that little chicken just out of an egg afraid to die? How is it that as soon as a duckling hatched by a hen comes near water it jumps into it and swims? It never swam before, nor saw anything swim. People call it instinct. It is a big word but it leaves us where we were before.

Let us study this phenomenon of instinct. A child begins to play on the piano. At first she must pay attention to every key she is fingering, and as she goes on and on for months and years, the playing becomes almost involuntary, instinctive. What was first done with conscious will does not require later on an effort of the will. This is not yet a complete proof. One half remains, and that is that almost all the actions which are now instinctive can be brought under the control of the will. Each muscle of the body can be brought under control. This is perfectly well known. So the proof is complete, by this double method, that what we now call instinct is the degeneration of voluntary actions. Therefore, if the analogy applies to the whole of creation, if all nature is uniform, then what is instinct in lower animals, as well as in men, must be the degeneration of will.

Applying the law that each involution presupposes an evolution, and each evolution an involution, we see that instinct is involved reason. What we call instinct in men or animals must therefore be involved, degenerated, voluntary actions, and voluntary actions are impossible without experience. Experience started that knowledge, and that knowledge is there. The fear of death, the duckling taking to the water, and all involuntary actions in the human being which have become instinctive, are the result of past experiences.

So far we have proceeded very clearly, and so far the latest science is with us. But here comes one more difficulty. The latest scieintific men are coming back to the ancient sages, and as far as they have done so, there is perfect agreement. They admit that each man and each animal is born with a fund of experience, and that all these actions in the mind are the result of past experience. 'But what', they ask, 'is the use of saying that the experience belongs to the soul? Why not say it belongs to the body and the body alone? Why not say it is hereditary transmission?' This is the last question. Why not say that all the experience with which I am born is the resultant of all the past experience of my ancestors? The sum total of the experience from the little protoplasm up to the highest human being is in me, but it has come from body to body in the course of hereditary transmission. Where will the difficulty be?

This question is very nice, and we admit some part of this hereditary transmission. How far? As far as furnishing the material. We, by our past actions, conform ourselves to a certain birth in a certain body, and the only suitable material for that body comes from the parents who have made themselves fit to have that soul as their offspring. But the simple hereditary theory takes for granted the most astonishing proposition without any proof, that mental experience can be recorded in matter, that mental experience can be involved in matter.

When I look at you, in the lake of my mind there is a wave. That wave subsides, but it remains in fine form, as an impression. We understand a physical impression's remaining in the body. But what proof is there for assuming that the mental impression can remain in the body, since the body goes to pieces? What carries it? Even granting it were possible for each mental impression to remain in the body, that every impression, beginning from the first man down to my father, was in my father's body, how could it be transmitted to me? Through the bioplasmic cell? How could that be? Because the father's body does not come to the child *in toto*. The same parents may have a number of children. Then, from this theory of hereditary transmission, where the impression and the impressed (this is to say, material) are one, it rigorously follows that, by the birth of every child, the parents would lose a part of their own impressions, or, if the parents should transmit the whole of their impressions, then, after the birth of the first child, their minds would be a vacuum.

Again, if in the bioplasmic cell the infinite amount of impressions from all time has entered, where and how is this? This is a most impossible position, and until these physiologists can prove how and where those impressions live in that cell, and what they mean by the mental impressions' sleeping in the physical cell, their position cannot be taken for granted.

So far it is clear, then, that these impressions are in the mind, that the mind comes to take its birth and rebirth and uses the material which is most proper for it, and that the mind which has made itself fit for only a particular kind of body will have to wait until it gets that material. This we understand.

The theory then comes to this, that there is hereditary transmission, so far as furnishing the material to the soul is concerned. But the soul migrates, and manufactures body after body; and each thought we think, and each deed we do, is stored in it in fine forms, ready to spring up again and take a new shape. When I look at you a wave rises in my mind. It dives down, as it were, and becomes finer and finer, but it does not die. It is ready to start up again as a wave in the shape of memory. So all these impressions are in the mind, and when I die the resultant force of them will be upon me. So what directs the soul when the body dies? The resultant, the sum total of all the works it has done, of the thoughts it has thought. If the resultant is such that it has to manufacture a new body for further experience, it will go to those parents who are ready to supply it with suitable material for that body.

Thus from body to body it will go, sometimes to a heaven, and back again to earth, becoming man or some lower animal. This way it will go on until it has finished its experience and completed the circle. It then knows its own nature, knows what it is, and ignorance vanishes. Its powers become manifest; it becomes perfect. No more is there any necessity for the soul to work through physical bodies, nor is there any necessity for it to work through finer or mental bodies. It shines in its own light and is free, no more to be born, no more to die.

We will not go now into the particulars of this. But I will bring before you one more point with regard to this theory of reincarnation. It is the theory that advances the freedom of the human soul. It is the one theory that does not lay the blame for all our weakness upon somebody else, which is a common human failing. Men in general lay all the blame of life on their fellow men, or, failing that, on God; or they conjure up a ghost and say it is fate.

Where is fate and who is fate? We reap what we sow. We are the makers of our own fate. None else has the blame, none else has the praise. The wind is blowing; those vessels whose sails are unfurled catch it and go forward on their way, but those which have their sails furled do not catch the wind. Is that the fault of the wind? Is it the fault of the merciful Father whose wind of mercy is blowing without ceasing, day and night, whose mercy knows no decay; is it his fault that some of us are happy and some unhappy?

We make our own destiny. His sun shines for the weak as well as for the strong. His wind blows for saint and sinner alike. He is the Lord of all, the Father of all, merciful and impartial. Do you mean to say that he, the Lord of creation, looks upon the petty things of our life in the same light as we do? What a degenerate idea of God that would be! We are like little puppies, making life-and-death struggles here and foolishly thinking that even God himself will take it as seriously as we do. He knows what the puppies' play means. Our attempts to lay the blame on him, making him the punisher and the rewarder, are only foolish. He neither punishes nor rewards any. His infinite mercy is open to everyone, at all times, in all places, under all conditions, unfailing, unswerving. Upon *us* depends how we use it. Upon *us* depends how we utilize it. Blame neither man nor God nor anyone in the world. When you find yourselves suffering, blame yourselves, and try to do better.

The infinite future is before you, and you must always remember that each word, each thought and deed, lays up a store for you, and that as the bad thoughts and bad works are ready to spring upon you like tigers, so also there is the inspiring hope that the good thoughts and good deeds are ready with the power of a hundred thousand angels to defend you always and for ever.

Section 7

Vedanta does not denounce the world. It really means deification of the world—giving up the world as we think of it, as we know it, as it appears to us—and to know what it really is. Deify it; it is God alone.

We have seen how the greater portion of our life must of necessity be filled with evils, however we may resist, and that this mass of evil is practically infinite for us. We have seen also that all religions propose a God as the way of escaping these difficulties. All religions tell us that if you take the world as it is, as most practical people would advise us to do in this age, then nothing would be left to us but evil. They further assert that there is something beyond this world. This life in the five senses, life in the material world, is not all; it is only a small portion, and merely superficial. Behind and beyond is the Infinite, in which there is no more evil. Some people call it God, some Allah, some Jehovah, Jove, and so on. The Vedantist calls it Brahman.

The first impression we get of the advice given by religions is that we had better terminate our existence. To the question as to how to cure the evils of life the answer apparently is, Give up life. It reminds me of the old story. A mosquito settled on the head of a man, and a friend, wishing to kill the mosquito, gave it such a blow that he killed both man and mosquito. The remedy of evil seems to suggest a similar course of action. Life is full of ills; the world is full of evil. That is a fact no one who is old enough to know the world can deny.

But what is the remedy proposed by all the religions? That this world is nothing; beyond this world is something which is very real. Here comes the difficulty. The remedy seems to destroy everything. I beg to state that in Vedanta alone we find a rational solution of the problem. I lay before you what Vedanta seeks to teach, and that is the deification of the world.

Vedanta does not in reality denounce the world. The ideal of renunciation nowhere attains such a height as in the teachings of Vedanta; but at the same time, dry suicidal advice is not intended. It really means deification of the world—giving up the world as we think of it, as we know it, as it appears to us—and knowing what it really is. Deify it; it is God alone.

We read at the commencement of one of the oldest of the Upanishads; 'Whatever exists in this universe is to be covered with the Lord.' We have to cover everything with the Lord himself, not by a false kind of optimism, not by blinding our eyes to the evil, but by really seeing God in everything. Thus we have to give up the world, and when the world is given up, what remains? God. What is meant? You can have your wife; it does not mean that you are to abandon her, but that you are to see God in the wife. Give up your children —what does that mean? To turn them out of doors, as some human brutes do in every country? Certainly not. That is diabolism; it is not religion. But see God in your children. So in everything. In life and in death, in happiness and in misery, the Lord is equally present. The whole world is full of the Lord. Open your eyes and see him. That is what Vedanta teaches.

Give up the world which you have conjectured, because your conjecture was based upon a very partial experience, upon very poor reasoning, and upon your own weakness. Give it up. The world we have been thinking of so long, the world to which we have been clinging to so long, is a false world of our own creation. Give that up. Open your eyes and see that, as such, it never existed; it was a dream, maya. What existed was the Lord himself. It is he who is in the child, in the **wife, and in the** husband; it is he who is in the good and in the bad. He is in the sin and in the sinner. He is in life and in death.

A tremendous assertion indeed! Yet that is the theme which Vedanta wants to demonstrate, to teach, and to preach.

Thus we avoid the dangers of life and its evils. Do not desire anything. What makes us miserable? The cause of all miseries from which we suffer is desire. You desire something, and the desire is not fulfilled; the result is distress. If there is no desire, there is no suffering. Here there is danger of my being misunderstood. So it is necessary to explain what I mean by giving up desire and becoming free from all misery. The walls have no desires and they never suffer. True, but they never evolve. This chair has no desires; it never suffers; but it is always a chair. There is glory in happiness; there is glory in suffering. If I may dare to say so, there is utility in evil too. The great lesson in misery we all know. There are hundreds of things we have done in our lives which we wish we had never done, but which, at the same time, have been great teachers. As for me, I am glad I have done something good and many things bad; glad I have done something right, and glad I have committed many errors; because every one of them has been a great lesson. I, as I am now, am the resultant of all I have done, all I have thought. Every action and thought have had their effect, and these effects are the sum total of my progress.

We all understand that desires are wrong, but what is meant by giving up desires? How could life go on? It would be the same suicidal advice—killing the desire and the man too. The solution is this: not that you should not have property, not that you should not have things which are necessary and things which are even luxuries. Have all that you want and more. Only know the truth and realize it. Wealth does not belong to anybody. Have no idea of proprietorship, possession. You are nobody, nor am I, nor anyone else. All belongs to the Lord. God is in the wealth that you enjoy. He is in the desire that rises in your mind. He is in the things you buy to satisfy your desire. He is in your beautiful attire, in your beautiful ornaments. This is the line of thought. All will be metamorphosed as soon as you begin to see things in that light. If you put God in your every move-ment, in your conversation, in your form, in everything, the whole scene changes, and the world, instead of appearing as one of woe and misery, will become a heaven.

If we understand the giving up of the world in its old, crude sense, then it would come to this, that we must not work, that we must be idle, sitting like lumps of earth, neither thinking nor doing anything, but must become fatalists, driven about by every circumstance, ordered about by the laws of nature, drifting from place to place. That would be the result. But that is not what is meant. We must work. Ordinary men, driven every-where by false desire—what do they know of work? The man impelled by his own feelings and his own senses—what does he know about work? He works who is not impelled by his own desires, by any selfishness whatsoever. He works who has no ulterior motive in view. He works who has nothing to gain from work.

Who enjoys the picture, the seller or the seer? The seller is busy with his accounts, computing what his gain will be, how much profit he will realize from the picture. His brain is full of that. He is looking at the hammer and watching the bids. He is intent on hearing how fast the bids are rising. That man is enjoying the picture who has gone there without any intention of buying or selling. He looks at the picture and enjoys it.

So do your work, says Vedanta. It first advises us how to work; by giving up—giving up the apparent, illusive world. What is meant by that? Seeing God everywhere. Thus do you work. Desire to live a hundred years; have all earthly desires, if you wish; only deify them, convert them into heaven. Have the desire to live a long life of helpfulness, of blissfulness and activity on this earth. Thus working, you will find the way out. There is no other way. If a man plunges headlong into foolish luxuries of the world without knowing the truth, he has missed his footing; he cannot reach the goal. And if a man curses the world, goes into a forest, mortifies his flesh, and kills himself little by little by starvation, makes his heart a barren waste, kills out all feeling, and becomes harsh, stern, and dried up, that man also has missed the way.

These are the two extremes, the two mistakes at either end. Both have lost the way, both have missed the goal.

So work, says Vedanta, putting God in everything and knowing him to be in everything. Work incessantly, holding life to be something deified, as God himself, and knowing that this is all we have to do, this is all we should ask for. God is in everything; where else shall we go to find him? He is already in every work, in every thought, in every feeling. Thus knowing, we must work. This is the only way; there is no other. Thus the effects of work will not bind us. We have seen how false desires are the cause of all the misery and evil we suffer; but when they are thus deified, purified, through God, they bring no evil, they bring no misery. Those who have not learned this secret will have to live in a demoniacal world until they discover it. Many do not know what an infinite mine of bliss is in them, around them, everywhere; they have not yet discovered it. What is a demoniacal world? Ignorance, says Vedanta.

More questions arise. It is very easy to talk. From my childhood I have heard of seeing God everywhere and in everything, and then I can really enjoy the world. But as soon as I mix with the world and get a few blows from it, the idea vanishes. I am walking in the street thinking that God is in every man, and a strong man comes along and gives me a push and I fall flat on the footpath. Then I rise up quickly with clenched fist, the blood has rushed to my head, and the reflection goes. Immediately I have become mad. Everything is forgotten; instead of encountering God I see the Devil. Ever since we were born we have been told to see God in all. Every religion teaches that—see God in everything and everywhere. We have all been taught that; but it is when we come to the practical side that the difficulty begins.

You remember how in *Aesop's Fables* a fine stag is looking at his form reflected in a lake and is saying to his young one, 'How powerful I am! Look at my splendid head; look at my limbs. How strong and muscular they are! And how swiftly I can run!' Then he hears the barking of dogs in the distance and immediately takes to his heels; and after he has run several miles he comes back panting.

The young one says, 'You just told me how strong

you were. How was it that when the dogs barked you ran away?'

'Yes, my son; but when the dogs bark all my confidence vanishes.'

Such is the case with us. We think highly of humanity, we feel ourselves strong and valiant, we make grand resolves; but when the dogs of trial and temptation bark, we are like the stag in the fable.

Then, if such is the case, what is the use of all these things? There is the greatest use. The use is this, that perseverance will finally conquer. The vast majority of persons are groping through this dark life without any ideal at all. If a man with an ideal makes a thousand mistakes, I am sure that the man without an ideal makes fifty thousand.

It is thought which is the propelling force in us. Fill the mind with the highest thoughts, hear them day after day, think them month after month. Never mind failure, they are quite natural. They are the beauty of life, these failures. What would life be without them? It would not be worth having if it were not for struggles. Where would be the poetry of life? Never mind the struggle, the mistakes. I never heard a cow tell a lie; but it is only a cow—never a man.

So never mind these failures, these little backslidings. Hold the ideal a thousand times, and if you fail a thousand times, make the attempt once more. The ideal of man is to see God in everything. But if you cannot see him in everything, see him in one thing, in that thing which you like best, and then see him in another. So on you can go. There is infinite life before the soul. Take your time and you will achieve your end.

3

SELF-REALIZATION THROUGH KNOWLEDGE

First, meditation should be of a negative nature. Think away everything. Analyse everything that comes in the mind by the sheer action of the will.

Next, assert what we really are—Existence, Knowledge, and Bliss—Being, Knowing, and Loving.

Meditation is the means of unification of the subject and object.

Meditate: Above it is full of me, below it is full of me, in the middle it is full of me. I am in all beings, and all beings are in me. *Om Tat Sat*, I am it. I am existence above mind. I am the one Spirit of the universe. I am neither pleasure nor pain.

The body drinks, eats, and so on. I am not the body. I am not the mind. I am He.

I am the witness. I look on. When health comes I am the witness. When disease comes I am the witness.

I am Existence, Knowledge, Bliss.

I am the essence and nectar of knowledge. Through eternity I change not. I am calm, resplendent, and unchanging.

Thus man, after this vain search after various gods outside himself, completes the circle and finds that the God whom he was imagining as sitting in heaven and ruling the world, is his own Self. None but I was God, and this little 'I' never existed.

FROM THE MOST ANCIENT times there have been various sects of thought in India, and as there never was a formulated or recognized church or body of men to designate the doctrines which should be believed by each school, people were very free to choose their own form, make their own philosophy, and establish their own sects.

The first school I will tell you about is styled the dualistic school. The dualists believe that God, who is the Creator of the universe and its Ruler, is eternally separate from nature, eternally separate from the human soul. God is eternal; nature is eternal; so are all souls. Nature and the souls become manifested and change, but God remains the same. According to the dualists, again this God is personal, in that he has qualities, not that he has a body. He has human attributes. He is merciful, he is just, he is powerful, he is almighty, he can be approached, he can be prayed to, he can be loved, he loves in return, and so forth. In one word, he is a human God, only infinitely greater than man; he has none of the evil qualities which man have. He cannot create without materials, and nature is the material out of which he creates the whole universe.

The vast mass of Indian people are dualists. All the

religions of Europe and western Asia are dualistic; they
have to be. The ordinary man cannot think of anything
which is not concrete. He naturally likes to cling to
that which his intellect can grasp. This is the religion
of the masses all over the world. They believe in a God
who is entirely separate from them, a great king, a
high, mighty monarch as it were. At the same time they
make him purer than the monarchs of the earth; they
give him all good qualities and remove the evil qualities
from him—as if it were ever possible for good to exist
without evil; as if there could be any conception of
light without a conception of darkness!

With all dualistic theories the first difficulty is: How
is it possible that, under the rule of a just and merciful
God, there can be so many evils in this world? This
question arose in all dualistic religions; but the Hindus
never invented a Satan as an answer to it. The Hindus
with one accord laid the blame on man, and it was easy
for them to do so. Why? Because they did not believe
that souls were created out of nothing.

We see in this life that we can shape and form our
future; every one of us, every day, is trying to shape
the morrow. Today we fix the fate of the morrow; tomorrow we shall fix the fate of the day after; and so
on. It is quite logical that this reasoning can be pushed
backwards too. If by our own deeds we shape our destiny
in the future, why not apply the same rule to the past?
If, in an infinite chain, a certain number of links are
alternately repeated, then if one of these groups of links
be explained, we can explain the whole chain. So in this
infinite length of time, if we can cut off one portion and
explain that portion and understand it, then, if it be true
that nature is uniform, the same explanation must apply

to the whole chain of time. If it be true that we are working out our own destiny here within this short space of time, if it be true that everything must have a cause, as we see it now, it must also be true that that which we are now is the effect of the whole of our past.

Therefore no other person is necessary to shape the destiny of mankind but man himself. The evils that are in the world are caused by none else but ourselves. We have caused all this evil; and just as we constantly see misery resulting from evil actions, so can we also see that much of the existing misery in the world is the effect of the past wickedness of man. Man alone, therefore, according to this theory, is responsible. God is not to blame. He, the eternally merciful Father, is not to blame at all. 'We reap what we sow.'

Another doctrine of the dualists is that every soul must eventually come to salvation. No one will be left out. Through various vicissitudes, through various sufferings and enjoyments, each one of them will come out in the end. Come out of what? The one common idea is that all souls have to get out of this universe. Neither the universe which we see and feel, nor even an imaginary one, can be right, the real one, because both are mixed up with good and evil. According to the dualists there is beyond this universe a place full of happiness and good only, and when that place is reached there will be no more necessity of being born and reborn, of living and dying; and this idea is very dear to them. No more disease there, and no more death. There will be eternal happiness, and they will be in the presence of God for all time and enjoy him for ever. They believe that all beings, from the lowest worm up to the highest angels and gods, will all, sooner or later, attain to that world where there will be no more misery. But our world will never end; it goes on infinitely, although moving in waves. Although moving in cycles, it never ends. The number of souls that are to be saved, that are to be perfected, is infinite.

The real Vedanta philosophy begins with those known as the qualified non-dualists. They make the statement that the effect is never different from the cause; the effect is but the cause reproduced in another form. If the universe is the effect and God the cause, it must be God himself—it cannot be anything but that. They start with the assertion that God is both the efficient and the material cause of the universe; that he himself is the Creator, and he himself is the material out of which the whole of nature is projected. The word 'creation' in your language has no equivalent in Sanskrit, because there is no sect in India which believes in creation, as it is regarded in the West, as something coming out of nothing. What we mean by creation is projection of that which already existed.

Now the whole universe, according to this sect, is God himself. He is the material of the universe. We read in the Vedas, 'As the spider spins the thread out of its own body, even so the whole universe has come out of that Being.' If the effect is the cause reproduced, the question is: How is it that we find this material, dull, unintelligent universe produced from God who is not material, but who is eternal intelligence; how, if the cause is pure and perfect, can the effect be quite different?

What do these qualified non-dualists say? Theirs is a very peculiar theory. They say that these three—God, nature, and the soul—are one. God is, as it were, the soul, and nature and souls are the body of God. Just as I have a body and I have a soul, so the whole universe and all souls are the body of God, and God is the Soul of souls. Thus, God is the material cause of the universe. The body may be changed—may be young or old, strong or weak—but that does not affect the soul at all. It is the same eternal existence, manifesting through the body. Bodies come and go, but the soul does not change. Even so the whole universe is the body of God, and in that sense it is God. But the change in the universe does not affect God. Out of this material he creates the universe, and at the end of a cycle his body becomes finer, it contracts; at the beginning of another cycle it becomes expanded again, and out of it evolve all these different worlds.

Now both the dualists and the qualified non-dualists admit that the soul is by its nature pure, but through its own deeds it becomes impure. The qualified non-dualists express it more beautifully than the dualists, by saying that the soul's purity and perfection become contracted and again become manifest, and that what we are now trying to do is to remanifest the intelligence, the purity, the power which is natural to the soul. Every wicked deed contracts the nature of the soul, and every good deed expands it; and these souls are all parts of God. 'As from a blazing fire fly millions of sparks of the same nature, even so from this infinite being, God, these souls have come.' Each has the same goal. The God of the qualified non-dualists is also a personal God, only he is interpenetrating everything in the universe. He is immanent in everything and is everywhere; and when the scriptures say that God is everything, it means that

God is interpenetrating everything, not that God has become the wall, but that God is in the wall. There is not a particle, not an atom in the universe, where he is not. Souls are all limited; they are not omnipresent. When they get expansion of their powers and become perfect, there is no more birth and death for them; they live with God for ever.

Now we come to advaitism, the last and what we think is the fairest flower of philosophy and religion that any country in any age has produced, where human thought attains its highest expression, and even goes beyond the mystery which seems to be impenetrable. That is the non-dualistic Vedanta. It is too abstruse, too elevated, to be the religion of the masses. Even in India, its birthplace, where it has been ruling supreme for the last three thousand years, it has not been able to permeate the masses.

As we go on we shall find that it is difficult for even the most thoughtful man and woman in any country to understand advaitism—we have made ourselves so weak; we have made ourselves so low. How many times I have been asked for a 'comfortable religion'! Very few men ask for the truth, fewer still dare to learn the truth, and fewest of all dare to follow it in all its practical bearings. It is not their fault; it is all weakness of the brain. Any new thought, especially of a high kind, creates a disturbance, tries to make a new channel, as it were, in the brain matter, and that unhinges the system, throws men off their balance. They are used to certain surroundings and have to overcome a huge mass of ancient superstitions, ancestral superstition, class superstition, city superstition, country superstition, and behind all, the vast mass of superstition that is innate in every human being. Yet there are a few brave souls in the world who dare to conceive the truth, who dare to take it up, and who dare to follow it to the end.

What does the advaitist declare? He says: If there is a God, that God must be both the material and the efficient cause of the universe. Not only is he the Creator, but he is also the created. He himself is this universe.

How can that be? God, the pure, the spirit, has become the universe? Yes—apparently so. That which all ignorant people see as the universe does not really exist. What are you and I and all these things we see? Mere self-hypnotism. There is but one Existence, the infinite, the ever-blessed One. In that Existence we dream all these various dreams. It is the Atman beyond all, the infinite, beyond the known, beyond the knowable; in and through that we see the universe. It is the only reality. It is this table; it is the wall; it is everything— minus the name and form. Take away the form of the table, take away the name; what remains is it. The Vedantist does not call it either he or she—these are fictions, delusions of the human brain. There is no sex in the soul. People who are under illusion, who have become like animals, see a woman or a man; living gods do not see men or women. How can they who are beyond everything have any sex idea? Everyone and everything is the Atman, the Self—sexless, pure, ever blessed. It is the name, the form, the body, which are material, and they make all this difference. If you take away these two differences of name and form, the whole universe is one; there are not two, but one everywhere. You and I are one. There is neither nature nor God nor the universe—only that one infinite Existence, out of which, through name and form, all these are manufactured.

How to know the Knower? It cannot be known. How can you see your own self? You can only reflect yourself. So all this universe is the reflection of that one eternal being, the Atman; and as the reflection falls upon good or bad reflectors, so good or bad images are cast up. Thus in the murderer the reflector is bad and not the Self. In the saint the reflector is pure. The Self, the Atman, is by its own nature pure. It is the same, the one Existence of the universe, that is reflecting itself from the lowest worm to the highest and most perfect being. The whole of this universe is one unity, one Existence, physically, mentally, morally, and spiritually. We are looking upon this one Existence in different forms and creating all these images upon it. To the being who has limited himself to the condition of man, it appears as the world of man. To the being who is on a higher plane of existence, it may seem like heaven. There is but one soul in the universe, not two. It neither comes nor goes. It neither is born nor dies nor reincarnates. How can it die? Where can it go? All these heavens, all these earths, are vain imaginations of the mind. They do not exist, never existed in the past, and never will exist in the future.

I am omnipresent, eternal. Where can I go? Where am I not already? I am reading this book of nature. Page after page I am finishing and turning over, and one dream of life after another goes away. Another page of life is turned over; another dream of life comes, and it goes away, rolling and rolling. And when I have finished my reading I let go and stand aside. I throw away the book, and the whole thing is finished.

What does the advaitist preach? He dethrones all the gods that ever existed or ever will exist in the universe and places on that throne the Self of man, the Atman, higher than the sun and the moon, higher than the heavens, greater than this great universe itself. No books, no scriptures, no science can ever imagine the glory of the Self that appears as man—the most glorious God that ever was, the only God that ever existed, exists, or ever will exist.

I am to worship, therefore, none but my Self. 'I worship my Self', says the advaitist. 'To whom shall I bow down? I salute my Self. To whom shall I go for help? Who can help me, the infinite Being of the universe?' These are foolish dreams, hallucinations. Who ever helped anyone? None. Wherever you see a weak man, a dualist, weeping and wailing for help from somewhere above the skies, it is because he does not know that the skies also are in him. He wants help from the skies, and the help comes. We see that it comes; but it comes from within himself, and he mistakes it as coming from without. Sometimes a sick man lying on his bed may hear a tap on the door. He gets up and opens it and finds no one there. He goes back to bed, and again he hears a tap. He gets up and opens the door. Nobody is there. At last he finds that it was his own heartbeat which he fancied was a knock at the door.

Thus man, after this vain search after various gods outside himself, completes the circle and comes back to the point from which he started—the human soul; and he finds that the God whom he was searching for over hill and dale, whom he was seeking in every brook, in every temple, in churches and heavens, that God whom he was even imagining as sitting in heaven and ruling the world, is his own Self. I am he, and he is I. None but I was God, and this little 'I' never existed.

Yet how could that perfect God have been deluded? He never was. How could a perfect God have been dreaming? He never dreamed. Truth never dreams. The very question as to whence this illusion arose is absurd. Illusion arises from illusion alone. There will be no illusion as soon as the truth is seen. Illusion always rests upon illusion; it never rests upon God, the Truth, the Atman. You are never in illusion; it is illusion that is in you, before you. A cloud is here; another comes and pushes it aside and take its place; still another comes and pushes that one away. As before the eternal blue sky clouds of various hue and colour come, remain for a short time and disappear, leaving it the same eternal blue, even so are you eternally pure, eternally perfect.

You are the veritable Gods of the universe. Nay, there are not two; there is but one. It is a mistake to say 'you' and 'I'. Say 'I'. It is I who am eating through millions of mouths; how can I be hungry? It is I who am working through an infinite number of hands; how can I be inactive? It is I who am living the life of the whole universe; where is death for me? I am beyond all life, beyond all death. Where shall I seek for freedom? For I am free by my nature. Who can bind me, the God of the universe? The scriptures of the world are but little maps, wanting to delineate my glory, who am the only Existence of the universe. Then what are these books to me? Thus says the advaitist.

'Know the truth and be free in a moment.' All the darkness will then vanish. When man has seen himself as one with the infinite Being of the universe; when all separateness has ceased; when all men and women, all gods and angels, all animals and plants, and the whole universe have melted into that Oneness, then all fear disappears. Can I hurt myself? Can I kill myself? Can I injure myself? Whom to fear? Can you fear yourself? Then will all sorrow disappear. What can cause me sorrow? I am the one Existence of the universe. Then all jealousies will disappear. Of whom to be jealous? Of myself? Then will all bad feelings disappear. Against whom can I have bad feeling? Against myself? There is none in the universe but me.

And this is the one way, says the Vedantist, to knowledge. Kill out this differentiation, kill out this superstition that there are many. 'He who in this world of many sees that One; he who in this mass of insentience sees that one sentient Being; he who in this world of shadows catches that Reality—unto him belongs eternal peace, unto none else, unto none else.'

These are the salient points of the three steps which Indian religious thought has taken in regard to God. We have seen that it began with the personal, the extra-cosmic God. It went from the external to the immanent God, God immanent in the universe. And it ended in identifying the soul itself with that God, and making one Soul, a unit, of all these various manifestations in the universe. This is the last word of the Vedas. Indian religious thought begins with dualism, goes through a qualified non-dualism, and ends in perfect non-dualism.

We know how very few in this world can come to the last, or even dare believe in it, and fewer still dare act according to it. Yet we know that therein lies the explanation of all ethics, of all morality, and of all spirituality in the universe. Why is it that everyone says, 'Do good to others'? Where is the explanation? Why is it that all great men have preached the brotherhood of mankind, and greater men, the brotherhood of all lives? Because, whether they were conscious of it or not, beyond all that, through all their irrational and personal superstitions, was peering forth the eternal light of the Self, denying all manifoldness, and asserting that the whole universe is but One.

Again, the last word gave us one universe, which through the senses we see as matter, through the intellect as souls, and through the Spirit as God. To the man who throws upon himself veils, which the world calls wickedness and evil, this very universe will change and become a hideous place; to another man, who wants enjoyments, this very universe will change in appearance and become a heaven; and to the perfect man the whole thing will vanish and become his own Self.

Now, as society exists at the present time, all these three stages are necessary. The one does not deny the other; one is simply the fulfilment of the other. The advaitist or the qualified advaitist does not say that dualism is wrong; it is a right view, but a lower one. It is on the way to truth. Therefore let everybody work out his own vision of this universe according to his own ideas. Injure none, deny the position of none. Take man where he stands, and if you can, lend him a helping hand and put him on a higher platform; but do not injure and do not destroy. All will come to truth in the long run. 'When all the desires of the heart will be vanquished, then this very mortal will become immortal.' Then the very man will become God.

Section 2

This is the only way to reach the goal, to tell ourselves and to tell everybody else that we are divine. And as we go on repeating this, strength comes.

Although all the systems agree that we had the empire and that we have lost it, they give us varied advice as to how to regain it. One says that you must perform certain ceremonies, pay certain sums of money to certain idols, eat certain sorts of food, live in a peculiar fashion, to regain that empire. Another says that if you weep and prostrate yourselves and ask pardon of some Being beyond nature, you will regain that empire. Again, another says if you love such a Being with all your heart, you will regain that empire.

But the last and the greatest counsel is that you need not weep at all. You need not go through all these ceremonies and need not take any notice of how to regain your empire, because you never lost it. Why should you go to seek for what you never lost? You are pure already, you are free already. If you think you are free, free you are this moment, and if you think you are bound, bound you will be.

This is a very bold statement. It may frighten you now, but when you think it over and realize it in your own life, then you will come to know that what I say is true. For, supposing that freedom is not your nature, by no manner of means can you become free. Supposing you were free and in some way you lost that freedom, that shows that you were not free to begin with. Had you been free, what could have made you lose it? The independent can never be made dependent; if it is really dependent, its independence was an hallucination.

Of the two sides, then, which will you take? If you say that the soul was by its own nature pure and free, it naturally follows that there was nothing in this universe which could make it bound or limited. But if there was anything in nature which could bind the soul, it naturally follows that it was not free, and your statement that it was free is a delusion. So if it is possible for us to attain to freedom, the conclusion is inevitable that the soul is by its nature free. It cannot be otherwise.

Freedom means independence of anything outside, and that means that nothing outside itself could work upon it as a cause. The soul is causeless, and from this follow all the great ideas that we have. You cannot establish the immortality of the soul unless you grant that it is by its nature free, or in other words, that it cannot be acted upon by anything outside. For death is an effect produced by some outside cause. I drink poison and I die, thus showing that my body can be acted upon by something outside that is called poison. But if it be true that the soul is free, it naturally follows that nothing can affect it and it can never die. Freedom, immortality, blessedness, all depend upon the soul being beyond the law of causation, beyond maya.

Of these two which will you take? Either make the first a delusion, or make the second a delusion. Certainly I will make the second a delusion. It is more consonant with all my feelings and aspirations. I am perfectly aware that I am free by nature, and I will not admit that this bondage is true and my freedom a delusion.

This discussion goes on in all philosophies, in some form or other. Even in the most modern philosophies you find the same discussion. There are two parties.

One says that there is no soul, that the idea of soul is a delusion produced by the repeated transit of particles of matter, bringing about the combination which you call the body or the brain; that the impression of freedom is the result of the vibrations and motions and continuous transit of these particles. There were Buddhist sects who held the same view and illustrated it by this example: If you take a torch and whirl it round rapidly, there will be a circle of light. That circle does not really exist, because the torch is changing place every moment. We are but bundles of little particles, which in their rapid whirling produce the delusion of a permanent soul.

The other party states that in the rapid succession of thought, matter occurs as a delusion, and does not really exist.

So we see one side claiming that spirit is a delusion and the other that matter is a delusion. Which side will you take? Of course we will take the spirit and deny matter. The arguments are similar for both, only on the spirit side the argument is a little stronger. For nobody has ever seen what matter is. We can only feel ourselves. I never knew a man who could feel matter by going outside of himself. Therefore the argument is a little stronger on the side of the spirit. Secondly, the spirit theory explains the universe, while materialism does not. Hence the materialistic explanation is illogical. If you boil down all the philosophies and analyse them, you will find that they are reduced to one or the other of these two positions.

So here, too, in a more intricate form, in a more philosophical form, we find the same question about freedom and bondage. One side says that the first is a delusion, and the other, that the second is a delusion.

And of course, we side with the second in believing that our bondage is a delusion.

The solution of Vedanta is that we are not bound, we are free already. Not only so, but to say or to think that we are bound is dangerous; it is a mistake, it is self-hypnotism. As soon as you say, 'I am bound', 'I am weak', 'I am helpless', woe unto you! You rivet one more chain upon yourself. Do not say it; do not think it. I have heard of a man who lived in a forest and used to repeat day and night, '*Shivoham*'—'I am the Blessed One' —and one day a tiger fell upon him and dragged him away to kill him. People on the other side of the river saw it and heard the voice, so long as voice remained in him, saying, 'Shivoham'—even in the very jaws of the tiger. There have been many such men. There have been men who, while being cut to pieces, have blessed their enemies. 'I am He, I am He; and so art thou. I am pure and perfect, and so are all my enemies. You are He, and so am I.' That is the position of strength.

There are great and wonderful things in the religions of the dualists. Wonderful is the idea of the Personal God apart from nature, whom we worship and love. Sometimes this idea is very soothing. But, says the Vedantist, that soothing is something like the effect that comes from an opiate, not natural. It brings weakness in the long run, and what this world wants today more than it ever did before is strength. It is weakness, says Vedanta, which is the cause of all misery in the world. Weakness is the one cause of suffering. We become miserable because we are weak. We lie, steal, kill, and commit other crimes because we are weak. We suffer because we are weak. We die because we are weak.

Where there is nothing to weaken us, there is no death or sorrow. We are miserable through delusion. Give up the delusion and the whole thing vanishes. It is plain and simple indeed. Through all these philosophical discussions and tremendous mental gymnastics we come to this one religious idea, the simplest in the whole world.

There is one idea which often militates against it. It is this: It is all very well to say, 'I am Pure, the Blessed', but I cannot show it always in my life. That is true; the ideal is always very hard. Every child that is born sees the sky overhead very far away, but is that any reason why we should not look towards the sky? Would it mend matters to go towards superstition? If we cannot get nectar, would it mend matters for us to drink poison? Would it be any help for us, because we cannot realize the truth immediately, to go into darkness and yield to weakness and superstition?

I have no objection to dualism in many of its forms. I like most of them, but I have objections to every form of teaching which inculcates weakness. This is the one question I put to every man, woman, or child who is in physical, mental, or spiritual training: 'Are you strong? Do you feel strength?'—for I know it is Truth alone that gives strength. I know that Truth alone gives life, and nothing but going towards Reality will make us strong, and that none will reach Truth until he is strong. Any system, therefore, which weakens the mind, makes one superstitious, makes one mope, makes one desire all sorts of wild impossibilities, mysteries, and superstitions, I do not like, because its effect is dangerous. Such systems never bring any good; such things create morbidity in the mind, make it weak, so weak that in course of time it will be almost impossible to receive Truth or live up to it.

Strength, therefore, is the one thing needful. Strength is the medicine for the world's disease. Strength is the medicine which the poor must have when tyrannized over by the rich. Strength is the medicine that the ignorant must have when oppressed by the learned; and it is the medicine that sinners must have when tyrannized over by other sinners. And nothing gives such strength as this idea of monism; nothing makes us so moral as this idea of monism. Nothing makes us work so well, at our best and highest, as when all the responsibility is thrown upon ourselves.

I challenge every one of you. How will you behave if I put a little baby in your hands? Your whole life will be changed for the moment; whatever you may be, you must become selfless for the time being. You will give up all your criminal ideas as soon as responsibility is thrown upon you; your whole character will change. So if the whole responsibility is thrown upon our own shoulders, we shall be at our highest and best. When we have nobody to grope towards, no Devil to lay our blame upon, no Personal God to carry our burdens, when we are alone responsible, then we shall rise to our highest and best. 'I am responsible for my fate, I am the bringer of good unto myself, I am the bringer of evil. I am the Pure and Blessed One.'

This, says Vedanta, is the only prayer that we should have. This is the only way to reach the goal, to tell ourselves and to tell everybody else that we are divine. And as we go on repeating this, strength comes. He who falters at first will get stronger and stronger, and the voice will increase in volume until the truth takes possession of our hearts and courses through our veins and permeates our bodies. Delusion will vanish as the light becomes more and more effulgent, load after load of ignorance will vanish, and then will come a time when all else has disappeared and the Sun alone shines.

Section 3

Are any practices necessary to realize this Oneness? Most decidedly. This delusion which says that you are Mr So-and-so or Mrs So-and-so can be got rid of by another delusion, and that is practice. Fire will eat fire, and you can use one delusion to conquer another delusion.

The Self, the Knower, the Lord of all, the real Being, is the cause of all the vision that is in the universe; but it is impossible for him to see himself, except through reflection. You cannot see your own face except in a mirror; and just so the Self cannot see its own nature until it is reflected; and this whole universe therefore is the Self trying to realize itself. This reflection is thrown back first from the protoplasm, then from plants and animals, and so on and on from better and better reflectors, until the best reflector—the perfect man—is reached; just as a man who, wanting to see his face, looks first in a little pool of muddy water, and sees just an outline, then comes to clear water and he sees a better image, then to a piece of shining metal and sees a still better image, and at last to a looking glass, and sees himself reflected as he is. Therefore the perfect man is the highest reflection of that Being, who is both subject and object.

You now find why man instinctively worships everything, and why perfect men are instinctively worshipped as God in every country. You may talk as you like, but it is they who are bound to be worshipped. That is why men worship Incarnations, such as Christ or Buddha. They are the most perfect manifestations of the eternal Self. They are much higher than all the conceptions of God that you or I can make. A perfect man is much higher than such conceptions. In him the circle becomes complete; the subject and the object become one. In him all delusions go away, and in their place comes the realization that he has always been that perfect Being.

I was once travelling in the desert in India. I travelled for over a month and always found the most beautiful landscapes before me, beautiful lakes and all that. One day I was very thirsty and I wanted to have a drink at one of these lakes, but when I approached that lake it vanished. Immediately with a blow came into my brain the idea that this was a mirage, about which I had read all my life; and then I remembered and smiled at my folly, that for the last month all the beautiful landscapes and lakes I had been seeing were this mirage, but I could not distinguish them then. The next morning I again began my march. There was the lake and the landscape, but with it immediately came the idea, 'This is a mirage.' Once known it had lost its power of illusion.

So this illusion of the universe will break one day. The whole of this will vanish, melt away. This is realization. Philosophy is no joke or talk. It has to be realized. This body will vanish, this earth and everything will vanish, this idea that I am the body or the mind will some time vanish. If the karma is ended it will disappear, never to come back; but if part of the karma remains, the body, even after the delusion has vanished, will continue to function for some time—like a potter's wheel, which keeps turning by its own momentum even after the pot has been shaped. Again this world will come, men and women and animals will come, just as the mirage came the next day, but not with the same force; along with it will come the idea that I know its nature now, and it will cause no bondage, no more pain or grief or misery. Whenever anything miserable will come, the mind will be able to say, 'I know you as hallucination.'

When a man has reached that state he is called *jivan-mukta*, 'living-free', free even while living. The aim and end in this life for the jnana-yogi is to become this jivan-mukta, 'living-free'. He is jivanmukta who can live in this world without being attached. He is like the lotus leaves in water, which are never wetted by the water. He is the highest of human beings, nay, the highest of all beings; for he has realized his identity with the Absolute, he has realized that he is one with God.

What will become of the world then? What good shall we do to the world? Such questions do not arise. 'What becomes of my ginger-bread if I become old?' says the baby. 'What becomes of my marbles if I grow up; so I will not grow up!' says the boy. 'What will become of my dolls if I grow old?' says the little child. It is the same question in connection with this world; it has no existence in the past, present, or future. If we have known the Atman as it is, if we have known that there is nothing else but this Atman, that everything else is but a dream, with no existence in reality, then this world with its poverties, its miseries, its wickedness, and its goodness will cease to disturb us. If they do not exist, for whom and for what shall we take trouble? This is what the jnana-yogis teach.

Before going into the practical part, we will take up one more intellectual question. So far the logic is tremendously rigorous. If man reasons, there is no place for him to stand until he comes to this: that there is but one Existence, that everything else is nothing. There is no other way left for rational mankind but to take this view. But how is it that what is infinite, ever perfect, ever blessed, Existence-Knowledge-Bliss Absolute, has come under these delusions? It is the same question that has been asked all the world over. In the vulgar form the question becomes, 'How did sin come into this world?' This is the most vulgar and sensuous form of the question, and the other is the most philosophic form; but the question is the same. The same question has been asked in various grades and fashions, but in its lower forms it finds no solution, because the stories of apples and serpents and women do not give the explanation. In that state the question is childish and so is the answer.

But the question has assumed a high philosophic form: 'How did this illusion come?' And the answer is as fine. The answer is that we cannot expect any answer to an impossible question. The very question is self-contradictory. You have no right to ask that question. Why? What is perfection? That which is beyond time, space, and causation. That is perfect. Then you ask how the perfect became imperfect. In logical language the question may be put in this form: 'How did that which is beyond causation become caused?' You contradict yourself. You first admit it is beyond causation and then ask what causes it. That question can only be asked within the limits of causation. As far as time and space and causation extend, so far can this question be asked. But beyond that it will be nonsense to ask it, because the question is illogical. Within time, space and causation it can never be answered, and what answer may lie beyond these limits can only be known when we have transcended them; therefore the wise will let this question rest. When a man is ill, he devotes himself to curing his disease, without insisting that he must first learn how he came to have it.

There is another answer on not quite such a highly philosophical plane. Can any reality produce delusion? Certainly not. We see that one delusion produces another, and so on. It is delusion always that produces delusion. It is disease that produces disease, and not health that produces disease. The wave is the same thing as the water; the effect is the cause in another form. The effect is delusion, and therefore the cause must be delusion. What produced this delusion? Another delusion. And so on without beginning. The only question that remains for you to ask is: Does not this break your monism, because you get two existences in the universe —one the Self, and the other the delusion? The answer is: Delusion cannot be called an existence. Thousands of dreams come into your life but do not form any part of your life. Dreams come and go; they have no existence. To call delusion existence will be sophistry. Therefore there is only one indivisible Existence in the universe, ever free and ever blessed, and that is what you are. This is the last conclusion reached by the advaitists.

It may then be asked: What becomes of all these various forms of worship? They will remain. They are simply groping in the dark for light, and through this groping light will come.

We have just seen that the Self cannot see itself. Our knowledge is within the network of maya, unreality, and beyond that is freedom. Within the network there is slavery; it is all under law. Beyond that there is no law. So far as the universe is concerned, existence is ruled by law; and beyond that is freedom. As long as you are in the network of time, space, and causation, to say you are free is nonsense, because in that network all is under rigorous law. Every thought that you think is caused, every feeling has been caused; to say that the will is free is sheer nonsense. It is only when the infinite Existence comes, as it were, into this network of maya that it takes the form of will. Will is a portion of that Being, caught in the network of maya; and therefore free will is a misnomer. It means nothing—sheer nonsense. So is all this talk about freedom. There is no freedom in maya. There is no freedom until you go beyond maya. That is the real freedom of the soul.

Men, however sharp and intellectual they may be, however clearly they see the force of the logic that nothing here can be free, are all compelled to think they are free; they cannot help it. No work can go on until we begin to say we are free. It means that the freedom we talk about is the glimpse of the blue sky through the clouds, and that the real freedom—the blue sky itself—is behind. True freedom cannot exist in the midst of this delusion, this hallucination, this nonsense of the world, this universe of the senses, body, and mind. All these dreams without beginning or end, uncontrolled and uncontrollable, ill-adjusted, broken, inharmonious, form our idea of this universe. In a dream, when you see a giant with twenty heads chasing you, and you are flying from him, you do not think it is inharmonious; you think it is proper and right. So is this law. All that you call law is simply chance without meaning. In this dream state you call it law. Within maya, so far as this law of time, space, and causation exists, there is no freedom; and all these various forms of worship are within this maya. The idea of God and the ideas of brute and of man are within this maya, and as such are equally hallucinations; all of them are dreams.

But you must take care not to argue like some extraordinary men of whom we hear at the present time. They say the idea of God is a delusion, but the idea of this world is true. Both ideas stand or fall by the same logic. He alone has the right to be an atheist who denies this world, as well as the other. The same argument applies to both. The same mass of delusion extends from God to the lowest animal, from a blade of grass to the Creator. They stand or fall by the same logic. The same person who sees falsity in the idea of God ought also to see it in the idea of his own body or his own mind. When God vanishes, then also vanish the body and mind, and when both vanish, that which is the real Existence remains for ever. 'There the eyes cannot go, nor the speech, nor the mind. We cannot see it, neither know it.' And we now understand that so far as speech and thought and knowledge and intellect go, it is all within this maya, within bondage. Beyond that is Reality. There neither thought nor mind nor speech can reach.

So far it is intellectually all right, but then comes the practice. The real work is in the practice. Are any practices necessary to realize this Oneness? Most decidedly. It is not that you become this Brahman. You are already that. It is not that you are going to become God or be perfect; you are already perfect, and whenever you think you are not, it is a delusion. This delusion which says that you are Mr So-and-so or Mrs So-and-so can be got rid of by another delusion, and that is practice. Fire will eat fire, and you can use one delusion to conquer another delusion. One cloud will come and brush away another cloud, and then both will go away.

What are these practices then? We must always bear in mind that we are not going to be free, but are free already. Every idea that we are bound is a delusion. Every idea that we are happy or unhappy is a tremendous delusion; and another delusion will come—that we have got to work and worship and struggle to be free; and this will chase out the first delusion, and then both will stop.

The fox is considered very unholy by the Mohammedans and by the Hindus. Also, if a dog touches any bit of food it has to be thrown out; it cannot be eaten by any man. In a certain Mohammedan house a fox entered and took a little bit of food from the table, ate it up, and fled. The man was a poor man and had prepared a very nice feast for himself, and that feast was made unholy and he could not eat it. So he went to a *mullah*, a priest, and said: 'This has happened to me: a fox came and took a mouthful out of my meal. What can be done? I had prepared a feast and wanted so much to eat it, and now comes this fox and destroys the whole affair.' The mullah thought for a minute and then found only one solution and said: 'The only way for you is to get a dog, and make him eat a bit out of the same plate, because dogs and foxes are eternally quarrelling. The food that was left by the fox will go into your stomach, and that left by the dog will go there too, and each impurity will cancel out the other.'

We are very much in the same predicament. This is an hallucination that we are imperfect, and we take up another, that we have to practise to become perfect. Then one will chase the other, as we can use one thorn to extract another and then throw both away. There are people for whom it is sufficient knowledge to hear, 'Thou art That.' With a flash this universe goes away and the real nature shines; but others have to struggle hard to get rid of this idea of bondage.

The first question is: Who are fit to become jnana-yogis? Those who are equipped with these requisites:

First, renunciation of all fruits of work and of all enjoyments in this life or another life. If you are the Creator of the universe, whatever you desire you will have, because you will create it for yourself; it is only a question of time. Some get it immediately; with others the past samskaras, impressions, stand in the way of getting their desires. We give the first place to desires for enjoyment, either in this or another life. Deny there is any life at all, because life is only another name for death. Deny that you are a living being. Who cares for life? Life is one of these hallucinations, and death is its counterpart. Joy is one part of these hallucinations, and misery the other part, and so on. What have you to do with life or death? These are all creations of the mind. This is called giving up desires of enjoyment either in this life or another.

Then comes controlling the mind, calming it so that it will not break into waves and have all sorts of desires, holding the mind steady, not allowing it to get into waves from external or internal causes, controlling the mind perfectly just by the power of will. The jnana-yogi does not take any one of the physical helps or external helps; simply philosophic reasoning, knowledge, and his own will—these are the instrumentalities he believes in.

Next comes *titiksha*, forbearance, bearing all miseries without murmuring, without complaining. When an injury comes, do not mind it. If a tiger comes, stand there. There are men who practise titiksha and succeed in it. There are men who sleep on the banks of the Ganges in the midsummer sun of India and in winter float in the waters of the Ganges for a whole day; they do not care. Men sit in the snow of the Himalayas and do not care to wear any garment. What is heat? What is cold? Let things come and go; what is that to me? I am not the body. It is hard to believe this in western countries; but it is good to know that it is done. Just as your people are brave enough to jump into the mouth of a cannon or into the midst of the battlefield, so our people are brave enough to think and act out their philosophy. They give up their lives for it. 'I am Existence-Knowledge-Bliss Absolute; I am He; I am He.' Just as the western ideal is to keep up luxury in practical life, so ours is to keep up the highest form of spirituality, to demonstrate that religion is not merely frothy words but can be carried out, every bit of it, in this life. This is titiksha, to bear everything, not to complain of anything. I myself have seen men who say: 'I am the Soul; what is the universe to me? Neither pleasure nor pain, nor virtue nor vice, nor heat nor cold, is anything to me.' That is titiksha—not running after the enjoyments of the body.

What is religion? To pray, 'Give me this and that'! Foolish ideas of religion! Those who believe in them have no true idea of God and soul. My Master used to say, the vulture rises higher and higher until he becomes a speck, but his eye is always on the piece of rotten carrion on earth. After all, what is the result of your ideas of religion? To cleanse the streets and have more bread and clothes? Who cares for bread and clothes? Millions come and go every minute. Who cares? Why care for the joys and vicissitudes of this little world? Go beyond that if you dare; go beyond law, let the whole universe vanish, and stand alone. 'I am Existence-Absolute, Knowledge-Absolute, Bliss-Absolute; I am He, I am He.'

Section 4

The jnani says: The mind does not exist, neither the body. His meditation therefore is the most difficult one, the negative; he denies everything, and what is left is the Self. The jnani wants to tear away the universe from the Self by the sheer force of analysis. The jnani seeks to tear himself away from this bondage of matter by the force of intellectual conviction. This is the negative way—the *neti, neti*—'not this, not this'.

Happiness is either in the body or in the mind or in the Atman. With animals, and in the lowest of human beings who are very much like animals, happiness is all in the body. No man can eat with the same pleasure as a famished dog or a wolf; so in the dog and the wolf the happiness is entirely in the body. In men we find a higher plane of happiness, that of thought. And in the jnani there is the highest plane of happiness in the Self, the Atman.

So to the philosopher this knowledge of the Self is of the highest utility, because it gives him the highest happiness possible. Sense gratification or physical things cannot be of the highest utility for him, because he does not find in them the same pleasure that he finds in knowledge itself; and after all, knowledge is the one goal and is really the highest happiness that we know. All the people that work and toil and labour like machines do not really enjoy life, but it is the wise man who enjoys. A rich man buys a picture, but it is the man who understands art that enjoys it. And if the rich man is without knowledge of art it is useless to him; he is only the owner. All over the world it is the wise man who enjoys the happiness of the world. The ignorant man never enjoys; he has to work for others unconsciously.

There is but one Atman; there cannot be two. We have seen how in the whole of this universe there is but one Existence; and that one Existence, when seen through the senses, is called the world, the world of matter. When it is seen through the mind, it is called the world of thoughts and ideas. And when it is seen as it is, then it is the one infinite Being. You must bear this in mind; it is not that there is a soul in man, although I had to take that for granted in order to explain it at first, but that there is only one Existence, and that one the Atman, the Self. When this is perceived through the senses, through sense imageries, it is called the body. When it is perceived through thought, it is called the mind. When it is perceived through its own nature, it is the Atman, the one only Existence.

So it is not that there are three things in one—the body, and the mind, and the Self, although that was a convenient way of putting it in the course of explanation; but all is that Atman, and that one Being is sometimes called the body, sometimes the mind, and sometimes the Self, according to different vision. There is but one Being, which the ignorant call the world.

Dualism and non-dualism are very good philosophic terms, but in perfect perception we never perceive the Real and the false at the same time. We are all born monists, we cannot help it. We always perceive the one. Suppose you see one of your friends coming at a distance in the street; you know him very well, but through the haze and mist that is before you, you think it is another man. When you see your friend as another man, you do not see your friend at all, he has vanished. You are perceiving only one. Suppose your friend is Mr A, but when you perceive Mr A as Mr B you do not see Mr A at all. In each case you perceive only one. When you see yourself as a body, you are body and nothing else, and that is the perception of the vast majority of mankind. They may talk of soul and mind and all these things, but what they perceive is physical form—touch, taste, vision, and so on.

Again, certain men, in certain states of consciousness, perceive themselves as thought. You know, of course, the story of Sir Humphry Davy, who was making experiments before his class with laughing gas; and suddenly one of the tubes broke, and the gas escaping, he breathed it in. For some moments he remained like a statue. Afterwards he told his class that when he was in that state, he actually perceived that the whole world is made up of ideas. The gas for a time made him forget the consciousness of the body, and that very thing which he was seeing as the body, he began to perceive as ideas.

When the consciousness rises still higher, when this little puny consciousness is gone for ever, that which is the Reality behind shines, and we see it as the one Existence-Knowledge-Bliss, the one Atman, the Universal. 'One that is only Knowledge itself, One that is Bliss itself, beyond all compare, beyond all limit, ever free, never bound, infinite as the sky, unchangeable as the sky: such a one will manifest himself in your heart in meditation.'

How does the advaitist theory explain these various phases of heavens and hells and these various ideas we find in all religions? When a man dies it is said that he goes to heaven or hell, goes here or there; or that when a man dies he is born again in another body, either in heaven or in another world or somewhere.

These are all hallucinations. Really speaking, nobody is ever born or dies. There is neither heaven nor hell nor this world; all three never really existed. Tell a child a lot of ghost stories, and let him go out into the street in the evening. There is a little stump of a tree. What does the child see? A ghost, with hands stretched out, ready to grab him. Suppose a man comes from the corner of the street, wanting to meet his sweetheart; he sees that stump of the tree as the girl. A policeman coming from the street corner sees the stump as a thief. The thief sees it as a policeman. It is the same stump of a tree that was seen in various ways. The stump is the reality, and the visions of the stump are the projections of the various minds.

There is one Being, this Self; it neither comes nor goes. When a man is ignorant, he wants to go to heaven or some such place; all his life he has been thinking and thinking of this, and when this earth-dream vanishes he sees this world as a heaven with angels flying about. If a man all his life desires to meet his forefathers he gets them all, from Adam downwards, because he creates them all. If a man is still more ignorant and has always been frightened by fanatics with ideas of hell, with all sorts of punishments when he dies, he will see this very world as hell. All that is meant by dying or being born is simply changes in the plane of vision. Neither do you move, nor does that move upon which you project your vision. You are the permanent, the unchangeable. How can you come and go? It is impossible; you are omnipresent.

You are where you are; these dreams, these various clouds move. One dream follows another without connection. There is no such thing as law or connection in this world, but we are thinking that there is a great deal of connection. All of you have probably read *Alice in Wonderland*. It is the most wonderful book for children that has been written in this century. When I read it I was delighted; it was always in my head to write that sort of a book for children. What pleased me most in it was what you think most incongruous; that there is no connection there. One idea comes and jumps into another, without any connection. When you were children you thought that the most wonderful connection. So this man brought back his thoughts of childhood, which were perfectly connected to him as a child, and composed this book for children. And all these books which men write, trying to make children swallow their own ideas as men, are nonsense. We too are grown-up children, that is all. The world is the same unconnected thing—*Alice in Wonderland*—with no connection whatever.

How? is the next question. How is it to be realized? How is this dream to be broken, how shall we wake up from this dream that we are little men and women, and all such things?

This slavery has to be broken. How? 'This Atman has first to be heard, then reasoned upon, and then meditated upon.' This is the method of the advaita jnani. The truth has to be heard, then reflected upon, and then to be constantly asserted. Think always: 'I am Brahman.'

Never say, 'O Lord, I am a miserable sinner.' Who will help you? You are the help of the universe. What in this universe can help you? Where is the man or the god or the demon to help you? What can prevail over you? You are the God of the universe; where can you seek for help? Never came help anywhere but from yourself. In your ignorance, every prayer was answered by some Being, but you answered the prayer yourself unknowingly. The help came from yourself, and you fondly imagined that some One was sending help to you. There is no help for you outside of yourself; you are the Creator of the universe. Like the silkworm you have built a cocoon around yourself. Who will save you? Burst your own cocoon and come out as the beautiful butterfly, as the free soul. Then alone you will see Truth. Ever tell yourself, 'I am He.' These are words that will burn up the dross that is in the mind, words that will bring out the tremendous energy which is within you already, the infinite power which is sleeping in your heart. This is to be brought out by constantly hearing the truth and nothing else. Wherever there is thought of weakness, approach not the place. Avoid all weakness if you want to be a jnani.

Before you begin to practise, clear your mind of all doubts. Fight and reason and argue, and when you have established it in your mind that this and this alone can be the truth and nothing else, do not argue any more; close your mouth. Hear not argumentation, neither argue yourself. What is the use of more arguments? You have satisfied yourself; you have decided the question. What remains? The truth has got to be realized; therefore why waste valuable time in vain arguments? The truth has now to be meditated upon, and every idea that strengthens you must be taken up and every thought that weakens you must be rejected.

The jnani says: The mind does not exist, neither the body. This idea of the body and of the mind must go, must be driven off; therefore it is foolish to think of them. It would be like trying to cure one ailment by bringing in another. His meditation therefore is the most difficult one, the negative; he denies everything, and what is left is the Self. This is the most analytical way. The jnani wants to tear away the universe from the Self by the sheer force of analysis. It is very easy to say, 'I am a jnani', but very hard to be really one. 'The way is long; it is, as it were, walking on the sharp edge of a razor, yet despair not. Awake, arise, and stop not until the goal is reached', say the Vedas.

So what is the meditation of the jnani? He wants to rise above every idea of body or mind, to drive away the idea that he is the body. For instance, when I say,

'I, Swami', immediately the idea of the body comes.
What must I do then? I must give the mind a hard blow
and say, 'No, I am not the body, I am the Self.' Who
cares if disease comes or death in the most horrible
form? I am not the body. Why make the body nice?
To enjoy the illusion once more? To continue the
slavery? Let it go. I am not the body. That is the way
of the jnani.

The jnani feels that he cannot wait, he must reach
the goal this very moment. He says, 'I am free through
eternity, I am never bound; I am the God of the universe
through all eternity. Who shall make me perfect? I am
perfect already.'

When a man is perfect he sees perfection in others.
When he sees imperfection, it is his own mind project-
ing itself. How can he see imperfection if he has not
got it in himself? So the jnani does not care for perfection. None exists for him. As soon as he is free, he does
not see good and evil. Who sees evil and good? He who
has it in himself. Who sees the body? He who thinks
he is the body. The moment you get rid of the idea
that you are the body, you do not see the world at all.
It vanishes for ever. The jnani seeks to tear himself
away from this bondage of matter by the force of intellectual conviction. This is the negative way—the *neti,
neti*—'not this, not this'.

4

SELF-REALIZATION THROUGH CONTROL OF MIND

Raja yoga is as much a science as any in the world. It is an analysis of the mind, a gathering of the facts of the supersensuous world and so building up the spiritual world. All the great spiritual teachers the world has known said, 'I see and I know.' Jesus, and Peter all claimed actual perception of the spiritual truths they taught.

This perception is obtained by yoga.

Neither memory nor consciousness can be the condition of existence. There is a superconscious state. Both it and the unconscious state are sensationless, but with a vast difference between them— the difference between ignorance and knowledge. Concentration of the mind is the source of all knowledge.

Yoga teaches us to make matter our slave, as it ought

to be. Yoga means 'yoke'—'to join'; that is, to join the soul of man with the supreme Soul or God.

This 'I' of ours covers just a little consciousness and a vast amount of unconsciousness, while over it, and mostly unknown to it, is the superconscious plane.

Through faithful practice, layer after layer of the mind opens before us, and each reveals new facts to us. We see as it were new worlds created before us, new powers are put into our hands, but we must not stop by the way, or allow ourselves to be dazzled by these beads of glass, when the mine of diamonds lies before us.

God alone is our goal.

Three things are necessary to the student who wishes to succeed. First. Give up all ideas of enjoyment in this world and the next; care only for God and Truth. We are here to know truth, not for enjoyment. Leave that to brutes who enjoy as we never can. Man is a thinking being and must struggle on until he conquers death, until he sees the light.

Second. Intense desire to know Truth and God. Be eager for them, long for them, as a drowning man longs for breath.

Third. Restrain the mind from going outward; restrain the senses; turn the mind inward; everything without murmuring; fasten the mind to one idea; think constantly of your real nature. Get rid of superstition. Do not hypnotize yourself into a belief in your own inferiority. Day and night tell yourself what you really are, until you realize, actually realize, your oneness with God.

Without these disciplines no results can be gained.

We can be conscious of the absolute, but we can never express it.

We have to go beyond sense limit and transcend even reason, and we have the power to do this.

Section 1

According to the raja-yogi, the external world is but the gross form of the internal, or subtle. The finer is always the cause, the grosser the effect. The man who has discovered and learned how to manipulate the internal forces will get the whole of nature under his control. The yogi proposes to himself no less a task than to master the whole universe, to control the whole of nature. He wants to arrive at the point where what we call nature's laws will have no influence over him, where he will be able to get beyond them all. He will be master of the whole of nature, internal and external.

ALL OUR KNOWLEDGE is based upon experience. What we call inferential knowledge, in which we go from the less to the more general or from the general to the particular, has experience as its basis. In what are called the exact sciences people easily find the truth, because it appeals to the experiences of every human being. The scientist does not tell you to believe in anything; but he has certain results which have come from his own experiences and, reasoning on them, when he asks us to believe in his conclusions, he appeals to some universal experience of humanity. In every exact science there is a basis which is common to all humanity, so that we can at once see the truth or the fallacy of the conclusions drawn therefrom. Now, the question is: Has religion any such basis or not? I shall have to answer the question both in the affirmative and in the negative.

Religion, as it is generally taught all over the world, is said to be based upon faith and belief, and in most cases consists only of different sets of theories; and that is the reason why we find all religions quarrelling with one another. These theories, again, are based upon belief. One man says there is a great Being sitting above the clouds and governing the whole universe, and he asks me to believe that solely on the authority of his assertion. In the same way I may have my own ideas, which I am asking others to believe; and if they ask a reason, I cannot give them any. This is why religion and metaphysical philosophy have a bad name nowadays. Every educated man seems to say, 'Oh, these religions are only bundles of theories without any standard to judge them by, each man preaching his own pet ideas.' Nevertheless there is a basis of universal belief in religion, governing all the different theories and all the varying ideas of different sects in different countries. Going to their basis, we find that they also are based upon universal experiences.

The Christian asks you to believe in his religion, to believe in Christ and to believe in him as the incarnation of God, to believe in a God, in a soul, and in a better state of that soul. If I ask him to reason, he says he believes in them. But if you go to the fountainhead of Christianity you will find that it is based upon experience. Christ said he saw God, the disciples said they felt God, and so forth. Similarly, in Buddhism, it is Buddha's experience. He experienced certain truths, saw them, came in contact with them, and preached them to the world. So with the Hindus. In their books the writers, who are called *rishis*, or sages, declare they experienced certain truths, and these they preach.

Thus it is clear that all the religions of the world have been built upon that one universal and adamantine foundation of all our knowledge—direct experience. The teachers all saw God; they all saw their own souls, they saw their future, they saw their eternity; and what they saw they preached. Only there is this difference, that by most of these religions, especially in modern times, a peculiar claim is made, namely, that these experiences are impossible at the present day; they were only possible with a few men, who were the founders of the religions that subsequently bore their names. At the present time these experiences have become obsolete, and therefore we have now to take religion on belief.

This I entirely deny. If there has been one experience in this world in any particular branch of knowledge, it absolutely follows that that experience has been possible millions of times before and will be repeated eternally. Uniformity is the rigorous law of nature; what once happened can happen always.

The teachers of the science of raja yoga, therefore, declare that religion is not only based upon the experience of ancient times, but that no man can be religious until he has the same perceptions himself. Raja yoga is the science which teaches us how to get these perceptions. It is not much use to talk about religion until one has felt it. Why is there so much disturbance, so much fighting and quarrelling in the name of God? There has been more bloodshed in the name of God than for any other cause, because people never went to the fountainhead; they were content to give only a mental assent to the customs of their forefathers, and wanted others to do the same. What right has a man to say he has a soul if he does not feel it, or that there is a God if he does not see him? If there is a God we must see him; if there is a soul we must perceive it; otherwise it is better not to believe. It is better to be an outspoken atheist than a hypocrite.

The modern idea, on the one hand, with the 'learned' is that religion and metaphysics and all search after a Supreme Being are futile; on the other hand, with the semi-educated the idea seems to be that these things really have no basis; their only value consists in the fact that they furnish strong motive powers for doing good to the world. If men believe in a God, they may become good and moral, and so make good citizens. We cannot blame them for holding such ideas, seeing that all the teaching these men get is simply to believe in an eternal rigmarole of words, without any substance behind them. They are asked to live upon words. Can they do it? If they could, I should not have the least regard for human nature. Man wants truth, wants to experience truth for himself. When he has grasped it, realized it, felt it within his heart of hearts, then alone, declare the Vedas, would all doubts vanish, all darkness be scattered, and all crookedness be made straight. 'Ye children of immortality, even those who live in the highest sphere, the way is found. There is a way out of all this darkness, and that is by perceiving Him who is beyond all darkness. There is no other way.'

The science of raja yoga proposes to put before humanity a practical and scientifically worked out method of reaching this truth. In the first place, every science must have its own method of investigation. If you want to become an astronomer, and sit down and cry, 'Astronomy! Astronomy!' you will never become one. If you want to be an astronomer you must go to an observatory, take a telescope, study the stars and planets, and then you will become an astronomer. Each science must have its own method. I could preach you thousands of sermons, but they would not make you religious until you practised the method. These are the truths of the sages of all countries, of all ages, of men pure and unselfish who had no motive but to do good to the world. They all declare that they have found some truth higher than what the senses can bring to us, and they invite verification. They ask us to take up the method and practise honestly. Then, if we do not find this higher truth, we shall have the right to say there is no truth in the claim; but before we have done that, we are not rational in denying the truth of their assertions. So we must work faithfully, using the prescribed methods, and light will come.

In acquiring knowledge we make use of generalization, and generalization is based upon observation. We first observe facts, then generalize, and then draw conclusions or principles. The knowledge of the mind, of the internal nature of man, of thought, can never be had until we have first the power of observing the facts that are going on within. It is comparatively easy to observe facts in the external world, for many instruments have been invented for the purpose; but in the internal world we have no instrument to help us. Yet we know we must observe in order to have a real science. Without proper analysis, any science will be hopeless, mere theorizing; and that is why all the psychologists have been quarrelling among themselves since the beginning of time, except those few who found out the means of observation.

The science of raja yoga, in the first place, proposes to give us such a means of observing the internal states. The instrument is the mind itself. The power of attention, when properly guided and directed towards the internal world, will analyse the mind and illumine facts for us. The powers of the mind are like rays of light dissipated; when they are concentrated they illumine. This is our only means of knowledge. Everyone is using it, both in the external and in the internal world; but, for the psychologist, the same minute observation has to be directed to the internal world which the scientific man directs to the external; and this requires a great deal of practice. From our childhood upwards we have been taught to pay attention only to things external, but never to things internal; hence most of us have nearly lost the faculty of observing the internal mechanism. To turn the mind, as it were, inside, stop it from going outside, and then to concentrate all its powers and throw them upon the mind itself, in order that it may know its own nature, analyse itself, is very hard work. Yet that is the only way to anything which will be a scientific approach to the subject.

What is the use of such knowledge? In the first place, knowledge itself is the highest reward of knowledge, and secondly, there is also utility in it. It will take away all our misery. When, by analysing his own mind, man comes face to face, as it were, with something which is never destroyed, something which is, by its own nature, eternally pure and perfect, he will no more be miserable, no more unhappy. All misery comes from fear, from unsatisfied desire. Man will find that he never dies, and then he will have no more fear of death. When he knows that he is perfect, he will have no more vain desires. And both these causes being absent, there will be no more misery; there will be perfect bliss, even while in this body.

There is only one method by which to attain this knowledge, that which is called concentration. The chemist in his laboratory concentrates all the energies of his mind into one focus and throws them upon the materials he is analysing, and so finds out their secrets. The astronomer concentrates all the energies of his mind and projects them through his telescope upon the skies; and the stars, the sun, and the moon give up their secrets to him.

How has all the knowledge in the world been gained but by the concentration of the powers of the mind? The world is ready to give up its secrets if we only know how to knock, how to give it the necessary blow. The strength and force of the blow come through concentration. There is no limit to the power of the human mind. The more concentrated it is, the more power is brought to bear on one point; that is the secret.

It is easy to concentrate the mind on external things; the mind naturally goes outward. But not so in the case of religion or psychology or metaphysics, where the subject and the object are one. The object is internal —the mind itself is the object—and it is necessary to study the mind itself, mind studying mind. We know that there is the power of the mind called reflection. I am talking to you. At the same time I am standing aside, as it were, a second person, and knowing and hearing what I am talking. You work and think at the same time, while a portion of your mind stands by and sees what you are thinking. The powers of the mind should be concentrated and turned back upon itself, and as the darkest places reveal their secrets before the penetrating rays of the sun, so will this concentrated mind penetrate its own innermost secrets. Thus will we come to the basis of belief, the real genuine religion. We will perceive for ourselves whether we have souls, whether life is of five minutes or of eternity, whether there is a God in the universe or none. It will all be revealed to us.

This is what raja yoga proposes to teach. The goal of all its teaching is how to concentrate the mind, then how to discover the innermost recesses of our own minds, then how to generalize their contents and form our own conclusions from them. It therefore never asks the question what our religion is—whether we are deists, or atheists, whether Christians, Jews, or Buddhists. We are human beings; that is sufficient. Every human being has the right and the power to seek for religion; every human being has the right to ask the reason why and to have his question answered by himself—if he only takes the trouble.

So far, then, we see that in the study of this raja yoga no faith or belief is necessary. Believe nothing until you find it out for yourself; that is what it teaches us. Truth requires no prop to make it stand. Do you mean to say that the facts of our awakened state require any dreams or imaginings to prove them? Certainly not. This study of raja yoga takes a long time and constant practice. A part of this practice is physical, but in the main it is mental. As we proceed we shall find how intimately the mind is connected with the body. If we believe that the mind is simply a finer part of the body, and that mind acts upon the body, then it stands to reason that the body must react upon the mind. If the body is sick, the mind becomes sick also. If the body is healthy, the mind remains healthy and strong. When one is angry the mind becomes disturbed. Similarly when the mind is disturbed, the body also becomes disturbed. With the majority of mankind the mind is greatly under the control of the body, their mind being very little developed. The vast mass of humanity is very little removed from the animals. Not only so, but in many instances the power of control in them is little higher than that of the lower animals. We have very little command of our minds.

Therefore to bring that command about, to get that control over body and mind, we must take certain physical helps. When the body is sufficiently controlled we can attempt the manipulation of the mind. By manipulating the mind, we shall be able to bring it under our control, make it work as we like, and compel it to concentrate its powers as we desire.

According to the raja-yogi, the external world is but the gross form of the internal, or subtle. The finer is always the cause, the grosser the effect. So the external world is the effect, the internal the cause. In the same way external forces are simply the grosser parts of that of which the internal forces are the finer. The man who has discovered and learned how to manipulate the internal forces will get the whole of nature under his control. The yogi proposes to himself no less a task than to master the whole universe, to control the whole of nature. He wants to arrive at the point where what we call nature's laws will have no influence over him, where he will be able to get beyond them all. He will be master of the whole of nature, internal and external. The progress and civilization of this human race simply mean controlling this nature.

Different races take to different processes of controlling nature. Just as in the same society some individuals want to control external nature, and others internal, so amongst races, some want to control external nature, and others internal. Some say that by controlling internal nature we control everything; others that by controlling external nature we control everything. Carried to the extreme both are right, because in nature there is no such division as internal or external. These are fictitious limitations that never existed. The externalists and the internalists are destined to meet at the same point, when both reach the extreme of their knowledge. Just as a physicist, when he pushes his knowledge to its limits, finds it melting away into metaphysics, so a metaphysician will find that what he calls mind and matter are but apparent distinctions, the reality being One.

The end and aim of all science is to find the unity, the One, out of which the manifold is being manufactured, that One existing as many. Raja yoga proposes to start from the internal world, to study internal nature, and through that, control the whole—both internal and external.

Section 2

Practice is absolutely necessary. You may sit down and listen to me by the hour every day, but if you do not practise, you will not get one step farther. It all depends on practice. We never understand

these things until we experience them. We will have
to see and feel them for ourselves. Simply listening
to explanations and theories will not do.

Raja yoga is divided into eight steps. The first is *yama*
—non-killing, truthfulness, non-stealing, continence, and
non-receiving of any gifts. Next is *niyama*—cleanliness,
contentment, austerity, study, and self-surrender to God.
Then come *asana*, or posture; *pranayama*, or control of
prana; *pratyahara*, or restraint of the senses from their
objects; *dharana*, or fixing the mind on a spot; *dhyana*,
or meditation; and *samadhi*, or superconsciousness.

Yama and niyama are moral trainings; without these
as the basis no practice of yoga will succeed. As these
two become established, the yogi will begin to realize
the fruits of his practice; without these it will never
bear fruit. A yogi must not think of injuring anyone,
by thought, word, or deed. Mercy shall not be for
men alone, but shall go beyond and embrace the whole
world.

The next step is asana, posture. A series of exercises,
physical and mental, is to be gone through every day
until certain higher states are reached. Therefore it is
quite necessary that we should find a posture in which
we can remain long. That posture which is the easiest
for one should be the one chosen. For thinking, a certain
posture may be very easy for one man, while for
another it may be very difficult. Nerve currents will
have to be displaced and given a new channel. New
sorts of vibrations will begin; the whole constitution will be remodelled, as it were. But the main
part of the activity will lie along the spinal column, so
that the one thing necessary for the posture is to hold

the spinal column free, sitting erect, holding the three parts—the chest, neck, and head—in a straight line. Let the whole weight of the body be supported by the ribs, and then you have an easy, natural posture with the spine straight. You will easily see that you cannot think very high thoughts with the chest in.

This portion of the yoga is a little similar to *hatha* yoga, which deals entirely with the physical body, its aim being to make the physical body very strong. We have nothing to do with it here, because its practices are very difficult and cannot be learned in a day and, after all, do not lead to much spiritual growth. The object in these is physical, not psychological. There is not one muscle in the body over which a man cannot establish a perfect control. The heart can be made to stop or go on at his bidding, and each part of the organism can be similarly controlled. The result of this branch of yoga is to make men live long; health is the chief idea, the one goal of the hatha-yogi. He is determined not to fall sick, and he never does. He lives long; a hundred years is nothing to him; he is quite young and fresh when he is a hundred and fifty, without one hair turned grey. But that is all. A banyan tree lives sometimes five thousand years, but it is a banyan tree and nothing more. So, if a man lives long, he is only a healthy animal.

Practice is absolutely necessary. You may sit down and listen to me by the hour every day, but if you do not practise, you will not get one step farther. It all depends on practice. We never understand these things until we experience them. We will have to see and feel them for ourselves. Simply listening to explanations and theories will not do.

There are several obstructions to practice. The first obstruction is an unhealthy body; if the body is not in a fit state, the practice will be obstructed. Therefore we have to keep the body in good health; we have to take care of what we eat and drink, and what we do. Always use a mental effort to keep the body strong. That is all—nothing further of the body. We must not forget that health is only a means to an end. If health were the end we would be like animals; animals rarely become unhealthy.

The second obstruction is doubt. We always feel doubtful about things we do not see. Man cannot live upon words, however he may try. So, doubt comes to us as to whether there is any truth in these things or not; even the best of us will doubt sometimes. With practice, within a few days, a little glimpse will come, enough to give one encouragement and hope. As a certain commentator on yoga philosophy says, 'When one proof is obtained, however little that may be, it will give us faith in the whole teaching of yoga.' These glimpses will come, by little bits at first, but enough to give you faith and strength and hope. For instance, if you concentrate your thoughts on the tip of your nose, in a few days you will begin to smell most beautiful fragrance, which will be enough to show you that there are certain mental perceptions that can be made obvious without the contact of physical objects. But we must always remember that these are only the means; the aim, the end, the goal, of all this training is liberation of the soul. Absolute control of nature, and nothing short of it, must be the goal. We must be the masters, and not the slaves, of nature; neither body nor mind must be our master, nor must we forget that the body is ours, and not we the body's.

A god and a demon went to learn about the Self from a great sage. They studied with him for a long time. At last the sage told them, 'You yourselves are the Being you are seeking.' Both of them thought that their bodies were the Self. They went back to their people quite satisfied and said, 'We have learned everything that was to be learned; eat, drink, and be merry; we are the Self; there is nothing beyond us.'

The nature of the demon was ignorant, clouded; so he never inquired any further, but was perfectly contented with the idea that he was God, that by the Self was meant the body. The god had a purer nature. He at first committed the mistake of thinking, 'I, this body, am Brahman; so keep it strong and in health, and well dressed, and give it all sorts of enjoyments.' But in a few days he found out that that could not be the meaning of the sage, their master; there must be something higher. So he came back and said, 'Sir, did you teach me that this body was the Self? If so, I see all bodies die; the Self cannot die.'

The sage said, 'Find it out; thou art That.' Then the god thought that the vital forces which work the body were what the sage meant. But after a time he found that if he ate, these vital forces remained strong, but if he starved, they became weak. The god then went back to the sage and said, 'Sir, do you mean that the vital forces are the Self?' The sage said, 'Find out for yourself; thou art That.'

The god returned home once more, thinking that it was the mind, perhaps, that was the Self. But in a short while he saw that thoughts were so various, now good,

again bad; the mind was too changeable to be the Self.
He went back to the sage and said, 'Sir, I do not think
that the mind is the Self; did you mean that?' 'No,'
replied the sage, 'thou art That; find out for yourself.'

The god went home and at last found that he was
the Self, beyond all thought, one, without birth or
death, whom the sword cannot pierce or the fire burn,
whom the air cannot dry or the water melt, the begin-
ningless and endless, the immovable, the intangible, the
omniscient, the omnipotent Being; that it was neither
the body nor the mind, but beyond them all. So he was
satisfied; but the poor demon did not get the truth,
owing to his fondness for the body.

This world has a good many of these demoniac natures,
but there are some gods too. If one proposes to teach
any science to increase the power of sense enjoyments,
one finds multitudes ready for it. If one undertakes to
show the supreme goal, one finds few to listen. Very
few have the power to grasp the highest, fewer still the
patience to attain to it. But there are a few also who
know that even if the body can be made to live for a
thousand years, the result in the end will be the same.
When the forces that hold it together go away, the
body must fall. No man was ever born who could stop
his body one moment from changing. Body is the name
of a series of changes. 'As in a river the masses of water
are changing before you every moment, and new masses
are coming, yet taking similar form, so is it with this
body.' Yet the body must be kept strong and healthy.
It is the best instrument we have.

Returning to our subject, we come next to pranayama,
control of the breathing. What has that to do with

concentrating the powers of the mind? Breath is like the flywheel of this machine, the body. In a big engine you find the flywheel first moving, and that motion is conveyed to finer and finer machinery until the most delicate and finest mechanism in the machine is in motion. The breath is that flywheel, supplying and regulating the motive power to everything in this body.

There was once a minister to a great king. He fell into disgrace. The king, as a punishment, ordered him to be shut up in the top of a very high tower. This was done, and the minister was left there to perish. He had a faithful wife, however, who came to the tower at night and called to her husband at the top to know what she could do to help him. He told her to return to the tower the following night and bring with her a long rope, some stout twine, packthread, silken thread, a beetle, and a little honey. Wondering much, the good wife obeyed her husband and brought him the desired articles. The husband directed her to attach the silken thread firmly to the beetle, then to smear its horns with a drop of honey and to set it free on the wall of the tower with its head pointing upward. She obeyed all these instructions, and the beetle started on its long journey. Smelling the honey ahead it slowly crept onward in the hope of reaching the honey, until at last it reached the top of the tower, when the minister grasped the beetle and got possession of the silk thread. He told his wife to tie the other end to the packthread, and after he had drawn up the packthread, he repeated the process with the stout twine, and lastly with the rope. Then the rest was easy. The minister descended from the tower by means of the rope and made his escape.

In this body of ours the breath motion is the silken thread; by laying hold of and learning to control it we grasp the packthread of the nerve currents, and from these the stout twine of our thoughts, and lastly the rope of prana, controlling which we reach freedom.

We do not know anything about our own bodies. We cannot know. At best we can take a dead body and cut it in pieces; and there are some who can take a live animal and cut it in pieces in order to see what is inside the body. Still, that has nothing to do with our own bodies. We know very little about them. Why is this? Because our attention is not discriminating enough to catch the very fine movements that are going on within. We can know of them only when the mind becomes more subtle and enters, as it were, deeper into the body. To get the subtle perception we have to begin with the grosser perceptions. We have to get hold of that which is setting the whole engine in motion. That is the prana, the most obvious manifestation of which is the breath. Then, along with the breath, we shall slowly enter the body, which will enable us to find out about the subtle forces, the nerve currents, that are moving all through the body. As soon as we perceive and learn to feel them, we shall begin to get control over them and over the body. The mind is also set in motion by these different nerve currents; so at last we shall reach the state of perfect control over the body and the mind, making both our servants. Knowledge is power. We have to get this power.

As soon as you begin to feel these currents in motion all over you, doubts will vanish; but it requires hard practice every day. You must practise at least twice every day, and the best times are towards the morning and the evening. When night passes into day, and day into night, a state of relative calmness ensues. The early morning and the early evening are the two periods of calmness. Your body will have a like tendency to become calm at those times. We should take advantage of that natural condition and begin to practise then. Make it a rule not to eat until you have practised; if you do this the sheer force of hunger will break your laziness. In India they teach children never to eat until they have practised or worshipped, and it becomes natural to them after a time; a boy will not feel hungry until he has bathed and practised.

Those of you who can afford it will do better to have a room for this practice alone. Do not sleep in that room; it must be kept holy. You must not enter the room until you have bathed and are perfectly clean in body and mind. Place flowers in that room always— they are the best surroundings for a yogi—and pictures that are pleasing. Burn incense morning and evening. Have no quarrelling or anger or unholy thought in that room. Only allow those persons to enter it who are of the same thought as you. Then gradually there will be an atmosphere of holiness in the room, so that when you are miserable, sorrowful, or doubtful, or when your mind is disturbed, the very fact of entering that room will make you calm. This was the idea of the temple and the church; and in some temples and churches you will find it even now; but in the majority of them the very idea has been lost. The fact is that by creating holy vibrations in a place it will become and remain holy. Those who cannot afford to have a room set apart can practise anywhere they like.

Sit in a straight posture, and the first thing to do is to send a current of holy thought to all creation. Mentally repeat: 'Let all beings be happy; let all beings be peaceful; let all beings be blissful.' So do to the east, south, north, and west. The more you do that the better you will feel yourself. You will find at last that the easiest way to make ourselves healthy is to see that others are healthy, and the easiest way to make ourselves happy is to see that others are happy. After doing that, those who believe in God should pray—not for money, not for health, nor for heaven: pray for knowledge and light; every other prayer is selfish. Then the next thing to do is to think of your own body, and see that it is strong and healthy; it is the best instrument you have. Think of it as being as strong as adamant, and that with the help of this body you will cross the ocean of life. Freedom is never to be reached by the weak. Throw away all weakness. Tell your body that it is strong, tell your mind that it is strong, and have unbounded faith and hope in yourself.

We have now to deal with the exercises in pranayama. The first step, according to the yogis, is to control the motion of the lungs. What we want to do is to feel the finer motions that are going on in the body. Our minds have become externalized and have lost sight of the fine motions inside. If we can begin to feel them, we can begin to control them. These nerve currents go on all over the body, bringing life and vitality to every muscle; but we do not feel them. The yogi says we can learn to do so. How? By taking up and controlling the motion of the lungs. When we have done that for a sufficient length of time we shall be able to control the finer motions.

Sit upright; the body must be kept straight. The spinal cord, although not attached to the vertebral column, is yet inside of it. If you sit crookedly you disturb this spinal cord; so let it be free. Any time that you sit crookedly and try to meditate you do yourself an injury. The three parts of the body—the chest, the neck, and the head—must be always held straight, in one line. You will find that by a little practice this will come to you as easily as breathing. The second thing is to get control of the nerves. The nerve centre that controls the respiratory organs has a sort of controlling effect on the other nerves, and rhythmical breathing is therefore necessary. The breathing that we generally use should not be called breathing at all; it is very irregular.

The first lesson is just to breathe, in a measured way, in and out. That will harmonize the system. When you have practised this for some time you will do well to join to it the repetition of some word as *Om*, or any other sacred word. In India we use certain symbolical words instead of counting one, two, three, four. That is why I advise you to join the mental repetition of the *Om* or some other sacred word to the pranayama. Let the word flow in and out with the breath, rhythmically, harmoniously, and you will find the whole body is becoming rhythmical. Then you will learn what rest is. Compared with it, sleep is no rest. Once this rest comes, the most tired nerves will be calmed down and you will find that you have never before really rested.

The first effect of this practice is perceived in the change of expression of one's face. Harsh lines disappear; with calm thought, calmness comes over the face. Next comes a beautiful voice. I never saw a yogi with a croaking voice. These signs come after a few months' practice.

The yogis claim that, of all the energies that are in the human body, the highest is what they call *ojas*. Now this ojas is stored up in the brain, and the more ojas is in a man's head, the more powerful he is, the more intellectual, the more spiritually strong. One man may speak beautiful language and beautiful thought, but they do not impress people. Another man speaks neither beautiful language nor beautiful thoughts, yet his words charm. Every movement of his is powerful. That is the power of ojas.

Now, in every man there is more or less of this ojas stored up. All the forces that are working in the body in their highest become ojas. You must remember that it is only a question of transformation. The same force which is working outside as electricity or magnetism will become changed into inner force; the same force that is working as muscular energy will be changed into ojas. The yogis say that that part of the human energy which is expressed through sexual action and sexual thought, when checked and controlled, easily becomes changed into ojas. It is only the chaste man or woman who can make the ojas rise and store it in the brain; that is why chastity has always been considered the highest virtue. A man feels that if he is unchaste, spirituality goes away; he loses mental vigour and moral stamina. That is why, in all the religious orders in the world which have produced spiritual giants, you will always find absolute chastity insisted upon. That is why monks came into existence, giving up marriage. There must be perfect chastity in thought, word, and deed. Without it the practice of raja yoga is dangerous and may lead to insanity. If people practise raja yoga and at the same time lead an impure life, how can they expect to become yogis?

The next step is called pratyahara. What is this? You know how perceptions come. First of all there are the external instruments, then the internal organs, acting in the body through the brain centres, and last there is the mind. When these come together and attach themselves to some external object, then we perceive it. At the same time it is a very difficult thing to concentrate the mind and attach it to one organ only; the mind is a slave.

We hear 'Be good', and 'Be good', and 'Be good', taught all over the world. There is hardly a child born in any country in the world who has not been told, 'Do not steal', 'Do not tell a lie'; but nobody tells the child how he can avoid doing them. Talking will not help him. Why should he not become a thief? We do not teach him how not to steal; we simply tell him, 'Do not steal.' Only when we teach him to control his mind do we really help him.

All actions, internal and external, occur when the mind joins itself to certain centres, called organs. Willingly or unwillingly it is drawn to join itself to the centres, and that is why people do foolish deeds and feel miserable, which, if the mind were under control, they would not do. What would be the result of controlling the mind? It then would not join itself to the centres of perception, and naturally feeling and willing would be under control.

It is clear so far. Is it possible? It is perfectly possible. You see it in modern times. The faith healers teach people to deny misery and pain and evil. Their philosophy is rather roundabout, but it is a part of yoga upon which they have somehow stumbled. Where they succeed in making a person throw off suffering by denying it, they really use a part of pratyahara, as they make the mind of the person strong enough to ignore the senses. The hypnotists, in a similar manner, by their suggestion excite in the patient a sort of morbid pratyahara for the time being. The so-called hypnotic suggestion can only act upon a weak mind; and until the operator, by means of fixed gaze or otherwise, has succeeded in putting the mind of the subject in a sort of passive, morbid condition, his suggestions never work.

Now, the control of the centres which is established for a time in a hypnotic patient or the patient of faith-healing, by the operator, is reprehensible, because it leads to ultimate ruin. It is not really controlling the brain centres by the power of one's own will, but is, as it were, stunning the patient's mind for a time by sudden blows which another's will delivers to it. It is not checking by means of reins and muscular strength the mad career of a fiery team, but rather by asking another to deliver heavy blows on the heads of the horses, to stun them for a time into gentleness. By each one of these processes the man operated upon loses a part of his mental energies, till at last the mind, instead of gaining the power of perfect control, becomes a shapeless, powerless mass and the only destination of the patient is the lunatic asylum.

Every attempt at control which is not voluntary, not made with the individual's own mind, not only is disastrous, but defeats its own end. The goal of each soul is freedom, mastery—freedom from the slavery of matter and thought, mastery of external and internal nature. Therefore, beware how you allow yourselves to be acted upon by others. Beware how you unknowingly bring another to ruin. True, some succeed in doing good to many, for a time, by giving a new trend to their propensities; but at the same time they bring ruin to millions by the unconscious suggestions they throw around, rousing in men and women that morbid, passive, hypnotic condition which makes them almost soulless at last.

Whosoever asks anyone to believe blindly, or drags people behind him by the controlling power of his superior will, does an injury to humanity, though he may not intend it. Therefore use your own minds, control body and mind yourselves, remember that unless you are a diseased person no extraneous will can work upon you. Avoid everyone, however great and good he may be, who asks you to believe blindly.

All over the world there have been dancing and jumping and howling sects, whose influence spreads like infection as they begin to sing and dance and preach; they also are a sort of hypnotist. They exercise a singular control for the time being over sensitive persons —alas! often, in the long run, to degenerate whole races. Aye, it is healthier for the individual or the race to remain wicked than be made apparently good by such morbid extraneous control. One's heart sinks to think of the amount of injury done to humanity by such irresponsible, yet well-meaning religious fanatics. They little know that the minds which attain to sudden spiritual upheaval under their suggestions, with music and prayers, are simply making themselves passive, morbid, and powerless; opening themselves to any other suggestion, be it ever so evil. Little do these ignorant, deluded persons

dream that, while they are congratulating themselves
upon their miraculous power to transform human hearts,
which power they think was poured upon them by
some Being above the clouds, they are sowing the seeds
of future decay, of crime, of lunacy, and of death.
Therefore, beware of everything that takes away your
freedom. Know that it is dangerous and avoid it by all
the means in your power.

He who has succeeded in attaching or detaching his
mind to or from the centres at will has succeeded in
pratyahara, which means 'gathering towards', checking
the outgoing powers of the mind, freeing it from the
thraldom of the senses. When we can do this we shall
really possess character. Then we shall have taken a
long step towards freedom; before that we are mere
machines.

How hard it is to control the mind! Well has it been
compared to the maddened monkey. There was a
monkey, restless by his own nature, as all monkeys are.
As if that were not enough, someone made him drink
freely of wine, so that he became still more restless.
Then a scorpion stung him. When a man is stung by a
scorpion he jumps about for a whole day; so the poor
monkey found his condition worse than ever. To
complete his misery a demon entered into him. What
language can describe the uncontrollable restlessness of
the monkey? The human mind is like that monkey,
incessantly active by its own nature. Then it becomes
drunk with the wine of desire, thus increasing its turbu-
lence. After desire has taken possession, comes the sting
of the scorpion of jealousy at the success of others; and
last of all the demon of pride enters the mind, making

it think itself all-important. How hard to control such a mind!

The first lesson, then, is to sit for some time and let the mind run on. The mind is bubbling up all the time. It is like that monkey jumping about. Let the monkey jump as much as he can; you simply wait and watch. Knowledge is power, says the proverb, and that is true. Until you know what the mind is doing you cannot control it. Give it the rein. Many hideous thoughts may come into it; you will be astonished that it was possible for you to think such thoughts. But you will find that each day the mind's vagaries are becoming less and less violent, that each day it is becoming calmer. In the first few months you will find that the mind will have a great many thoughts; later you will find that they have somewhat decreased, and in a few more months they will be fewer and fewer, until at last the mind will be under perfect control. But you must patiently practise every day. As soon as the steam is turned on, the engine must run; as soon as things are before us, we must perceive. So a man, to prove that he is not a machine, must demonstrate that he is under the control of nothing. This controlling of the mind and not allowing it to join itself to the centres is pratyahara. How is this practised? It is a tremendous work, not to be done in a day. Only after a patient, continuous struggle for years can we succeed.

After you have practised pratyahara for a time, take the next step, the dharana, holding the mind to certain points. What is meant by holding the mind to certain points? Forcing the mind to feel certain parts of the body to the exclusion of others. For instance, try to feel only the hand, to the exclusion of other parts of the body. When the *chitta*, or mind-stuff, is confined and limited to a certain place, it is dharana. This dharana is of various sorts, and along with it, it is better to have a little play of the imagination. For instance, the mind should be made to think of one point in the heart. That is very difficult; an easier way is to imagine a lotus there. That lotus is full of light, effulgent light. Put the mind there. Or think of the lotus in the brain as full of light.

The yogi must always practise. He should try to live alone; the companionship of different sorts of people distracts the mind. He should not speak much, because to speak distracts the mind; the mind cannot be controlled after a whole day's hard work. One observing the above rules becomes a yogi.

Such is the power of yoga that even the least of it will bring a great amount of benefit. It will not hurt anyone but will benefit everyone. First of all, it will tone down nervous excitement, bring calmness, enable us to see things more clearly. The temperament will be better and the health will be better.

When one begins to concentrate, the dropping of a pin will seem like a thunderbolt going through the brain. As the organs get finer, the perceptions get finer. These are the stages through which we have to pass, and all those who persevere will succeed. Give up all argumentation and other distractions. Is there anything in dry intellectual jargon? It only throws the mind off its balance and disturbs it. Things of subtler planes have to be realized. Will talking do that? So give up all vain talk. Read only those books which have been written by persons who have had realization.

Those who really want to be yogis must give up,

once for all, this nibbling at things. Take up one idea. Make that one idea your life; think of it; dream of it; live on that idea. Let the brain, muscles, nerves, every part of your body, be full of that idea, and just leave every other idea alone. This is the way to success, and this is the way great spiritual giants are produced.

Section 3

All the different steps in yoga are intended to bring us scientifically to the superconscious state, or samadhi. Inspiration is as much in every man's nature as it was in that of the ancient prophets. These prophets were not unique; they were men as you and I. They were great yogis. They had gained this superconsciousness, and you and I can do the same. The very fact that one man ever reached that state proves that it is possible for every man to do so. Not only is it possible, but every man must eventually get to that state—and that is religion.

We have taken a cursory view of the different steps in raja yoga except the finer ones, the training in concentration, which is the goal to which raja yoga will lead us. We see, as human beings, that all our knowledge which is called rational is referred to consciousness. My consciousness of this table, and of your presence, makes me know that the table and you are here. At the same time, there is a very great part of my existence of which I am not conscious. All the different organs inside the body, the different parts of the brain—nobody is conscious of these.

When I eat food I do it consciously; when I assimilate it I do it unconsciously. When the food is manufactured into blood, it is done unconsciously. When out of the blood all the different parts of my body are strengthened, it is done unconsciously. And yet it is I who am doing all this; there cannot be twenty people in this one body. How do I know that I do it, and nobody else? It may be urged that my business is only in eating and assimilating the food, and that strengthening the body by the food is done for me by somebody else. That cannot be, because it can be demonstrated that almost every action of which we are now unconscious can be brought up to the plane of consciousness. The heart is beating apparently without our control; none of us can control the heart; it goes on its own way. But by practice men can bring even the heart under control, until it will just beat at will, slowly, or quickly, or almost stop. Nearly every part of the body can be brought under control. What does this show? That the functions which are beneath consciousness are also performed by us, only we are doing it unconsciously.

We have, then, two planes in which the human mind works. First is the conscious plane, in which all work is always accompanied by the feeling of ego. Next comes the unconscious plane, where the work is unaccompanied by the feeling of ego. That part of the mind's work which is unaccompanied by the feeling of ego is unconscious work, and that part which is accompanied by the feeling of ego is conscious work. In the lower animals this unconscious work is called instinct. In higher animals, and in the highest of all animals, man, what is called conscious work prevails.

But it does not end here. There is a still higher plane

on which the mind can work. It can go beyond consciousness. Just as unconscious work is beneath consciousness, so there is another work which is above consciousness and which also is not accompanied by the feeling of ego. The feeling of ego is only on the middle plane. When the mind is above or below that line there is no feeling of 'I', and yet the mind works. When the mind goes beyond this line of self-consciousness it is called samadhi, or superconsciousness.

How, for instance, do we know that a man in samadhi has not gone below consciousness, has not degenerated instead of going higher? In both cases the works are unaccompanied by ego. The answer is, by the effects, by the results of the work, we know that which is below, and that which is above. When a man goes into deep sleep he enters a plane beneath consciousness. He works the body all the time; he breathes, he moves the body perhaps in his sleep, without any accompanying feeling of ego. He is unconscious, and when he returns from his sleep he is the same man who went into it. The sum total of the knowledge which he had before he went into the sleep remains the same; it does not increase at all. No enlightenment comes. But when a man goes into samadhi, if he goes into it a fool, he comes out a sage.

What makes the difference? From one state a man comes out the very same man that he went in, and from the other state the man comes out enlightened: a sage, a prophet, a saint—his whole character changed, his life changed, illumined. These are the two effects. Now the effects being different, the causes must be different. As this illumination with which a man comes back from samadhi is much higher than can be got from unconsciousness, or much higher than can be got by reasoning in a conscious state, it must therefore be superconsciousness, and samadhi is called the super-conscious state.

This, in short, is the idea of samadhi. What is its application? The application is here. The field of reason, or the conscious working of the mind, is narrow and limited. There is a little circle within which human reason must move. It cannot go beyond. Every attempt to go beyond is impossible, yet it is beyond this circle of reason that there lies all that humanity holds most dear. All these questions—whether there is an immortal Soul, whether there is a God, whether there is any supreme Intelligence guiding this universe or not—are beyond the field of reason.

All our ethical theories, all our moral attitudes, all that is good and great in human nature, have been moulded upon answers that have come from beyond the circle. It is very important, therefore, that we should have answers to these questions. If life is only a short play, if the universe is only a 'fortuitous combination of atoms', then why should I do good to another? Why should there be mercy, justice, or fellow-feeling?

All ethics, all human action, and all human thought hang upon this one idea of unselfishness. The whole idea of human life can be put into that one word, *unselfishness*. Why should we be unselfish? Where is the necessity, the force, the power, that compels me to be unselfish? You call yourself a rational man, a utilitarian, but if you do not show me a reason for utility, I say you are irrational. Show me the reason why I should not be selfish. The answer is that this world is only one drop in an infinite ocean, one link in an infinite chain. Where did those who preached unselfishness, and taught it to the human race, get this idea? We know it is not instinctive; the animals, which have instinct, do not know it. Neither is it reason; reason does not know anything about these ideas. Whence then did they come?

We find, in studying history, one fact held in common by all the great teachers of religion the world ever had. They all claim to have got their truths from beyond; only many of them did not know where they got them from. For instance, one would say that an angel came down, in the form of a human being with wings, and said to him, 'Hear, O man, this is the message.' Another says that a *deva*, a bright being, appeared to him. A third says he dreamed that his ancestor came and told him certain things; he did not know anything beyond that. But this is common, that all claim that this knowledge has come to them from beyond, not through their reasoning power. What does the science of yoga teach? It teaches that they were right in claiming that all this knowledge came to them from beyond reasoning, but that it came from within themselves.

The yogi teaches that the mind itself has a higher state of existence, beyond reason, a superconscious state, and when the mind gets to that higher state, then this knowledge, beyond reasoning, comes to man. Metaphysical and transcendental knowledge comes to that man. This state of going beyond reason, transcending ordinary human nature, may sometimes come by chance to a man who does not understand its science; he, as it were, stumbles upon it. When he stumbles upon it, he generally interprets it as coming from outside. So this explains why an inspiration, or transcendental knowledge, may be the same in different countries, but in one country it will seem to come through an angel, and then in another through a deva, and in a third through God. What does it mean? It means that the mind brought the knowledge by its own nature and that the finding of the knowledge was interpreted according to the beliefs and education of the person through whom it came. The real fact is that these various men, as it were, stumbled upon this super-conscious state.

The yogi says there is a great danger in stumbling upon this state. In a good many cases there is the danger of the brain's being deranged; and as a rule you will find that all those men, however great they were, who had stumbled upon this superconscious state without understanding it groped in the dark and generally had, along with their knowledge, some quaint superstitions. They opened themselves to hallucination. Mohammed spoke some wonderful truths. If you read the Koran, you find the most wonderful truths mixed with super-stitions. How will you explain it? That man was inspired, no doubt, but that inspiration was, as it were, stumbled upon. He was not a trained yogi and did not know the reason for what he was doing. Think of the good Mohammed did to the world, and think of the great evil that has been done through his fanaticism! Think of the millions massacred through his teachings—mothers bereft of their children, children made orphans, whole countries destroyed, millions upon millions of people killed!

So we see this danger by studying the lives of great teachers like Mohammed and others. Yet we find, at the same time, that they were all inspired. Whenever a prophet got into the superconscious state by heightening his emotional nature, he brought away from it not only some truths but some fanaticism also, some superstition which injured the world as much as the greatness of the teaching helped. To get any reason out of the mass of incongruity we call human life, we have to transcend our reason; but we must do it scientifically, slowly, by regular practice, and we must cast off all superstition. We must take up the study of the superconscious state just as any other science. On reason we must lay our foundation. We must follow reason as far as it leads, and when reason fails, reason itself will show us the way to the highest plane. When you hear a man say, 'I am inspired', and then talk irrationally, reject it. Why? Because these three states—instinct, reason, and super-consciousness, or the unconscious, conscious, and super-conscious states—belong to one and the same mind. There are not three minds in one man, but one state of it develops into the others. Instinct develops into reason, and reason into the transcendental consciousness; therefore not one of the states contradicts the others. Real inspiration never contradicts reason, but fulfils it. Just as you find the great prophets saying, 'I come not to destroy but to fulfil', so inspiration always comes to fulfil reason and is in harmony with it.

All the different steps in yoga are intended to bring us scientifically to the superconscious state, or samadhi. Furthermore, this is a most vital point to understand, that inspiration is as much in every man's nature as it was in that of the ancient prophets. These prophets were not unique; they were men as you or I. They were great yogis. They had gained this superconsciousness, and you and I can do the same. They were not peculiar

people. The very fact that one man ever reached that
state proves that it is possible for every man to do so.
Not only is it possible, but every man must eventually
get to that state—and that is religion. Experience is the
only teacher we have. We may talk and reason all our
lives, but we shall not understand a word of truth until
we experience it ourselves.

In order to reach the superconscious state in a scientific
manner it is necessary to pass through the various steps
of raja yoga I have been teaching. After pratyahara
and dharana, we come to dhyana, meditation. When the
mind has been trained to remain fixed on a certain
internal or external location, there comes to it the
power of flowing in an unbroken current, as it
were, towards that point. This state is called dhyana.
When one has so intensified the power of dhyana
as to be able to reject the external part of perception
and remain meditating only on the internal part, the
meaning, that state is called samadhi. That is, if the
mind can first concentrate upon an object, and then is
able to continue in that concentration for a length of
time, and then, by continued concentration, to dwell
only on the internal part of the perception of which the
object was the effect, everything comes under the
control of such a mind.

This meditative state is the highest state of existence.
So long as there is desire no real happiness can come. It
is only the contemplative, witness-like study of objects
that brings to us real enjoyment and happiness. The
animal has its happiness in the senses, the man in his
intellect, and the god in spiritual contemplation. It is
only to the soul that has attained to this contemplative

state that the world really becomes beautiful. To him who desires nothing and does not mix himself up with them, the manifold changes of nature are one panorama of beauty and sublimity.

When, by the previous preparations, it becomes strong and controlled, and has the power of finer perception, the mind should be employed in meditation. This meditation must begin with gross objects and slowly rise to finer and finer, until it becomes objectless. The mind should first be employed in perceiving the external causes of sensations, then the internal motions, and then its own reaction. When it has succeeded in perceiving the external causes of sensations by themselves, the mind will acquire the power of perceiving all fine material existences, all fine bodies and forms. When it can succeed in perceiving the motions inside by themselves, it will gain the control of all mental waves, in itself or in others, even before they have translated themselves into physical energy. And when he will be able to perceive the mental reaction by itself, the yogi will acquire the knowledge of everything, as every sensible object, and every thought, is the result of this reaction. Then will he have seen the very foundations of his mind, and it will be under his perfect control. Different powers will come to the yogi; if he yields to the temptations of any one of these the road to his further progress will be barred. Such is the evil of running after enjoyments. But if he is strong enough to reject even these miraculous powers, he will attain to the goal of yoga, the complete suppression of the waves in the ocean of the mind. Then the glory of the Soul, undisturbed by the distractions of the mind or motions of the body, will shine in its full effulgence; and the yogi will find himself as he is and as he always was, the essence of Knowledge, the Immortal, the All-pervading.

Samadhi is the property of every human being—nay, of every animal. From the lowest animal to the highest angel, some time or other each one will have to come to that state; and then, and then alone, will real religion begin for him. Until then we only struggle towards that stage. There is no difference now between us and those who have no religion, because we have no experience. What is concentration good for, save to bring us to this experience? Each one of the steps to attain samadhi has been reasoned out, properly adjusted, scientifically organized, and, when faithfully practised, will surely lead us to the desired end. Then will all sorrows cease, all miseries vanish; the seeds for actions will be burned, and the soul will be free for ever.

There was a great god-sage called Narada. Just as there are sages among mankind, great yogis, so there are great yogis among the gods. Narada was a good yogi and very great. He travelled everywhere. One day he was passing through a forest and saw a man who had been meditating until the white ants had built a huge mound round his body—so long had he been sitting in that position. He said to Narada, 'Where are you going?'

Narada replied, 'I am going to heaven.'

'Then ask God when he will be merciful to me, when I shall attain freedom.'

Farther on Narada saw another man. He was jumping about, singing and dancing, and said, 'O, Narada, where are you going?' His voice and his gestures were wild.

Narada said, 'I am going to heaven.'

'Then ask when I shall be free.'

Narada went on. In the course of time he came again by the same road, and there was the man who had been meditating with the ant hill around him. He said, 'O Narada, did you ask the Lord about me?'

'Oh, yes.'

'What did he say?'

'The Lord told me that you would attain freedom in four more births.'

Then the man began to weep and wail, and said, 'I have meditated until an ant hill has grown around me, and I have four more births yet!'

Narada went to the other man.

'Did you ask my question?'

'Oh, yes. Do you see this tamarind tree? I have to tell you that as many leaves as there are on that tree, so many times you shall be born, and then you shall attain freedom.'

The man began to dance for joy, and said, 'I shall have my freedom after such a short time!'

A voice came, 'My child, you will have freedom this minute.'

That was the reward for his perseverance. He was ready to work through all those births; nothing discouraged him. But the first man felt that even four more births were too long. Only perseverance like that of the man who was willing to wait aeons brings about the highest result.

5

SELF-REALIZATION
THROUGH SELFLESS WORK

The highest man *cannot* work, for there is no
binding element, no attachment, no ignorance in
him. A ship is said to have passed by a mountain of
magnetic ore, and all the bolts and bars were drawn
out, and it went to pieces. It is in ignorance that
struggle remains, because we are all really atheists.
Real theists cannot work. We are atheists more or
less. We do not see God or believe in him. He is
G. O. D. to us, and nothing more. There are
moments when we think he is near, but then we
fall down again. When you see him, who struggles
for whom? Help the Lord! There is a proverb in
our language 'Shall we teach the Architect of the
universe how to build?' So those are the highest of
mankind who do not work. The next time you
see these silly phrases about the world and how we
must all help God and do this or that for him,
remember this. Do not think such thoughts; they
are too selfish.

All the work you do is subjective, is done for your own benefit. God has not fallen into a ditch for you and me to help him out by building a hospital or something of that sort.

He *allows* you to work. He allows you to exercise your muscles in this great gymnasium, not in order to help him but that you may help yourself. Do you think even an ant will die for want of your help? Most arrant blasphemy! The world does not need you at all. The world goes on; you are like a drop in this ocean. A leaf does not move, the wind does not blow, without him.

Blessed are we that we are given the privilege of working for him, not of helping him. Cut out this word 'help' from your mind. You cannot help; it is blaspheming. You are here yourself at his pleasure. Do you mean to say you help him? You worship. When you give a morsel of food to the dog, you worship the dog as God. God is in that dog. God is the dog. He is all and in all. We are allowed to worship him.

Stand in that reverent attitude to the whole universe, and then will come perfect non-attachment. This should be your duty. This is the proper attitude of work. This is the secret taught by karma yoga.

Section 1

The karma yogi is the man who understands that the highest ideal is non-resistance. Before reaching this highest ideal man's duty is to resist evil. Let him work, let him fight, let him strike straight from the shoulder. Then only, when he has gained the power to resist, will non-resistance be a virtue.

HUMAN SOCIETY is a graded organization. We all know about morality and we all know about duty; but at the same time we find that in different countries the significance of morality varies greatly. What is regarded as moral in one country may in another be considered perfectly immoral. For instance, in one country cousins may marry; in another, it is thought to be very immoral. In one, men may marry their sisters-in-law; in another, it is regarded as immoral. In one country people may marry only once; in another, many times; and so forth. Similarly, in all other departments of morality we find the standard varies greatly; yet we have the idea that there must be a universal standard of morality.

So it is with duty. The idea of duty varies much among different nations. In one country, if a man does not do certain things, people will say he has acted wrongly, while if he does those very things in another country, people will say that he did not act rightly— and yet we know that there must be some universal idea of duty. In the same way, one class of society thinks that certain things are among its duties, while another class thinks quite the opposite and would be horrified if it had to do those things.

Two ways are left open to us: the way of the ignorant, who think that there is only one way to truth and that all the rest are wrong; and the way of the wise, who admit that, according to our mental constitution or the different planes of existence in which we are, duty and morality may vary. The important thing is to know that there are gradations of duty and of morality —that the duty of one state of life, in one set of circumstances, will not and cannot be that of another.

To illustrate, all great teachers have taught, 'Resist not evil'—that non-resistance is the highest moral ideal. But we all know that if a certain number of us attempted to put that maxim fully into practice, the whole social fabric would fall to pieces; the wicked would take possession of our properties and our lives and would do whatever they liked with us. Even if only one day of such non-resistance were practised it would lead to disaster. Yet intuitively, in our heart of hearts, we feel the truth of the teaching, 'Resist not evil.' This seems to us to be the highest ideal; yet to teach this doctrine only would be equivalent to condemning a vast portion of mankind. Not only so; it would be making men feel that they were always doing wrong and cause in them scruples of conscience in all their actions; it would weaken them, and that constant self-disapproval would breed more vice than any other weakness would.

To the man who has begun to hate himself the gate to degeneration has already opened; and the same is true of a nation. Out first duty is not to hate ourselves; to advance we must have faith in ourselves first and then in God. He who has no faith in himself can never have faith in God.

Therefore, the only alternative remaining to us is to

recognize that duty and morality vary under different circumstances; not that the man who resists evil is doing what is always and in itself wrong, but that in the different circumstances in which he is placed it may become even his duty to resist evil.

In reading the Bhagavad-Gita, many may have felt astonished at the second chapter, wherein Sri Krishna calls Arjuna a hypocrite and a coward because of his refusal to fight, or offer resistance, on account of his adversaries being his friends and relatives, Arjuna making the plea that non-resistance was the highest ideal of love. This is a great lesson for us all to learn, that in all matters the two extremes are alike. The extreme positive and the extreme negative are always similar. When the vibrations of light are too slow we do not see them, nor do we see them when they are too rapid. So with sound; when very low in pitch we do not hear it, when very high we do not hear it either. Of like nature is the difference between resistance and non-resistance. One man does not resist because he is weak, lazy, and cannot, not because he will not; the other man knows that he can strike an irresistible blow if he likes; yet he not only does not strike, but blesses his enemies. The one who from weakness resists not commits a sin, and as such cannot receive any benefit from the non-reistance; while the other would commit a sin by offering resistance.

Buddha gave up his throne and renounced his position; that was true renunciation. But there cannot be any question of renunciation in the case of a beggar who has nothing to renounce. So we must always be careful about what we really mean when we speak of non-resistance and ideal love. We must first take care to understand whether we have the power of resistance or not. Then, having the power, if we renounce it and do not resist, we are doing a grand act of love; but if we cannot resist, and yet, at the same time, try to deceive ourselves into the belief that we are actuated by motives of the highest love, we are doing the exact opposite. Arjuna became a coward at the sight of the mighty array against him; his 'love' made him forget his duty towards his country and king. That is why Sri Krishna told him that he was a hypocrite; 'Thou talkest like a wise man, but thy actions betray thee to be a coward; therefore, stand up and fight!'

Such is the central idea of karma yoga. The karma-yogi is the man who understands that the highest ideal is non-resistance, and who also knows that his non-resistance is the highest manifestation of power; but he knows too that what is called the resisting of evil is a step on the way towards the manifestation of this highest power, namely, non-resistance. Before reaching this highest ideal man's duty is to resist evil. Let him work, let him fight, let him strike straight from the shoulder. Then only, when he has gained the power to resist, will non-resistance be a virtue.

I once met a man in my country whom I had known before as a very stupid, dull person, who knew nothing and had not the desire to know anything and was living the life of a brute. He asked me what he should do to know God, how he was to get free.

'Can you tell a lie?' I asked him.

'No', he replied.

'Then you must learn to do so. It is better to tell a lie than to be a brute or a log of wood. You are inactive; you certainly have not reached the highest state, which is beyond all actions, calm and serene. You are too dull even to do something wicked.'

That was an extreme case, of course, and I was joking with him; but what I meant was that a man must be active in order to pass through activity to perfect calmness. Inactivity should be avoided by all means. Activity always means resistance. Resist all evils, mental and physical; and when you have succeeded in resisting, then will calmness come.

It is very easy to say, 'Hate nobody, resist not evil', but we know what that kind of advice generally means in practice. When the eyes of society are turned towards us we may make a show of non-resistance, but in our hearts it is canker all the time. We feel the utter want of the calm of non-resistance; we feel that it would be better for us to resist. If you desire wealth, and know at the same time that the whole world regards him who aims at wealth as a very wicked man, you perhaps will not dare to plunge into the struggle for wealth; yet your mind will be running day and night after money. This is hypocrisy and will serve no purpose. Plunge into the world, and then, after a time, when you have suffered and enjoyed all that is in it, will renunciation come; then will calmness come. So fulfil your desire for power and everything else, and after you have fulfilled the desire will come the time when you will know that they are all very little things. But until you have fulfilled this desire, until you have passed through that activity, it is impossible for you to come to the state of calmness, serenity, and self-surrender. These ideas of serenity and renunciation have been preached for thousands of years; everybody has heard of them from childhood; and yet we see very few in the world who have really reached that stage. I do not know if I have seen twenty persons in my life who are really calm and non-resisting, and I have travelled over half the world.

Every man should take up his own ideal and endeavour to accomplish it. That is a surer way to progressing than taking up other men's ideals, which he can never hope to accomplish. For instance, we take a child and at once give him the task of walking twenty miles. Either the little one dies or one in a thousand crawls the twenty miles to reach the end exhausted and half dead. That is what we generally try to do with the world. Not all the men and women in any society are of the same mind, capacity, or power to do things; they must have different ideals, and we have no right to sneer at any ideal. Let everyone do the best he can to realize his own ideal. Nor is it right that I should be judged by your standard or you by mine. The apple tree should not be judged by the standard of the oak, nor the oak by that of the apple. To judge the apple tree you must take the apple standard, and for the oak, its own standard.

Unity in variety is the plan of creation. However men and women may vary individually, there is unity in the background. The different individual characters and classes of men and women are natural variations in creation. Hence we ought not to judge them by the same standard or put the same ideal before them. Such a course creates only an unnatural struggle, and the result is that a man begins to hate himself and is hindered from becoming religious and good. Our duty is to encourage everyone in his struggle to live up to his own highest ideal, and strive at the same time to make that ideal as near as possible to the truth.

The life of every individual, according to the Hindu scriptures, has its peculiar duties apart from those which are common to humanity. The Hindu begins life as a student; then he marries and becomes a householder; in old age he retires; and lastly he gives up the world and becomes a sannyasin. To each of these stages of life certain duties are attached. No one of these stages is intrinsically superior to another. The life of the married man is quite as great as that of the celibate who has devoted himself to religious work. The scavenger in the street is quite as great and glorious as the king on his throne. Take the king off his throne, make him do the work of the scavenger, and see how he fares. Take up the scavenger and see how he will rule. It is useless to say that the man who lives out of the world is a greater man than he who lives in the world; it is much more difficult to live in the world and worship God than to give it up and live a free-and-easy life.

The four stages of life in India have in later times been reduced to two—that of the householder and that of the monk. The householder marries and carries on his duties as a citizen; the duty of the other is to devote his energies wholly to religion, to preach and to worship God.

The householder is the basis, the prop, of the whole of society. He is the principal earner. The poor, the weak, the children and the women who do not work— all live upon the householder. So there must be certain duties that he has to perform, and these duties must make him feel strong to perform them, and not make him think that he is doing things beneath his ideal. At the same time, he must struggle hard to acquire these things: first, knowledge, and second, wealth. It is his duty, and if he does not do his duty he is nobody. A householder who does not struggle to get wealth is immoral. If he is lazy and content to lead an idle life, he is immoral, because upon him depend hundreds. If he gets riches, hundreds of others will be thereby supported.

Going after wealth in such a case is not bad, because that wealth is for distribution. The householder is the centre of life and society. It is a worship for him to acquire and spend wealth nobly; for the householder who struggles to become rich by good means and for good purposes is doing practically the same thing for the attainment of salvation as the anchorite does in his cell when he is praying; for in them we see only the different aspects of the same virtue of self-surrender and self-sacrifice prompted by the feeling of devotion to God and to all that is his.

If a man retires from the world to worship God, he must not think that those who live in the world and work for the good of the world are not worshipping God; neither must those who live in the world, for wife and children, think that those who give up the world are low vagabonds. Each is great in his own place. This thought I will illustrate by a story.

A certain king used to inquire of all the sannyasins that came to his country, 'Which is the greater man— he who gives up the world and becomes a sannyasin or he who lives in the world and performs his duties as a householder?' Many wise men sought to solve the problem. Some asserted that the sannyasin was the greater, upon which the king demanded that they should prove their assertion. When they could not, he ordered them to marry and become householders. Then others came and said, 'The householder who performs his duties is the greater man.' Of them, too, the king demanded proofs. When they could not give them, he made them also settle down as householders.

At last there came a young sannyasin, and the king similarly inquired of him also. He answered, 'Each, O king, is equally great in his place.'

'Prove this to me', demanded the king.

'I will prove it to you', said the sannyasin, 'but you must first come and live as I do for a few days, that I may be able to prove to you what I say.'

The king consented and followed the sannyasin out of his own territory and passed through many other countries until they came to a great kingdom. In the capital of that kingdom a ceremony was going on. The king and the sannyasin heard the noise of drums and music, and heard also the criers; the people were assembled in the streets in gala dress, and a proclamation was being made. The king and the sannyasin stood there to see what was going on. The crier was proclaiming loudly that the princess, daughter of the king of that country, was about to choose a husband from among those assembled before her.

It was an old custom in India for princesses to choose husbands in this way. Each princess had certain ideas of the sort of man she wanted for a husband. Some would have the handsomest man, others would have only the most learned, others again the richest, and so on. All the princes of the neighbourhood would put on their bravest attire and present themselves before her. Sometimes they too had their own criers to enumerate their advantages and the reasons why they hoped the princess would choose them. The princess would be taken round on a throne, in the most splendid array, and would look at and hear about them. If she was not pleased with what she saw and heard, she would say to her bearers, 'Move on', and no more notice was taken of the rejected suitors. If, however, the princess was pleased with any one of them she would throw a garland of flowers over him and he became her husband.

The princess of the country to which our king and sannyasin had come was having one of these interesting ceremonies. She was the most beautiful princess in the world, and her husband would be ruler of the kingdom after her father's death. The idea of this princess was to marry the handsomest man, but she could not find the right one to please her. Several times these meetings had taken place, but the princess could not select a husband. This meeting was the most splendid of all; more people than ever had come to it. The princess came in on a throne, and the bearers carried her from place to place. She did not seem to care for anyone, and everyone became disappointed that this meeting also was going to be a failure.

Just then came a young man, a sannyasin, handsome as if the sun had come down to the earth, and stood in one corner of the assembly, watching what was going on. The throne with the princess came near him, and as soon as she saw the beautiful sannyasin, she stopped and threw the garland over him.

The young sannyasin seized the garland and threw it off, exclaiming: 'What nonsense is this? I am a sannyasin. What is marriage to me?'

The king of that country thought that perhaps this man was poor and so dared not marry the princess, and said to him, 'With my daughter goes half my kingdom now, and the whole kingdom after my death!' and put the garland again on the sannyasin.

The young man threw it off once more, saying, 'Nonsense! I do not want to marry', and walked quickly away from the assembly.

Now the princess had fallen so much in love with this young man that she said, 'I must marry this man or I shall die'; and she went after him to bring him back. Then our other sannyasin, who had brought the king there, said to him, 'King, let us follow this pair.' So they walked after them, but at a good distance behind. The young sannyasin who had refused to marry the princess walked out into the country for several miles. When he came to a forest and entered into it, the princess followed him, and the other two followed them. Now this young sannyasin was well acquainted with that forest and knew all the intricate paths in it. He suddenly passed into one of these and disappeared, and the princess could not discover him. After trying for a long time to find him, she sat down under a tree and began to weep; for she did not know the way out. Then our king and the other sannyasin came up to her and said, 'Do not weep; we shall show you the way out of this forest, but it is too dark for us to find it now. Here is a big tree; let us rest under it, and in the morning we shall go early and show you the road.'

Now, a little bird and his wife and their three little ones lived on that tree, in a nest. This little bird looked down and saw the three people under the tree and said to his wife. 'My dear, what shall we do? Here are some guests in the house, and it is winter, and we have no fire.' So he flew away and got a bit of burning firewood in his beak and dropped it before the guests, to which they added fuel and made a blazing fire. But the little bird was not satisfied. He said again to his wife, 'My dear, what shall we do? There is nothing to give these people to eat, and they are hungry. We are householders; it is our duty to feed anyone who comes to the house. I must do what I can, I will give them my body.' So he plunged into the midst of the fire and perished. The guests saw him falling and tried to save him, but he was too quick for them.

The little bird's wife saw what her husband did, and she said: 'Here are three persons and only one little bird for them to eat. It is not enough; it is my duty as a wife not to let my husband's effort go in vain; let them have my body also.' Then she fell into the fire and was burned to death.

Then the three baby birds, when they saw what was done and that there was still not enough food for the three guests, said: 'Our parents have done what they could and still it is not enough. It is our duty to carry on the work of our parents; let our bodies go too.' And they all dashed down into the fire also.

Amazed at what they saw, the three people could not of course eat these birds. They passed the night without food, and in the morning the king and the sannyasin showed the princess the way, and she went back to her father.

Then the sannyasin said to the king, 'King, you have seen that each is great in his own place. If you want to live in the world, live like those birds, ready at any moment to sacrifice yourself for others. If you want to renounce the world, be like that young man to whom that most beautiful woman and a kingdom was as nothing. If you want to be a householder, hold your life a sacrifice for the welfare of others; and if you choose the life of renunciation do not even look at beauty and money and power. Each is great in his own place, but the duty of the one is not the duty of the other.'

Section 2

The whole gist of this teaching is that you should work like a master and not as a slave; work incessantly, but do not do slave's work. Work through freedom! Work through love!

Helping others physically, by removing their physical needs, is indeed great; but the help is greater according as the need is greater and according as the help is far-reaching. If a man's wants can be removed for an hour, it is helping him indeed; if his wants can be removed for a year, it will be more help to him; but if his wants can be removed for ever, it is surely the greatest help that can be given him.

Spiritual knowledge is the only thing that can destroy miseries for ever; any other knowledge satisfies wants only for a time. It is only with the knowledge of the Spirit that the root cause of want is annihilated for ever; so helping man spiritually is the highest help that can be given to him. He who gives man spiritual knowledge is the greatest benefactor of mankind, and as such we always find that those were the most powerful of men who helped man in his spiritual needs, because spirituality is the true basis of all our activities in life. A spiritually strong and sound man will be strong in every other respect, if he so wishes. Until there is spiritual strength in man even physical needs cannot be well satisfied.

Next to spiritual comes intellectual help. The gift of knowledge is a far higher gift than that of food and clothes; it is even higher than giving life to a man, because the real life of man consists of knowledge. Ignorance is death, knowledge is life. Life is of very little value if it is a life in the dark, groping through ignorance and misery.

Next in order comes, of course, helping a man physically.

Therefore, in considering the question of helping others, we must always strive not to commit the mistake of thinking that physical help is the only help that can be given. It is not only the last but the least, because it cannot bring about permanent satisfaction. The misery that I feel when I am hungry is satisfied by eating, but hunger returns; my misery can cease only when I am satisfied beyond all want. Then hunger will not make me miserable; no distress, no sorrow, will be able to move me. So that help which tends to make us strong spiritually is the highest; next to it comes intellectual help, and after that physical help.

The miseries of the world cannot be cured by physical help only. Until man's nature changes, these physical needs will always arise and miseries will always be felt, and no amount of physical help will cure them completely. The only solution of this problem is to make mankind pure. Ignorance is the mother of all the evil and all the misery we see. Let men have light, let them be pure and spiritually strong and educated; then alone will misery cease in the world, not before. We may convert every house in the country into a charity asylum; we may fill the land with hospitals; but the misery of man will still continue to exist until man's character changes.

We read in the Bhagavad-Gita again and again that we must all work incessantly. All work is by nature composed of good and evil. We cannot do any work which will not do some good somewhere; there cannot be any work which will not cause some harm somewhere. Every work must necessarily be a mixture of good and evil. Yet we are commanded to work incessantly. Good and evil will both have their results, will produce their karma. Good action will entail upon us good effect; bad action, bad. But good and bad are both bondages of the soul. The solution reached in the Gita in regard to this bondage-producing nature of work is that, if we do not attach ourselves to the work we do, it will not have any binding effect on our soul. This is the one central idea in the Gita: work incessantly, but be not attached to it.

Every work that we do, every movement of the body, every thought that we think, leaves an impression on the mind-stuff, and even when such impressions are not obvious on the surface they are sufficiently strong to work beneath the surface, subconsciously. What we are every moment is determined by the sum total of these impressions on the mind. What I am just at this moment is the effect of the sum total of all the impressions of my past life.

This is really what is meant by character; each man's character is determined by the sum total of these impressions. If good impressions prevail, the character becomes good; if bad, it becomes bad. If a man continuously hears bad words, thinks bad thoughts, does bad actions, his mind will be full of bad impressions; and they will influence his thought and work without his being conscious of the fact. In fact, these bad impressions are always working, and their resultant must be evil; and that man will be a bad man; he cannot help it. The sum total of these impressions in him will create the strong motive power for doing bad actions. He will be like a machine in the hands of his impressions, and they will force him to do evil. Similarly, if a man thinks good thoughts and does good works, the sum total of these impressions will be good; and they, in a similar manner, will force him to do good even in spite of himself. When a man has done so much good work and thought so many good thoughts, there is an irresistible tendency in him to do good. In spite of himself and even if he wishes to do evil, his mind, as the sum total of his tendencies, will not allow him to do so: the tendencies will turn him back; he is completely under the influence of the good tendencies. When such is the case, a man's good character is said to be established.

There is a still higher state than having this good tendency, and that is the desire for liberation. You must remember that freedom of the soul is the goal of all yogas, and each one equally leads to the same result. By work alone men may get to where Buddha got largely by meditation or Christ by prayer. Buddha was a working jnani; Christ was a bhakta; but the same goal was reached by both of them. The difficulty is here. Liberation means entire freedom—freedom from the bondage of good as well as from the bondage of evil. A golden chain is as much a chain as an iron one. There is a thorn in my finger. I use another to take the first one out, and when I have taken it out I throw both of them aside; I have no necessity for keeping the second thorn, because both are thorns after all. So the bad tendencies are to be counteracted by the good ones, and the bad impressions on the mind should be removed by the fresh waves of good ones, until all that is evil almost disappears or is subdued and held in control in a corner of the mind. But after that the good tendencies have also to be conquered. Thus the 'attached' becomes the 'unattached'. Work, but let not the action or the thought of it produce a deep impression on the mind. Let the ripples come and go, let huge actions proceed from the muscles and the brain, but let them not make any deep impressions on the soul.

How can this be done? We see that the impression of any action to which we attach ourselves remains. I may meet hundreds of persons during the day, and among them meet also one whom I love; and when I retire at night I may try to think of all the faces I saw, but only that face comes before the mind—the face which I met perhaps only for one minute, and which I loved. All the others have vanished. My attachment to this particular person caused a deeper impression on my mind than all the other faces. Physiologically, the impressions have all been the same; every one of the faces that I saw pictured itself on the retina, and the brain took the pictures in, and yet there was no similarity of effect upon the mind.

Therefore, be unattached. Let things work; let brain centres work; work incessantly, but let not a ripple conquer the mind. Work as if you were a stranger in this land, a sojourner. Work incessantly, but do not bind yourselves; bondage is terrible. This world is not our habitation, it is only one of the many stages through which we are passing. 'The whole of nature is for the soul, not the soul for nature.' The very reason of nature's existence is for the education of the soul; it has no other meaning. It is there because the soul must have knowledge, and through knowledge free itself. If we remember this always, we shall never be attached to nature; we shall know that nature is a book in which we are to read and that when we have gained the required knowledge the book is of no more value to us.

The whole gist of this teaching is that you should work like a master and not as a slave; work incessantly, but do not do slave's work. Do you not see how everybody works? Nobody can be altogether at rest. Ninety-nine per cent of mankind work like slaves, and the result is misery; it is all selfish work. Work through freedom! Work through love!

The word *love* is very difficult to understand. Love never comes until there is freedom. There is no true love possible in the slave. If you buy a slave and tie him down in chains and make him work for you, he will work like a drudge, but there will be no love in him. So when we ourselves work for the things of the world as slaves, there can be no love in us, and our work is not true work. This is true of work done for relatives and friends, and is true of work done for our own selves. Selfish work is slave's work. And here is a test: Every act of love brings happiness; there is no act of love which does not bring peace and blessedness as its reaction.

Therefore true love can never react so as to cause pain either to the lover or to the beloved. Suppose a man loves a woman; he wishes to have her all to himself and feels extremely jealous about her every movement; he wants her to sit near him, to stand near him, and to eat and move at his bidding. He is a slave to her and wishes to have her as his slave. That is not love; it is a kind of morbid affection of the slave, insinuating itself as love. It cannot be love, because it is painful; if she does not do what he wants, it brings him pain. With love there is no painful reaction; love only brings a reaction of bliss. If it does not, it is not love; it is mistaking something else for love. When you have succeeded in loving your husband, your wife, your children, the whole world, the universe, in such a manner that there is no reaction of pain or jealousy, no selfish feeling, then you are in a fit state to be unattached.

Krishna says: 'Look at me, Arjuna! If I stop from work for a moment the whole universe will die. I have nothing to gain from work; I am the one Lord. But why do I work? Because I love the world.' God is unattached because he loves. That real love makes us unattached.

To attain this non-attachment is almost a life work; but as soon as we have reached this point we have attained the goal of love and become free. The bondage of nature falls from us, and we see nature as she is; she forges no more chains for us. We stand entirely free and take not the results of work into consideration; who then cares for what the results may be?

Do you ask anything from your children in return for what you have given them? It is your duty to work for them, and there the matter ends. In whatever you do for a particular person, city, or state, assume the same attitude towards it as you have towards your children—expect nothing in return. If you can invariably take the position of a giver, in which everything given by you is a free offering to the world, without any thought of return, then will your work bring you no attachment. Attachment comes only where we expect a return.

If working like slaves results in selfishness and attachment, working as masters of our own minds gives rise to the bliss of non-attachment. We often talk of right and justice, but we find that in the world right and justice are mere baby's talk. There are two things which guide the conduct of men; might and mercy. The exercise of might is invariably the exercise of selfishness. Men and women try to make the most of whatever power or advantage they have. Mercy is heaven itself; to be good we have all to be merciful. Even justice and right should stand on mercy. All thought of obtaining return for the work we do hinders our spiritual progress; nay, in the end it brings misery.

There is another way in which this idea of mercy and selfless charity can be put into practice; that is by looking upon work as worship, in case we believe in a Personal God. Here we give up all the fruits of our work unto the Lord; and, worshipping him thus, we have no right to expect anything from mankind for the work we do. The Lord himself works incessantly and is ever without attachment. Just as water cannot wet the lotus leaf, so work cannot bind the unselfish man by giving rise to attachment to results.

Now you see what karma yoga means: even at the point of death to help anyone, without asking questions.

Be cheated millions of times and never ask a question, and never think of what you are doing. Never vaunt of your gifts to the poor or expect their gratitude, but rather be grateful to them for giving you the occasion of practising charity upon them.

It is necessary in the study of karma yoga to know what duty is. If I have to do something, I must first know that it is my duty, and then I can do it. We find that there are varied ideas of duty, differing according to different states in life, different historical periods, and different nations.

The term *duty*, like every other universal, abstract term, is impossible clearly to define; we can only get an idea of it by knowing its practical operations and results. The ordinary idea of duty everywhere is that every good man follows the dictates of his conscience. But what is it that makes an act a duty? If a Christian finds a piece of beef before him and does not eat it to save his own life, or will not give it to save the life of another man, he is sure to feel that he has not done his duty. But if a Hindu dares to eat that piece of beef or to give it to another Hindu, he is equally sure to feel that he too has not done his duty; the Hindu's training and education make him feel that way. In the last century there were notorious bands of robbers in India called thugs. They thought it their duty to kill any man they could and take away his money; the larger the number of men they killed, the better they thought they were. Ordinarily, if a man goes out into the street and shoots down another man, he is apt to feel sorry for it, thinking that he has done wrong. But if the very same man, as a soldier in his regiment, kills not one but twenty, he is certain to feel glad and think that he has done his duty remarkably well.

Therefore we see that it is not the thing done that defines a duty. To give an objective definition of duty is thus entirely impossible. Yet there is duty from the subjective side. Any action that makes us go Godward is a good action and is our duty; any action that makes us go downward is evil and is not our duty. From the subjective standpoint we may see that certain acts have a tendency to exalt and ennoble us, while certain other acts have a tendency to degrade and to brutalize us. But it is not possible to make out with certainty which acts have which kind of tendency in relation to all persons, of all sorts and conditions. There is, however, only one idea of duty which has been universally accepted by all mankind, of all ages and sects and countries, and that has been summed up in a Sanskrit aphorism thus: 'Do not injure any being. Not injuring any being is virtue; injuring any being is sin.'

The Bhagavad-Gita frequently alludes to duties dependent upon birth and position in life. Birth and position in life and in society largely determine the mental and moral attitude of individuals towards the various activities of life. It is therefore our duty to do that work which will exalt and ennoble us in accordance with the ideals and activities of the society in which we are born. But it must be particularly remembered that the same ideals and activities do not prevail in all societies and countries; our ignorance of this is the main cause of much of the hatred of one nation towards another. When I came to this country and was going through the Chicago Fair, a man from behind pulled at my turban. I looked back and saw that he was a very gentlemanly looking man, neatly dressed. I spoke to him and when he found that I knew English he became very much abashed. On another occasion in the same Fair another man gave me a push. When I asked him the reason, he also was ashamed and stammered out an apology saying, 'Why do you dress that way?' The sympathies of these men were limited within the range of their own fashion of dress.

Much of the oppression of weaker nations by powerful ones is caused by this prejudice. It dries up their fellow-feeling for fellow men. That very man who asked me why I did not dress as he did and wanted to ill-treat me because of my dress may have been a very good man, a good father and a good citizen; but the kindliness of his nature died out as soon as he saw a man in a different dress. Strangers are exploited in all countries, because they do not know how to defend themselves; thus they carry home false impressions of the peoples they have seen. Sailors, soldiers, and traders behave in foreign lands in very queer ways, although they would not dream of doing so in their own country; perhaps this is why the Chinese call Europeans and Americans 'foreign devils'. They could not have done this if they had met the good, the kindly, sides of western life.

Therefore the one point we ought to remember is that we should always try to see the duty of others through their own eyes and never judge the customs of other peoples by our own standard. I am not the standard of the universe. I have to accommodate myself to the world, and not the world to me. So we see that environments change the nature of our duties, and doing the duty which is ours at any particular time is the best thing we can do in this world. Let us do that duty which is ours by birth; and when we have done that, let us do the duty which is ours by our position in life and in society. There is, however, one great danger in human nature—that man never examines himself. He thinks he is quite as fit to be on the throne as the king. Even if he is, he must first show that he has done the duty of his own position; and then higher duties will come to him. When we begin to work earnestly in the world, nature gives us blows right and left and soon enables us to find out our position. No man can long occupy satisfactorily a position for which he is not fit. There is no use in grumbling against nature's adjustment. He who does the lower work is not therefore a lower man. No man is to be judged by the mere nature of his duties, but all should be judged by the manner and the spirit in which they perform them.

Later on we shall find that even this idea of duty undergoes change, and that the greatest work is done only when there is no selfish motive to prompt it. Yet it is work through the sense of duty that leads us to work without any idea of duty. Then work will become worship—nay, something higher; then will work be done for its own sake. We shall find that the philosophy of duty, whether it be in the form of ethics or of love, is the same as in every other yoga—the object being the attenuating of the lower self, so that the real higher Self may shine forth; to lessen the frittering away of energies on the lower plane of existence, so that the soul may manifest itself on the higher ones.

Duty is seldom sweet. It is only when love greases its wheels that it runs smoothly; it is a continuous friction otherwise. How else could parents do their duties to their children, husbands to their wives, and vice versa? Do we not meet with cases of friction every day in our lives? Duty is sweet only through love, and love shines alone in freedom. Yet is it freedom to be a slave to the senses, to anger, to jealousies, and to a hundred other petty things that must occur every day in human life? In all these little roughnesses that we meet with in life, the highest expression of freedom is to forbear. Women who are slaves to their own irritable, jealous tempers are apt to blame their husbands and assert their own 'freedom'—as they think—not knowing that thereby they only prove that they are slaves. So it is with husbands who eternally find fault with their wives.

The only way to rise is by doing the duty next to us, and thus gathering strength, go on until we reach the highest state.

A young sannyasin went to a forest; there he meditated, worshipped, and practised yoga for a long time. After years of hard work and practice he was one day sitting under a tree, when some dry leaves fell upon his head. He looked up and saw a crow and a crane fighting on the top of the tree, which made him very angry. He said, 'What! Dare you throw these dry leaves upon my head!' As with these words he angrily glanced at them, a flash of fire went out—such was the yogi's power—and burnt the birds to ashes. He was very glad, almost overjoyed, at this development of power; he could burn the crow and the crane by a look!

After a time he had to go to the town to beg his bread. He went, stood at a door, and said, 'Mother, give me food.'

A voice came from inside the house, 'Wait a little, my son.'

The young man thought, 'You wretched woman, how dare you make me wait! You do not know my power.'

While he was thinking thus the voice came again: 'Boy, don't be thinking too much of yourself. Here is neither crow nor crane.'

He was astonished. Still he had to wait. At last the woman came, and he fell at her feet and said, 'Mother, how did you know that?'

She said: 'My boy, I do not know your yoga or your practices. I am a common, everyday woman. I made you wait because my husband is ill and I was nursing him. All my life I have struggled to do my duty. When I was unmarried, I did my duty to my parents; now that I am married, I do my duty to my husband. That is all the yoga I practise. But by doing my duty I have become illumined; thus I could read your thoughts and know what you had done in the forest. If you want to know something higher than this, go to the market of such and such a town where you will find a *vyadha* [one belonging to the lowest class of people in India, who were hunters and butchers] who will tell you something that you will be very glad to learn.'

The sannyasin thought, 'Why should I go to that town and to a vyadha!' But after what he had seen, his mind opened a little, so he went. When he came near the town he found the market, and there saw, at a distance, a big fat vyadha cutting meat with big knives, talking and bargaining with different people. The young man said: 'Lord help me! Is this the man from whom I am going to learn? He is the incarnation of a demon, if he is anything.'

In the meantime the man looked up and said: 'O

Swami, did that lady send you here? Take a seat until I have done my business.'

The sannyasin thought, 'What comes to me here?' He took his seat.

The man went on with his work, and after he had finished he took his money and said to the sannyasin, 'Come, sir, come to my home.' On reaching home the vyadha gave him a seat, saying, 'Wait here', and went into the house. He then bathed his old father and mother, fed them, and did all he could to please them, after which he came to the sannyasin and said, 'Now, sir, you have come here to see me. What can I do for you?'

The sannyasin asked him a few questions about soul and about God, and the vyadha gave him a lecture which forms a part of the Mahabharata. It contains one of the highest flights of the Vedanta.

When the vyadha finished his teaching the sannyasin felt astonished. He said: 'Why are you in that body? With such knowledge as yours why are you in a vyadha's body, and doing such filthy, ugly work?'

'My son', replied the vyadha, 'no duty is ugly, no duty is impure. My birth placed me in these circumstances and this environment. In my boyhood I learnt the trade. I am unattached and I try to do my duty well. I try to do my duty as a householder, and I try to do all I can to make my father and mother happy. I neither know your yoga, nor have I become a sannyasin, nor did I go out of the world into a forest. Nevertheless all that you have heard and seen has come to me through the unattached doing of the duty which belongs to my position'.

There is a sage in India, a great yogi, one of the most

wonderful men I have ever seen in my life. He is a peculiar man; he will not teach anyone. If you ask him a question he will not answer. It is too much for him to take up the position of a teacher; he will not do it. If you ask a question and wait for some days, in the course of conversation he will bring up the subject, and wonderful light will he throw on it. He told me once the secret of work: 'Let the end and the means be joined into one.' When you are doing any work, do not think of anything beyond. Do it as worship, as the highest worship, and devote your whole life to it for the time being. In the story the vyadha and the woman did their duty with cheerfulness and whole-heartedness; and the result was that they became illumined, thus clearly showing that the right performance of the duties of any station in life, without attachment to results, leads us to the highest realization of the perfection of the soul.

It is the worker who is attached to results that grumbles about the nature of the duty which has fallen to his lot; to the unattached worker all duties are equally good and form efficient instruments with which selfishness and sensuality may be killed and the freedom of the soul secured. We are all apt to think too highly of ourselves. Our duties are determined by our deserts to a much larger extent than we are willing to grant. Competition rouses envy, and it kills the kindliness of the heart. To the grumbler all duties are distasteful; nothing will ever satisfy him, and his whole life is doomed to failure. Let us work on, doing as we go whatever happens to be our duty, and being ever ready to put our shoulders to the wheel. Then surely shall we see the Light!

Section 3

The main effect of work done for others is to purify ourselves. By means of the constant effort to do good to others we are trying to forget ourselves; this forgetfulness of self is the one great lesson we have to learn in life. Every act of charity, every thought of sympathy, every action of help, every good deed, takes so much of self-importance away from our little selves and makes us think ourselves as the lowest and the least; and therefore they are all good.

Our duty to others means helping others; doing good to the world. Why should we do good to the world? Apparently to help the world. That should be the highest motive in us. But if we consider well, we find that the world does not require our help at all. This world was not made that you or I should come and help it. I once read a sermon in which it was said: 'All this beautiful world is very good, because it gives us time and opportunity to help others.' Apparently this is a very beautiful sentiment; but is it not a blasphemy to say that the world needs our help? We cannot deny that there is much misery in it; to go out and help others is, therefore, the best thing we can do, although, in the long run, we shall find that helping others is only helping ourselves. As a boy I had some white mice. They were kept in a little box in which there were little wheels, and when the mice tried to cross the wheels, the wheels turned and turned, and the mice never got anywhere. So it is with the world and our helping it. The only help is that we get moral exercise.

This world is neither good nor evil; each man manufactures a world for himself. If a blind man begins to think of the world, it is either as soft or hard, or as cold or hot. We are a mass of happiness or misery; we have seen that hundreds of times in our lives. As a rule the young are optimistic and the old pessimistic. The young have life before them. The old complain their day is gone; hundreds of desires, which they cannot fulfil, struggle in their hearts. Both are foolish nevertheless. Life is good or evil according to the state of mind in which we look at it; it is neither in itself. Fire, in itself, is neither good nor evil. When it keeps us warm we say, 'How beautiful is fire!' When it burns our fingers we blame it. Still, in itself it is neither good nor bad; according as we use it, it produces in us the feeling of good or bad. So also is this world. It is perfect. By perfection is meant that it is perfectly fitted to meet its ends. We may all be perfectly sure that it will go on beautifully well without us, and we need not bother our heads wishing to help it.

Yet we must do good; the desire to do good is the highest motive power we have, if we know all the time that it is a privilege to help others. Do not stand on a high pedestal and take five cents in your hand and say, 'Here, my poor man.' But be grateful that the poor man is there, so that by making a gift to him you are able to help yourself. It is not the receiver that is blessed, but it is the giver. Be thankful that you are allowed to exercise your power of benevolence and mercy in the world, and thus become pure and perfect. All good acts tend to make us pure and perfect. What can we do at best? Build a hospital, make roads, or erect charity asylums! We may organize a charity and collect two or three millions of dollars, build a hospital with one million, with the second give balls and drink champagne, and of the third let the officers steal half, and leave the rest finally to reach the poor; but what are all these? One mighty wind in five minutes can break all your buildings up. What shall we do then? One volcanic eruption may sweep away all our roads and hospitals and cities and buildings.

Let us give up all this foolish talk of doing good to the world. It is not waiting for your or my help. Yet we must work and constantly do good, because it is a blessing to ourselves. That is the only way we can become perfect. No beggar whom we have helped has ever owed a single cent to us; we owe everything to him, because he has allowed us to exercise our charity on him. It is entirely wrong to think that we have done, or can do, good to the world, or to think that we have helped people. It is a foolish thought, and all foolish thoughts bring misery. We think that we have helped some man and expect him to thank us; and because he does not, unhappiness comes to us. Why should we expect anything in return for what we do? Be grateful to the man you help, think of him as God. Is it not a great privilege to be allowed to worship God by helping our fellow man? If we were really unattached, we should escape all this pain of vain expectation and could cheerfully do good work in the world. Never will unhappiness or misery come through work done without attachment. The world will go on with its happiness and misery through eternity.

There was a poor man who wanted some money, and somehow he had heard that if he could get hold of a ghost, he might command him to bring money or anything else he liked; so he was very anxious to get hold of a ghost. He went about searching for a man who would give him a ghost, and at last he found a sage with great powers and besought his help. The sage asked him what he would do with a ghost. 'I want a ghost to work for me. Teach me how to get hold of one, sir; I desire it very much', replied the man.

But the sage said, 'Don't disturb yourself; go home.'

The next day the man went again to the sage and began to weep and pray, 'Give me a ghost; I must have a ghost, sir, to help me.'

At last the sage was disgusted and said: 'Take this charm, repeat this magic word, and a ghost will come, and whatever you say to him he will do. But beware; they are terrible beings and must be kept continually busy. If you fail to give him work he will take your life.'

The man replied, 'That is easy; I can give him work for all his life.'

Then he went to a forest, and after long repetition of the magic word a huge ghost appeared before him, and said, 'I am a ghost. I have been conquered by your magic; but you must keep me constantly employed. The moment you fail to give me work I will kill you.'

The man said, 'Build me a palace.'

The ghost said, 'It is done; the palace is built.'

'Bring me money', said the man.

'Here is your money', said the ghost.

'Cut this forest down and build a city in its place.'

'That is done', said the ghost. 'Anything more?'

Now the man began to be frightened and thought he could give him nothing more to do; he did everything in a trice.

The ghost said, 'Give me something to do or I will eat you up.'

The poor man could find no further occupation for him and was frightened. So he ran and ran and at last reached the sage, and said, 'Oh, sir, protect my life!'

The sage asked him what the matter was, and the man replied: 'I have nothing to give the ghost to do. Everything I tell him to do he does in a moment, and he threatens to eat me up if I do not give him work.'

Just then the ghost arrived, saying, 'I'll eat you up', and was about to swallow the man. The man began to shake, and begged the sage to save his life.

The sage said: 'I will find you a way out. Look at that dog with a curly tail. Draw your sword quickly and cut the tail off and give it to the ghost to straighten out.'

The man cut off the dog's tail and gave it to the ghost, saying, 'Straighten that out for me.'

The ghost took it and slowly and carefully straightened it out, but as soon as he let it go, it instantly curled up again. Once more he laboriously straightened it out, only to find it again curled up as soon as he attempted to let go of it. Again he patiently straightened it out, but as soon as he let it go it curled up again. So he went on for days and days, until he was exhausted and said: 'I was never in such trouble before in my life. I am an old, veteran ghost, but never before was I in such trouble. I will make a compromise with you. You let me off and I will let you keep all I have given you and will promise not to harm you.'

The man was much pleased and accepted the offer gladly.

This world is like a dog's curly tail, and people have

been striving to straighten it out for hundreds of years; but when they let it go, it has curled up again. How could it be otherwise? One must first know how to work without attachment, then one will not be a fanatic. When we know that this world is like a dog's curly tail and will never get straightened, we shall not become fanatics. If there were no fanaticism in the world it would make much more progress than it does now. It is a mistake to think that fanaticism can make for the progress of mankind. On the contrary, it is a retarding element creating hatred and anger, and causing people to fight each other, and making them unsympathetic. We think that whatever we do or possess is the best in the world, and what we do not do or possess is of no value. So always remember the instance of the curly tail of the dog whenever you have a tendency to become a fanatic. You need not worry or make yourself sleepless about the world; it will go on without you. When you have avoided fanaticism, then alone will you work well. It is level-headed man, the calm man of good judgement and cool nerves, of great sympathy and love, who does good work and so does good to himself. The fanatic is foolish and has no sympathy; he can never straighten the world, nor himself become pure and perfect.

Just as every action that emanates from us comes back to us as reaction, even so our actions may act on other people and theirs on us. Perhaps all of you have observed it as a fact that when persons do evil actions they become more and more evil, and when they begin to do good they become stronger and stronger and learn to do good at all times.

This intensification of the influence of action cannot be

explained on any other ground than that we can act and react upon each other. When I am doing a certain action, my mind may be said to be in a certain state of vibration; all minds which are in similar circumstances will have the tendency to be affected by my mind. Suppose there are different musical instruments tuned alike in one room; you may have noticed that when one is struck the others have the tendency to vibrate so as to give the same note. So all minds that have the same tension, so to say, will be equally affected by the same thought. Of course, this influence of thought on mind will vary, according to distance and other causes, but the mind is always open to being affected. Suppose I am doing an evil act, my mind is in a certain state of vibration, and all minds in the universe which are in a similar state have the possibility of being affected by the vibration of my mind. So, when I am doing a good action, my mind is in another state of vibration; and all minds similarly strung have the possibility of being affected by my mind; and this power of mind upon mind is more or less according as the force of the tension is greater or less.

Following this simile further, it is quite possible that, just as light waves may travel for millions of years before they reach any object, so thought waves may also travel hundreds of years before they meet an object with which they will vibrate in unison. It is quite possible, therefore, that this atmosphere of ours is full of such thought pulsations, both good and evil. Every thought projected from every brain goes on pulsating, as it were, until it meets a fit object that will receive it. Any mind which is open to receive some of these impulses will take them immediately. So when a man is doing evil actions he has brought his mind to a certain state of tension, and all the waves which correspond to that state of tension, which may be said to be already in the atmosphere, will struggle to enter into his mind.

We run, therefore, a twofold danger in doing evil: first, we open ourselves to all the evil influences surrounding us; secondly, we create evil which affects others, may be hundreds of years hence. In doing evil we injure ourselves and others also. In doing good we do good to ourselves and to others as well; and like all other forces in man, these forces of good and evil also gather strength from outside.

According to karma yoga, the action one has done cannot be destroyed until it has borne its fruit; no power in nature can stop it from yielding its results. If I do an evil action, I must suffer for it; there is no power in this universe to stop or stay it. Similarly, if I do a good action, there is no power in the universe which can stop its bearing good results. The cause must have its effect; nothing can prevent or restrain this.

Now comes a very fine and serious point in karma yoga, namely, that these actions of ours, both good and evil, are intimately connected with each other. We cannot draw a line of demarcation and say this action is entirely good and this entirely evil. There is no action which does not bear good and evil fruits at the same time. To take the nearest example: I am talking to you, and some of you, perhaps, think I am doing good; and at the same time I am, perhaps, killing thousands of microbes in the atmosphere. I am thus doing evil to something else. When an action does good to those whom we know and who are fond of us, we say that it is very good action. For instance, you may call my speaking to you very good, but the microbes will not;

the microbes you do not see, but yourselves you do see. The way in which my talk affects you is obvious to you, but how it affects the microbes is not so obvious. And so, also, if we analyse our evil actions, we may find that some good possibly results from them somewhere. He who in good action sees that there is something evil in it, and in the midst of evil sees that there is something good in it somewhere, has known the secret of work.

But what follows from this? That howsoever we may try, there cannot be any action which is perfectly pure or any which is perfectly impure, taking purity and impurity in the sense of injury and non-injury. We cannot breathe or live without injuring others, and every bit of the food we eat is taken away from another's mouth. Our very lives are crowding out other lives. It may be men or animals or small microbes, but some one or other of these we have to crowd out. That being the case, it naturally follows that perfection can never be attained by work. We may work through all eternity, but there will be no way out of this intricate maze. You may work on and on and on; there will be no end to this inevitable association of good and evil in the results of work.

The second point to consider is, What is the end of work? We find the vast majority of people in every country believing that there will be a time when this world will become perfect, when there will be no disease or death or unhappiness or wickedness. That is a very good idea, a very good motive power to inspire and uplift the ignorant; but if we think for a moment we shall find on the very face of it that it cannot be so. How can it be, seeing that good and evil are the obverse and reverse of the same coin? How can you have good without evil at the same time? What is meant by perfection? A perfect life is a contradiction in terms. Life itself is a state of continuous struggle between ourselves and everything outside. Every moment we are actually fighting with external nature, and if we are defeated our life has to go. There is, for instance, a continuous struggle for food and air. If food or air fails we die. Life is not a simple and smoothly flowing thing, but it is a compound effect. This complex struggle between something inside and the external world is what we call life. So it is clear that when this struggle ceases there will be an end of life. What is meant by ideal happiness is that—the cessation of this struggle. But then life will cease, for the struggle can only cease when life itself has ceased.

We have seen already that in helping the world we help ourselves. The main effect of work done for others is to purify ourselves. By means of the constant effort to do good to others we are trying to forget ourselves; this forgetfulness of self is the one great lesson we have to learn in life. Man thinks foolishly that he can make himself happy, and after years of struggle finds out at last that true happiness consists in killing selfishness and that no one can make him happy except himself. Every act of charity, every thought of sympathy, every action of help, every good deed, takes so much of self-importance away from our little selves and makes us think of ourselves as the lowest and the least; and therefore they are all good.

Here we find that jnana, bhakti, and karma all come to one point. The highest ideal is eternal and entire self-abnegation, where there is no 'I', but all is 'Thou'; and whether he is conscious or unconscious of it, karma yoga leads to that end.

However much their systems of philosophy and religion may differ, all mankind stand in reverence and awe before the man who is ready to sacrifice himself for others: Here it is not at all any question of creed or doctrine. Even men who are very opposed to all religious ideas feel, when they see one of these acts of complete self-sacrifice, that they must revere it. Have you not seen even a most bigoted Christian, when he reads Edwin Arnold's *The Light of Asia*, stand in reverence of Buddha, who preached no God, preached nothing but self-sacrifice? The only thing is that the bigot does not know that his own end and aim in life is exactly the same as that of those from whom he differs.

The worshipper, by keeping constantly before him the idea of God and a surrounding of good, comes to the same point at last and says, 'Thy will be done', and keeps nothing for himself. That is self-abnegation. So karma, bhakti, and jnana all meet here; and this is what was meant by all the great preachers of ancient times, when they taught that God is not the world. They very rightly said that the world is one thing and God is another. What they mean by the world is selfishness. Unselfishness is God. One may live on a throne, in a golden palace, and be perfectly unselfish; then he is in God. Another may live in a hut and wear rags and have nothing in the world; yet if he is selfish he is intensely merged in the world.

To come back to one of our main points, we say that we cannot do good without at the same time doing some evil, or do evil without doing some good. Knowing this, how can we work? There have therefore been sects in this world who have in an astoundingly preposterous way preached slow suicide as the only means to get out of the world; because, if a man lives, he has to kill poor little animals and plants or do injury to something or someone. So according to them the only way out of the world is to die. The Jains have preached this doctrine as their highest ideal. This teaching seems to be very logical.

But the true solution is found in the Gita. It is the theory of non-attachment—to be attached to nothing while doing our work of life. Know that you are separated entirely from the world, that you are in the world but that whatever you may be doing in it, you are not doing for your own sake. Any action that you do for yourself will bring its effect to bear upon you. If it is a good action you will have to take the good effect, and if bad, you will have to take the bad effect; but any action that is not done for your own sake, whatever it be, will have no effect on you. There is to be found a very expressive sentence in our scriptures embodying this idea: 'Even if he kill the whole universe, or be himself killed, he is neither the killer nor the killed, when he knows that he is not acting for himself at all.'

Therefore karma yoga teaches, 'Do not give up the world. Live in the world, imbibe its influences as much as you can. But if it be for your own enjoyment's sake, work not at all.' Enjoyment should not be the goal. First kill your self and then take the whole world as yourself. As the old Christians used to say, 'The old man must die.' This old man is the selfish idea that the whole world is made for our enjoyment. Foolish parents teach their children to pray, 'O Lord, thou hast created this sun for me and this moon for me'—as if the Lord has had nothing else to do than to create everything for these babies. Do not teach your children such nonsense. This world is not for our sake. Millions pass out of it every year; the world does not feel it; millions of others are supplied in their place. Just as much as the world is for us, so we also are for the world.

There was a great sage in India called Vyasa. This Vyasa is known as the author of the Vedanta Aphorisms and was a holy man. His father had tried to become a very perfect man and had failed. His grandfather had also tried and failed. His great-grandfather had similarly tried and failed. He himself did not succeed perfectly, but his son, Shuka, was born perfect. Vyasa taught his son wisdom; and after himself teaching him the knowledge of Truth, he sent him to the court of King Janaka. Janaka was a great king and was called Janaka Videha. Videha means 'without a body'. Although a king, he had entirely forgotten that he had a body; he felt all the time that he was Spirit. This boy Shuka was sent to be taught by him.

The king knew that Vyasa's son was coming to him to learn wisdom; so he made certain arrangements beforehand. When the boy presented himself at the gates of the palace, the guards took no notice of him whatsoever. They only gave him a seat, and he sat there for three days and nights, nobody speaking to him, nobody asking him who he was or whence he came. He was the son of a very great sage, his father was honoured by the whole country, and he himself was a most respectable person; yet the low, vulgar guards of the palace would take no notice of him. After that, suddenly, the ministers of the

king and all the big officials came there and received him
with the greatest honours. They conducted him in and
showed him into splendid rooms, gave him the most
fragrant baths and wonderful dress, and for eight days
they kept him there in all kinds of luxury. That solemnly
serene face of Shuka did not change even to the smallest
extent by the change in the treatment accorded to him;
he was the same in the midst of this luxury as when
waiting at the door.

Then he was brought before the king. The king was
on his throne, music was playing, and dancing and other
amusements were going on. The king then gave him a
cup of milk, full to the brim, and asked him to go seven
times round the hall without spilling even a drop. The
boy took the cup and proceeded in the midst of the
music and the attraction of the beautiful faces. As desired
by the king, seven times did he go round, and not a
drop of the milk was spilt. The boy's mind could not
be attracted by anything in the world unless he allowed
it to affect him. And when he brought the cup to the
king, the king said to him, 'What your father has taught
you, and what you have learned yourself, I can only
repeat. You have known the Truth. Go home.'

Thus the man that has practised control over himself
cannot be acted upon by anything outside; there is no
more slavery for him; his mind has become free. Such a
man alone is fit to live well in the world. We generally
find men holding two opinions regarding the world.
Some are pessimists and say, 'How horrible this world is,
how wicked!' Some others are optimists and say, 'How
beautiful this world is, how wonderful!' To those who
have not controlled their own minds, the world is either
full of evil or at best a mixture of good and evil.

This very world will become to us a happy world when we become masters of our own minds. Nothing will then work upon us as good or evil; we shall find everything to be in its proper place, to be harmonious. Often men who begin by saying that the world is a hell end by saying that it is a heaven, when they succeed in the practice of self-control. If we want to be genuine karma-yogis and wish to train ourselves to the attainment of this state, wherever we may begin we are sure to end in perfect self-abnegation; and as soon as this seeming self has gone, the whole world, which at first appears to us to be filled with evil, will appear to be heaven itself and full of blessedness. Its very atmosphere will be blessed; every human face there will be good. Such is the end and aim of karma yoga, and such is its perfection in practical life.

Our various yogas do not conflict with each other; each of them leads us to the same goal and makes us perfect. Only each has to be strenuously practised. The whole secret is in practising. First you have to hear, then think, and then practise. This is true of every yoga. You have first to hear about it and understand what it is; and many things which you do not understand will be made clear to you by constant hearing and thinking.

It is hard to understand everything at once. The explanation of everything is after all in yourself. No one was ever really taught by another; each of us has to teach himself. The external teacher offers only the suggestion which rouses the internal teacher to work to understand things. Then things will be made clearer to us by our own power of perception and thought, and we shall realize them in our own souls; and that realization will grow into the intense power of will. First it is feeling, then it becomes willing, and out of that willing comes the tremendous force for work that will go through every vein and nerve and muscle, until the whole mass of the body is changed into an instrument of the yoga of unselfish work, and the desired result of perfect self-abnegation and utter unselfishness is duly attained.

This attainment does not depend on any dogma or doctrine or belief. Whether one is a Christian or Jew or Gentile, it does not matter. Are you unselfish? That is the question. If you are, you will be perfect without reading a single religious book, without going into a single church or temple. Each one of our yogas is fitted to make man perfect even without the help of the others, because they have all the same goal in view. The yogas of work, wisdom, and devotion are all capable of serving as direct and independent means for the attainment of moksha. 'Fools alone say that work and philosophy are different, not the learned.' The learned know that, though apparently different from each other, they at last lead to the same goal of human perfection.

Section 4

The world's wheel within a wheel is a terrible mechanism. There are only two ways out of it. One is to give up all concern with the machine, to let it go and stand aside—to give up our desires. That is very easy to say, but is almost impossible to do. The other way is to plunge into the world and learn the secret of work. Do not fly away from the wheels of the world-machine, but stand inside it and learn the secret of work. Through proper work done inside, it is also possible to come out.

This universe is only a part of infinite Existence, thrown into a peculiar mould, composed of space, time, and causation. It necessarily follows that law is possible only within this conditioned universe; beyond it there cannot be any law. When we speak of the universe we only mean that portion of Existence which is limited by our minds—the universe of the senses, which we can see, feel, touch, hear, think of, imagine. This alone is under law; but beyond it Existence cannot be subject to law, because causation does not extend beyond the world of our minds. Anything beyond the range of our mind and our senses is not bound by the law of causation, as there is no mental association of things in the region beyond the senses, and no causation without association of ideas. It is only when Being or Existence gets moulded into name and form that it obeys the law of causation and is said to be subject to law—because all law has its essence in causation.

Therefore we see at once that there cannot be any such thing as free-will; the very words are contradiction, because the will is what we know, and everything that we know is within our universe, and everything within our universe is moulded by the conditions of space, time, and causation. Everything that we know, or can possibly know, must be subject to causation, and that which obeys the law of causation cannot be free. It is acted upon by other agents and becomes a cause in its turn. But that which has become converted into the will, which was not the will before, but which, when it fell into this mould of space, time, and causation, became converted into the human will, is free; and when this will gets out of the mould of space, time, and causation, it will be free again. From freedom it comes, and becomes moulded into this bondage, and it gets out and goes back to freedom again.

The question has been raised as to from whom this universe comes, in whom it rests, and to whom it goes; and the answer has been given that from freedom it comes, in bondage it rests, and goes back into that freedom again. So when we speak of man as no other than that infinite Being which is manifesting itself, we mean that only one very small part thereof is man; this body and this mind which we see are only one part of the whole, only one spot of the infinite Being. This whole universe is only one speck of the infinite Being; and all our laws, our bondages, our joys and our sorrows, our happinesses and our expectations, are only within this small universe; all our progression and regression are within its small compass.

To acquire freedom we have to get beyond the limitations of this universe; it cannot be found here. Perfect equilibrium, or what the Christians call the peace that passeth all understanding, cannot be had in this universe, nor in heaven, nor in any place where our mind and thoughts can go, where the senses can feel, or which the imagination can conceive. No such place can give us that freedom, because all such places would be within our universe, and it is limited by space, time, and causation. There may be places that are more ethereal than this earth of ours, where enjoyments may be keener; but even those places must be in the universe, and therefore in bondage to law. So we have to go beyond, and real religion begins where this little universe ends. These little joys and sorrows and this knowledge of things end there, and Reality begins. Until we give up the thirst after life, the strong attachment to this our transient, conditioned existence, we have no hope of catching even a glimpse of that infinite freedom beyond.

It stands to reason then that there is only one way to attain to that freedom which is the goal of all the noblest aspirations of mankind, and that is by giving up this little life, giving up this little universe, giving up this earth, giving up heaven, giving up the body; giving up the mind, giving up everything that is limited and conditioned. If we give up our attachment to this little universe of the senses and of the mind, we shall be free immediately. The only way to come out of bondage is to go beyond the limitations of law, to go beyond causation.

But it is a most difficult thing to give up the clinging to this universe; few ever attain to that. There are two ways to do it mentioned in our books. One is called the *Neti, neti* ('Not this, not this'); the other is called *Iti* ('This'); the former is the negative, and the latter is the positive, way. The negative way is the more difficult. It is only possible for men of the very highest, exceptional minds and gigantic wills, who simply stand up and say, 'No, I will not have this', and the mind and body obey their will, and they come out successful. But such people are very rare. The vast majority of mankind choose the positive way, the way through the world, making use of all the bondages themselves to break those very bondages. This is also a kind of giving up; only it is done slowly and gradually, by knowing things, enjoying things, and thus obtaining experience and knowing the nature of things until the mind lets them all go at last and becomes unattached.

The former way of obtaining non-attachment is by reasoning, and the latter way is through work and experience. The first is the path of jnana yoga, and is characterized by the refusal to do any work; the second is that of karma yoga, in which there is no cessation from work. Everyone must work in the universe. Only those who are perfectly satisfied with the Self, whose desires do not go beyond the Self, whose mind never strays out of the Self, to whom the Self is all in all—only those do not work. The rest must work.

A current, rushing down of its own nature, falls into a hollow and makes a whirlpool, and after running a little in that whirlpool, it emerges again in the form of the free current to go on unchecked. Each human life is like that current. It gets into the whirl, gets involved in this world of space, time, and causation, whirls round a little, crying out, 'my father, my brother, my name, my fame', and so on, and at last emerges out of it and regains its original freedom. The whole universe is doing that. Whether we know it or not, whether we are conscious or unconscious of it, we are all working to get out of the dream of the world. Man's experience in the world is to enable him to get out of its whirpool.

What is karma yoga? The knowledge of the secret of work. We see that the whole universe is working. For what? For salvation, for liberty. From the atom to the highest being, working for the one end: liberty for the mind, for the body, for the spirit. All things are always trying to get freedom, flying away from bondage. The sun, the moon, the earth, the planets—all are trying to fly away from bondage. The centrifugal and the centripetal forces of nature are indeed typical of our universe.

To find the way out of the bondages of the world we have to go through it slowly and surely. There may be those exceptional persons about whom I just spoke, those who can stand aside and give up the world as a snake casts off its skin and stands aside and looks at it. There are, no doubt, these exceptional beings; but the rest of mankind have to go slowly through the world of work. Karma yoga shows the process, the secret and the method of doing it to the best advantage.

What does it say? Work incessantly, but give up all attachment to work. Do not identify yourself with anything. Hold your mind free. All this that you see—the pains and the miseries—are but the necessary conditions of this world. Poverty and wealth and happiness are but momentary; they do not belong to our real nature at all. Our nature is far beyond misery and happiness, beyond every object of the senses, beyond the imagination. And yet we must go on working all the time. Misery comes through attachment, not through work. As soon as we identify ourselves with the work we do, we feel miserable; but if we do not identify ourselves with it we do not feel that misery. If a beautiful picture belonging to another is burnt, a man does not generally become miserable; but when his own picture is burnt how miserable he feels! Why? Both were beautiful pictures, perhaps copies of the same original; but in one case very much more misery is felt than in the other. It is because in one case he identifies himself with the picture, and not in the other.

This 'I and mine' causes the whole misery. With the sense of possession comes selfishness, and selfishness brings on misery. Every act of selfishness or thought of selfishness makes us attached to something, and immediately we are made slaves. Therefore, karma yoga tells us to enjoy the beauty of all the pictures in the world, but not to identify ourselves with any of them. Never say 'mine'. Whenever we say a thing is 'mine', misery will immediately come. Do not even say 'my child' in your mind. If you do, then will come the misery. Do not say 'my house', do not say 'my body'. The whole difficulty is there. The body is neither yours, nor mine, nor anybody's. These bodies are coming and going by the laws of nature, but we are free, standing as witness. This body is no more free than a picture or a wall. Why should we be attached so much to a body? If somebody paints a picture, he does it and passes on. Do not project that tentacle of selfishness, 'I must possess it.' As soon as that is projected, misery will begin.

Here are the two ways of giving up all attachment. The one is for those who do not believe in God or in any outside help. They are left to their own devices; they have simply to work with their own will, with the powers of their mind and discrimination, saying, 'I must be non-attached.' For those who believe in God there is another way, which is much less difficult. They give up the fruits of work unto the Lord; they work and are never attached to the results. Whatever they see, feel, hear, or do, is for him. For whatever good work we may do, let us not claim any praise or benefit. It is the Lord's; give up the fruits unto him. Let us stand aside and think that we are only servants obeying the Lord, our master, and that every impulse for action comes from him every moment. Whatever thou worshippest, whatever thou perceivest, whatever thou doest—give up all unto him and be at rest.

Let us be at peace, perfect peace, with ourselves, and give up our whole body and mind and everything as an eternal sacrifice unto the Lord. Instead of the sacrifice of pouring oblations into the fire, perform this one great sacrifice day and night—the sacrifice of your little self. 'I searched for wealth in this world; Thou art the only wealth I have found; I sacrifice myself unto Thee. I searched for someone to love; Thou art the only beloved I have found; I sacrifice myself unto Thee.' Let us repeat this day and night and say: 'Nothing for me. No matter whether the thing is good, bad, or indifferent, I do not care for it. I sacrifice all unto Thee.' Day and night let us renounce our seeming self until it becomes a habit with us to do so, until it gets into the blood, the nerves, and the brain, and the whole body is every moment obedient to this idea of self-renunciation. Go then into the midst of the battlefield, with the roaring cannon and the din of war, and you will find yourself to be free and at peace.

Karma yoga teaches us that the ordinary idea of duty is on the lower plane; nevertheless, all of us have to do our duty. Yet we may see that this peculiar sense of duty is very often a great cause of misery. Duty becomes a disease with us. It catches hold of us and makes our whole life miserable. It is the bane of human life. This duty, this idea of duty is the midday summer sun, which scorches the innermost soul of mankind. Look at those poor slaves to duty! Duty leaves them no time to say prayers, no time to bathe. Duty is ever on them. They go out and work. Duty is on them! It is living a slave's life, at last dropping down in the street and dying in harness, like a horse. This is duty as it is understood.

The only true duty is to be unattached and to work as free beings, to give up all work unto God. All our duties are his. Blessed are we that we are ordered out here. We serve our time; whether we do it ill or well, who knows? If we do it well, we do not get the fruits. If we do it ill, neither do we care. Be at rest, be free, and work.

What is duty after all? It is really the impulsion of the flesh, or our attachment. And when an attachment has become established, we call it duty. For instance, in countries where there is no marriage, there is no duty between husband and wife. When marriage comes, husband and wife live together on account of attachment; and that kind of living together becomes settled after generations; and when it becomes so settled, it becomes a duty. It is, so to say, a sort of chronic disease. When attachment becomes chronic, we baptize it with the high-sounding name of duty. We strew flowers upon it, trumpets sound for it, sacred texts are said over it, and then the whole world fights and men earnestly rob each other for this duty's sake.

Duty is good to the extent that it checks brutality. To the lowest kinds of men, who cannot have any other ideal, it is of some good; but those who want to be karma-yogis must throw this idea of duty overboard. There is no duty for you and me. Whatever you have to give to the world do give by all means, but not as a duty. Do not take any thought of that. Be not compelled. Why should you be compelled? Everything that you do under compulsion goes to build up attachment. Why should you have any duty? Resign everything unto God. In this tremendous fiery furnace where the fire of duty scorches everybody, drink this cup of nectar and be happy.

We are all simply working out His will and have nothing to do with rewards and punishments. If you want the reward you must also have the punishment; the only way to get out of the punishment is to give up the reward. The only way of getting out of misery is by giving up the idea of happiness, because these two are linked to each other. On one side there is happiness; on the other there is misery. On one side there is life; on the other there is death. The only way to get beyond is to give up the love of life. Life and death are the same thing looked at from different points. So the idea of happiness without misery, or of life without misery, or of life without death, is very good for schoolboys and children; but the thinker sees that it is all a contradiction in terms and gives up both. Seek no praise, no reward for anything you do. No sooner do we perform a good action than we begin to desire credit for it. No sooner do we give money to some charity than we want to see our names blazoned in the papers. Misery must come as the result of such desires.

In the presence of an ever-active Providence, who notes even the sparrow's fall, how can man attach any importance to his own work? Will it not be a blasphemy to do so when we know that He is taking care of the minutest things in the world? We have only to stand in awe and reverence before Him saying, 'Thy will be done.'

The highest men cannot work, for in them there is no attachment. Those who have become ever associated with the Self, for them there is no work. Such are indeed the highest of mankind; but apart from them everyone else has to work. In so working we should never think that we can help even the least thing in this universe. We cannot. We only help ourselves in this gymnasium of the world. This is the proper attitude for work. Give up all fruits of work; do good for its own sake; then alone will come perfect non-attachment. The bonds of the heart will thus break, and we shall reap perfect freedom. This freedom is indeed the goal of karma yoga.

The next idea we take up is the idea of equality. This promise of a millennium has been a great incentive to work. Many religions preach this as one of their doctrines—that God is coming to rule the universe, and that then there will be no difference at all in conditions. The people who preach this doctrine are mere fanatics, and fanatics are indeed the sincerest of mankind. Christianity was preached precisely on the basis of the fascination of this fanaticism, and that is what made it so attractive to the Greek and Roman slaves. They believed that under the millennial religion there would be no more slavery, that there would be plenty to eat and drink; and therefore they flocked round the Christian standard. Those who preached the idea first were of course ignorant fanatics, but very sincere. In modern times this millennial aspiration is expressed in terms of equality—of liberty, equality, and fraternity. This also is fanaticism.

True equality has never been and never can be on earth. How can we all be equal here? This impossible kind of equality implies total death. What makes this world what it is? Lost balance. In the primal state, which is called chaos, there is perfect balance. How do all the

formative forces of the universe come then? By struggling, competition, conflict. Suppose that all the particles
of matter were held in equilibrium; would there be then
any process of creation? We know from science that
it is impossible. Disturb a sheet of water, and you find
every particle of the water trying to become calm again,
one rushing against the other; and in the same way all
the phenomena which we call the universe—all things
therein—are struggling to get back to the state of perfect
balance. Again a disturbance comes, and again we have
combination and creation. Inequality is the very basis of
creation. At the same time, the forces struggling to
obtain equality are as much a necessity of creation as
those which destroy it.

Absolute equality, that which means a perfect balance
of all the struggling forces in all the planes, can never
be in this world. Before you attain that state, the world
will have become quite unfit- for any kind of life, and
no one will be here. We find, therefore, not only that
all these ideas of the millennium and of absolute equality
are impossible, but also that, if we try to carry them
out, they will lead us surely enough to the day of destruction. What makes the difference between man and
man? It is largely the difference in the brain. Nowadays
no one but a lunatic will say that we are all born with
the same brain power. We come into the world with
unequal endowments; we come as greater men or as
lesser men, and there is no getting away from that pre-
natally determined condition. The American Indians
were in this country for thousands of years, and a few
handfuls of your ancestors came to their land. What a
difference they have caused in the appearance of the
country! Why did not the Indians make improvements

and build cities, if all were equal? With your ancestors a different sort of brain power came into the land, different bundles of past impressions came, and they manifested themselves. Absolute non-differentiation is death. So long as this world lasts, differentiation there will and must be, and the millennium of perfect equality will come only when a cycle of creation comes to its end. Before that, equality cannot be.

Yet this idea of realizing the millennium is a great motive power. Just as inequality is necessary for creation itself, so the struggle to limit it is also necessary. If there were no struggle to become free and get back to God, there would be no creation either. It is the difference between these two forces that determines the nature of the motives of men. There will always be these motives to work, some tending towards bondage and others towards freedom.

This world's wheel within a wheel is a terrible mechanism. If we put our hands in it, as soon as we are caught we are gone. We all think that when we have done a certain duty we shall be at rest; but before we have done a part of that duty another is already waiting. We are all being dragged along by this mighty, complex world-machine. There are only two ways out of it. One is to give up all concern with the machine, to let it go and stand aside—to give up our desires. That is very easy to say, but is almost impossible to do. I do not know whether in twenty millions of men one can do that. The other way is to plunge into the world and learn the secret of work, and that is the way of karma yoga. Do not fly away from the wheels of the world-machine, but stand inside it and learn the secret of work.

Through proper work done inside, it is also possible to come out. Through this machinery itself is the way out.

We have now seen what work is. It is a part of nature's foundation, and goes on always. Those who believe in God understand this better, because they know that God is not such an incapable being as will need our help. Although this universe will go on always, our goal is freedom, our goal is unselfishness; and according to karma yoga that goal is to be reached through work. All ideas of making the world perfectly happy may be good as motive powers for fanatics; but we must know that fanaticism brings forth as much evil as good. The karma-yogi asks why you require any motive to work other than the inborn love of freedom. Be beyond the common 'worthy' motives. 'To work you have the right, but not to the fruits thereof.' Man can train himself to know and practise that, says the karma-yogi. When the idea of doing good becomes a part of his very being, then he will not seek for any motive outside. Let us do good because it is good to do good; he who does good work even in order to get to heaven binds himself down, says the karma-yogi. Any work that is done with even the least selfish motive, instead of making us free, forges one more chain for our feet.

So the only way is to give up all the fruits of work, to be unattached to them. Know that this world is not we, nor are we this world; that we are really not the body; that we really do not work. We are the Self, eternally at rest and at peace. Why should we be bound by anything? It is very good to say that we should be perfectly non-attached; but what is the way to be so? Every good work we do without any ulterior motive, instead of forging a new chain, will break one of the links in the existing chains. Every good thought that we send to the world, without thinking of any return, will be stored up and break one link in the chain, and make us purer and purer, until we become the purest of mortals.

Let me tell you in conclusion a few words about one man who actually carried this teaching of karma yoga into practice. That man is Buddha. He is the one man who ever carried this into perfect practice. Buddha is the only prophet who said, 'I do not care to know your various theories about God. What is the use of discussing all the subtle doctrines about the soul? Do good and be good, and this will take you to freedom and to whatever truth there is.' He was, in the conduct of his life, absolutely without personal motives; and what man worked more than he? Show me in history one character who has soared so high. The whole human race has produced but one such character, such high philosophy, such wide sympathy.

This great philosopher, preaching the highest philosophy, yet had the deepest sympathy for the lowest of animals and never put forth any claims for himself. He is the ideal karma-yogi, acting entirely without motive. He is the first great reformer the world has seen. He was the first who dared to say, 'Believe not because some old manuscripts are produced; believe not because it is your national belief, because you have been made to believe it from your childhood; but reason it all out, and after you have analysed it, then, if you find that it will do good to one and all, believe it, live up to it, and help others to live up to it.'

He works best who works without any motive—

neither for money, nor for fame, nor for anything else. And when a man can do that, he will be a Buddha and out of him will come the power to work in such a manner as will transform the world. This man represents the very highest ideal of karma yoga.

6

SELF-REALIZATION THROUGH LOVE OF GOD

The best definition given of bhakti yoga is perhaps embodied in the verse: 'May that love undying which the non-discriminating have for the fleeting objects of the senses never leave this heart of mine—of me who seek after Thee!'

We see what a strong love men, who do not know any better, have for sense objects, for money, dress, their wives, children, friends, and possessions. What a tremendous clinging they have to all these things! So in the above prayer the sage says, 'I will have that attachment—that tremendous clinging—only to Thee.'

This love, when given to God, is called bhakti. Bhakti is not destructive; it teaches that no one of the faculties we have has been given in vain, that through them is the natural way to come to liberation. Bhakti does not kill out our tendencies, it does not go against nature, but only gives it a higher and more powerful direction. When the same kind of love that has been given to sense objects is given to God, it is called bhakti.

The chief thing is to *want* God. It is only when we have become satiated with everything here that we look beyond for a supply. Have done with this child's play of the world as soon as you can and then you will find the necessity for something beyond the world, and the first step in religion will come.

There is a form of religion which is fashionable. My friend has much furniture in her parlour; it is the fashion to have a Japanese vase, so she must have one, even if it costs a thousand dollars. In the same way she will have a little religion, and join a church.

Bhakti is not for such. That is not 'want'. Want is that without which we cannot live. We want breath, we want food, we want clothes; without them we cannot live. When a man loves a woman in this world, there are times when he feels that without her he cannot live, although that is a mistake. When a husband dies the wife thinks she cannot live without him; but she lives all the same.

That is the secret of necessity; it is that without which we cannot live; it must come to us or we die. When the time comes that we feel the same about God, or in other words, we want something beyond this world, something above all material forces, then we may become bhaktas.

Section 1

We plainly see that bhakti is a series or succession
of mental efforts at religious realization, beginning
with ordinary worship and ending in a supreme
intensity of love for the *Ishvara* [Personal God].

BHAKTI YOGA is a real, genuine search after the
Lord, a search beginning, continuing, and ending in
love. One single moment of the madness of extreme love
to God brings us eternal freedom. 'Bhakti', says Narada
in his explanation of the Bhakti Aphorisms, 'is intense
love to God.' 'When a man gets it he loves all, hates
none; he becomes satisfied for ever.' 'This love cannot
be reduced to any earthly benefit'—because so long as
worldly desires last that kind of love does not come.
'Bhakti is greater than karma, greater than [raja] yoga,
because these are intended for an object in view, while
bhakti is its own fruition, its own means, and its own
end.'

There is not really so much difference between knowledge (jnana) and love (bhakti) as people sometimes
imagine. We shall see, as we go on, that in the end they
converge and meet at the same point. So also is it with
raja yoga, which, when pursued as a means to attain
liberation, and not (as unfortunately it frequently
becomes in the hands of charlatans and mystery-
mongers) as an instrument to hoodwink the unwary,
leads us also to the same goal.

The one great advantage of bhakti is that it is the
easiest and the most natural way to reach the great divine
end in view. Its great disadvantage is that in its lower

forms it oftentimes degenerates into hideous fanaticism. The fanatical crew in Hinduism or Mohammedanism or Christianity have always been almost exclusively recruited from these worshippers on the lower planes of bhakti. The singleness of attachment to a loved object, without which no genuine love can grow, is very often also the cause of the denunciation of everything else. All the weak and undeveloped minds in every religion or country have only one way of loving their own ideal, i.e. by hating every other ideal. Herein is the explanation of why the same man who is so lovingly attached to his own ideal of God, so devoted to his own ideal of religion, becomes a howling fanatic as soon as he sees or hears anything of any other ideal. This kind of love is somewhat like the canine instinct of guarding the master's property from intrusion; only the instinct of the dog is better than the reason of man, for the dog never mistakes its master for an enemy, in whatever dress he may come before it. Again, the fanatic loses all power of judgment. Personal considerations are in his case of such absorbing interest that to him it is no question at all what a man says—whether it is right or wrong; but the one thing he is always particularly careful to know is, who says it. The same man who is kind, good, honest, and loving to people of his own opinion will not hesitate to do the vilest deeds against persons beyond the pale of his own religious brotherhood.

But this danger exists only in that stage of bhakti which is called the preparatory. When bhakti has become ripe and has passed into that form which is called the supreme, no more is there any fear of these hideous manifestations of fanaticism. That soul which is overpowered by this higher form of Bhakti is too near the

God of love to become an instrument for the diffusion of hatred.

It is not given to all of us to be harmonious in the building up of our characters in this life; yet we know that that character is of the noblest type in which all these three—knowledge and love and raja yoga—are harmoniously fused. Three things are necessary for a bird to fly: the two wings, and the tail as a rudder for steering. Jnana is the one wing, bhakti is the other, and raja yoga is the tail that keeps up the balance. For those who cannot pursue all these three forms of worship together in harmony, and take up, therefore, bhakti alone as their way, it is necessary always to remember that forms and ceremonials, though absolutely necessary for the progressing soul, have no other value than taking us on to that state in which we feel the most intense love to God.

We plainly see, therefore, that bhakti is a series or succession of mental efforts at religious realization, beginning with ordinary worship and ending in a supreme intensity of love for the *Ishvara* [Personal God].

It has always to be understood that the Personal God worshipped by the bhakta is not separate or different from Brahman. All is Brahman, the One without a second; only Brahman, as Unity or Absolute, is too much of an abstraction to be loved and worshipped. So the bhakta chooses the relative aspect of Brahman, that is, Ishvara, the Supreme Ruler. To use a simile: Brahman is as the clay or substance out of which an infinite variety of articles are fashioned. As clay, they are all one; but form or manifestation differentiates them. Before every one of them was made, they all existed potentially in the clay; and, of course, they are identical substantially. But when formed, and so long as the form remains, they are separate and different. The clay mouse can never become a clay elephant, because, as manifestations, form alone makes them what they are, though as unformed clay they are all one. Ishvara is the highest manifestation of the Absolute Reality, or in other words, the highest possible reading of the Absolute by the human mind. Creation is eternal, and so also is Ishvara.

Bhakti yoga, as we have said, is divided into the preparatory and the supreme forms. We shall find, as we go on, how in the preparatory stage we unavoidably stand in need of many concrete helps to enable us to get on. And indeed the mythological and symbolical parts of all religions are natural growths which early environ the aspiring soul and help it Godward. It is also a significant fact that spiritual giants have been produced only in those systems of religion where there is an exuberant growth of rich mythology and ritualism. The dry, fanatical forms of religion, which attempt to eradicate all that is poetical, all that is beautiful and sublime, all that gives a firm grasp to the infant mind tottering in its Godward way—the forms which attempt to break down the very ridgepoles of the spiritual roof, and in their ignorant and superstitious conceptions of truth try to drive away all that is life-giving, all that furnishes the formative material to the spiritual plant growing in the human soul—such forms of religion too soon find that all that is left to them is but an empty shell, a contentless frame of words and sophistry, with perhaps a little flavour of a kind of social scavenging or the so-called spirit of reform.

The vast mass of those whose religion is like this are conscious or unconscious materialists—the end and aim of their lives here and hereafter being enjoyment, which, indeed, is to them the alpha and the omega of human life. Work like street-cleaning and scavenging, intended for the material comfort of man, is, according to them, the be-all and end-all of human existence. And the sooner the followers of this curious mixture of ignorance and fanaticism come out in their true colours, and join, as they well deserve to do, the ranks of atheists and materialists, the better will it be for the world. One ounce of the practice of righteousness and of spiritual self-realization outweighs tons and tons of frothy talk and nonsensical sentiments. Show us one, but one, gigantic spiritual genius growing out of all this dry dust of ignorance and fanaticism; and if you cannot, close your mouths, open the windows of your hearts to the clear light of truth, and sit like children at the feet of those who know what they are talking about—the sages of India. Let us, then, listen attentively to what they say.

Section 2

'Take the sweetness of all, sit with all, take the name of all, say yea, yea—but keep your seat firm.'

Every soul is destined to be perfect, and every being, in the end, will attain the state of perfection. Whatever we are now is the result of our acts and thoughts in the past; and whatever we shall be in the future will be the result of what we think and do now. But this, the shaping of our own destinies, does not preclude our receiving help from outside; nay, in the vast majority of cases such help is absolutely necessary. When it comes, the higher powers and possibilities of the soul are quickened, spiritual life is awakened, growth is animated, and man becomes holy and perfect in the end.

This quickening impulse cannot be derived from books. The soul can only receive impulse from another soul, and from nothing else. We may study books all our lives, we may become very intellectual, but in the end we find that we have not developed at all spiritually. It is not true that a higher order of intellectual development always goes hand in hand with a proportionate development of the spiritual side in man. In studying books we are sometimes deluded into thinking that thereby we are being spiritually helped; but, if we analyse the effect of the study of books on ourselves, we shall find that at the utmost it is only our intellect that derives profit from such studies, and not our inner spirit. This inadequacy of books to quicken spiritual growth is the reason why, although almost every one of us can *speak* most wonderfully on spiritual matters, when it comes to action and the living of a truly spiritual life, we find ourselves so awfully deficient. To quicken the spirit, the impulse must come from another soul.

The person from whose soul such an impulse comes is called the *guru*, the teacher; and the person to whose soul the impulse is conveyed is called the student. To convey such an impulse to any soul, in the first place, the soul from which it proceeds must possess the power of transmitting it, as it were, to another; and in the second place, the soul to which it is transmitted must be fit to receive it. The seed must be a living seed, and the field must be ready ploughed; and when both these conditions are fulfilled, a wonderful growth of genuine religion takes place.

Such alone are the real teachers, and such alone are also the real students, the real aspirants. All others are only playing with spirituality. They have just a little curiosity awakened, just a little intellectual aspiration kindled in them, but are merely standing on the outward fringe of the horizon of religion. There is, no doubt, some value even in that, as it may, in course of time, result in the awakening of a real thirst for religion; and it is a mysterious law of nature that as soon as the field is ready, the seed must and does come; as soon as the soul earnestly desires to have religion, the transmitter of the religious force must and does appear to help that soul. When the power that attracts the light of religion in the receiving soul is full and strong, the power which answers to that attraction and sends in light does come as a matter of course.

There are, however, certain great dangers in the way. There is, for instance, the danger to the receiving soul of its mistaking momentary emotions for real religious yearning. We may study that in ourselves. Many a time in our lives somebody dies whom we loved. We receive a blow; we feel that the world is slipping between our fingers, that we want something surer and higher, and that we must become religious. In a few days that wave of feeling has passed away, and we are left stranded just where we were before. All of us often mistake such impulses for real thirst after religion; but as long as these momentary emotions are thus mistaken, that continuous, real craving of the soul for religion will not come, and we shall not find the true transmitter of spirituality. So whenever we are tempted to complain that our search after the truth that we desire so much is proving vain, instead of so complaining, our first duty ought to be to look into our own souls and find whether the craving in the heart is real. Then, in the vast majority of cases, it would be discovered that we were not fit to receive the truth, that there was no real thirst for spirituality.

There are still greater dangers in regard to the transmitter, the guru. There are many who, though immersed in ignorance, yet, in the pride of their hearts, fancy they know everything and not only do not stop there, but offer to take others on their shoulders; and thus, the blind leading the blind, both fall into the ditch. The world is full of these. Everyone wants to be a teacher; every beggar wants to make a gift of a million dollars! Just as these beggars are ridiculous, so are these teachers.

How are we to know a teacher, then? The sun requires no torch to make it visible; we need not light a candle in order to see it. When the sun rises, we instinctively become aware of the fact, and when a teacher of men comes to help us, the soul will instinctively know that the truth has already begun to shine upon it. Truth stands on its own evidence; it does not require any other testimony to prove it true. It is self-effulgent. It penetrates into the innermost corners of our nature, and in its presence the whole universe stands up and says, 'This is truth.' The teachers whose wisdom and truth shine like the light of the sun are the very greatest the world has known, and they are worshipped as God by the major portion of mankind. But we may get help from comparatively lesser ones also; only we ourselves do not possess intuition enough to judge properly of the man from whom we receive teaching and guidance. So there ought to be certain tests, certain conditions, for the teacher to satisfy, as also for the taught.

The conditions necessary for the taught are purity, a real thirst after knowledge, and perseverance.

With regard to the teacher, we must see that he knows the spirit of the scriptures. The whole world reads Bibles, Vedas, and Korans; but they are all only words, syntax, etymology, philology—the dry bones of religion. The teacher who deals too much in words and allows the mind to be carried away by the force of words loses the spirit. Those who employ such methods to impart religion to others, are only desirous to show off their learning, so that the world may praise them as great scholars. You will find that not one of the great teachers of the world ever went into these various explanations of the texts; there is with them no attempt at 'text-torturing', no eternal playing upon the meaning of words and their roots. Yet they nobly taught, while others who have nothing to teach have taken up a word sometimes, and written a three-volume book on its origin, on the man who used it first, and on what that man was accustomed to eat, and how long he slept, and so on.

Bhagavan Ramakrishna used to tell a story of some men who went into a mango orchard and busied themselves in counting the leaves, the twigs, and the branches, examining their colour, comparing their size, and noting down everything most carefully, and then got up a learned discussion on each of these topics, which were undoubtedly highly interesting to them. But one of them, more sensible than the others, did not care for any of this and instead began to eat the mango fruit. And was he not wise?

17

The second condition necessary in the teacher is sinlessness. He must be perfectly pure, and then alone his words come to have value, because he is only then the true transmitter. What can he transmit if he has no spiritual power in himself? There must be the worthy vibration of spirituality in the mind of the teacher so that it may be sympathetically conveyed to the mind of the taught. The function of the teacher is indeed an affair of the transference of something, and not one of mere stimulation of the existing intellectual or other faculties in the taught. Something real and appreciable as an influence comes from the teacher and goes to the taught. Therefore the teacher must be pure.

The third condition is in regard to the motive. The teacher must not teach with any ulterior, selfish motive —for money, name, or fame; his work must be simply out of love, out of pure love for mankind at large. The only medium through which spiritual force can be transmitted is love. Any selfish motive, such as the desire for gain or for name, will immediately destroy this conveying medium. God is love, and only he who has known God as love, can be a teacher of godliness and God to man.

When you see that in your teacher these conditions are all fulfilled, you are safe. If they are not, it is unsafe to allow yourself to be taught by him, for there is the great danger that, if he cannot convey goodness to your heart, he may convey wickedness. This danger must by all means be guarded against. 'He who is learned in the scriptures, sinless, unpolluted by lust, and is the greatest knower of Brahman is the real teacher.'

This eye-opener of the aspirant after religion is the teacher. With the teacher, therefore, our relationship is the same as that between an ancestor and his descendant. Without faith, humility, submission, and veneration in our hearts towards our religious teacher, there cannot be any growth of religion in us. It is a significant fact that where this kind of relation between the teacher and the taught prevails, there alone do gigantic spiritual men grow, while in those countries which have neglected to keep up this kind of relation, the religious teacher has become a mere lecturer—the teacher expecting his five dollars and the person taught expecting his brain to be filled with the teacher's words, and each going his own way after this much has been done. Under such circumstances spirituality becomes almost an unknown quantity. There is none to transmit it and none to have it transmitted to. Religion with such people becomes a business; they think they can obtain it with their dollars. Would to God that religion could be obtained so easily! But unfortunately it cannot be.

Religion, which is the highest knowledge and the highest wisdom, cannot be bought, nor can it be acquired from books. You may thrust your head into all the corners of the world, you may explore the Himalayas, the Alps, and the Caucasus, you may sound the bottom of the sea and pry into every nook of Tibet and the desert of Gobi, but you will not find it anywhere until your heart is ready for receiving it and your teacher has come. And when that divinely appointed teacher comes, serve him with childlike confidence and simplicity, freely open your heart to his influence, and see in him God manifested. Those who come to seek truth with such a spirit of love and veneration, to them the Lord of truth reveals the most wonderful things regarding truth, goodness, and beauty.

Wherever His name is spoken, that very place is holy. How much more so is the man who speaks His name, and with what veneration ought we to approach that man out of whom comes to us spiritual truth! Such great teachers of spiritual truth are indeed very few in number in this world; but the world is never altogether without them. They are always the fairest flowers of human life—'an ocean of mercy without any motive'.

Higher and nobler than all ordinary ones, are another set of teachers, the *avataras*. They can transmit spirituality with a touch, even with a mere wish. The lowest and most degraded characters in one second become saints at their command. They are the teachers of all teachers, the highest manifestations of God through man. We cannot see God except through them. We cannot help worshipping them. And indeed they are the only ones whom we are bound to worship.

God understands human failings and becomes man to do good to humanity. 'Whenever virtue subsides and wickedness prevails I manifest Myself. To establish virtue, to destroy evil, to save the good, I come from age to age.' 'Fools deride me who have assumed the human form, without knowing my real nature as the Lord of the universe.' Such is Sri Krishna's declaration in the Gita on the Incarnation. 'When a huge tidal wave comes,' says Bhagavan Sri Ramakrishna, 'all the little brooks and ditches become full to the brim without any effort or consciousness on their own part; so when an Incarnation comes, a tidal wave of spirituality breaks upon the world, and people feel spirituality in the very air.'

One who aspires to be a bhakta must know that 'so

many opinions are so many ways.' He must know that all the various sects of the different religions are the various manifestations of the glory of the same Lord. 'They call You by so many names; they divide You, as it were, by different names; yet in each one of these is to be found Your omnipotence.... You reach the worshipper through all of these; neither is there any special time so long as the soul has intense love for You. You are so easy to approach; it is my misfortune that I cannot love You.' Not only this. The bhakta must take care not to hate, or even to criticize, those radiant sons of light who are the founders of various sects; he must not even hear them· spoken ill of.

Very few, indeed, are those who are at once the possessors of an extensive sympathy and power of appreciation as well as an intensity of love. We find, as a rule, that liberal and sympathetic sects lose the intensity of religious feeling, and in their hands, religion is apt to degenerate into a kind of politico-social club life. On the other hand, intensely narrow sectarians, while displaying a very commendable love of their own ideals, are seen to have acquired every particle of that love by hating everyone who is not of exactly the same opinions as themselves. Would to God that this world was full of men who were as intense in their love as world-wide in their sympathies! But such are only few and far between.

Yet we know that it is practicable to educate large numbers of human being into the ideal of a wonderful blending of both the width and the intensity of love; and the way to do that is by this path of the 'chosen ideal'. Every sect of every religion presents only one ideal of its own to mankind; but the eternal Vedantic religion opens to mankind an infinite number of doors for ingress into the inner shrine of Divinity, and places before humanity an almost inexhaustible array of ideals, there being in each of them a manifestation of the Eternal One.

Bhakti yoga, therefore, lays on us the imperative command not to hate or deny any one of the various paths that lead to salvation. Yet the growing plant must be hedged round to protect it until it has grown into a tree. The tender plant of spirituality will die if exposed too early to the action of a constant change of ideas and ideals. Many people, in the name of what may be called religious liberalism, may be seen feeding their idle curiosity with a continuous succession of different ideals. With them, hearing new things grows into a kind of a disease, a sort of religious drink-mania. They want to hear new things just by way of getting a temporary nervous excitement, and when one such exciting influence has had its effect on them, they are ready for another.

Devotion to one ideal is absolutely necessary for the beginner in the practice of religious devotion. He must say with Hanuman in the Ramayana, 'Though I know that the Lord of Sri [Vishnu] and the Lord of Janaki [Rama] are both manifestations of the same Supreme Being, yet my all in all is the lotus-eyed Rama.' Or, as was said by the sage Tulsidas; 'Take the sweetness of all, sit with all, take the name of all, say yea, yea—but keep your seat firm.' Then, if the devotional aspirant is sincere, out of this little seed will come a gigantic tree, like the Indian banyan, sending out branch after branch and root after root to all sides, till it covers the entire field of religion. Thus will the true devotee realize that He who was his own Ideal in life is worshipped in all Ideals, by all sects, under all names, and through all forms.

With regard to the method and the means of bhakti yoga we read in the commentary of Bhagavan Ramanuja on the Vedanta Sutras: 'The attaining of bhakti comes through discrimination, controlling the passions, practice, sacrificial work, purity, strength, and suppression of excessive joy.'

Viveka, or discrimination, is, according to Ramanuja, discriminating, among other things, pure food from the impure. 'When the food is pure the sattva element gets purified and the memory becomes unwavering.'

The question of food has always been one of the most vital with the bhaktas. Apart from the extravagance into which some of the bhakti sects have run, there is a great truth underlying this question of food. The materials which we receive through our food into our body structure go a great way to determine our mental constitution; therefore the food we eat has to be particularly taken care of.

This discrimination of food is, after all, of secondary importance. The very same passage quoted above is explained by Shankara in a different way, by giving an entirely different meaning to the word *ahara*, translated generally as 'food'. According to him, 'That which is gathered in is Ahara. The knowledge of the various sensations such as sound, is gathered in for the enjoyment of the enjoyer; the purification of this knowledge gathered in by the senses is called the purification of the food (ahara). The purification of food means the acquiring of the knowledge of sensations untouched by the defects of attachment, aversion, and delusion. Such is the meaning. Therefore such knowledge, or Ahara, being purified, the sattva material of its possessor—the internal organ—will become purified, and the sattva being purified, an unbroken memory of the Infinite One will result.'

These two explanations are apparently conflicting; yet both are true and necessary. The manipulating and controlling of what may be called the finer body, that is to say, the mind, are no doubt higher functions than the controlling of the grosser body of flesh. But the control of the grosser is absolutely necessary to enable one to .arrive at the control of the finer. The beginner, therefore, must pay particular attention to all such dietetic rules as have come down from the line of the accredited teachers. But the extravagant, meaningless fanaticism, which has driven religion entirely to the kitchen, as may be noticed in many of our sects, is a peculiar sort of pure and simple materialism. It is neither jnana nor bhakti nor karma; it is a special kind of lunacy. So it stands to reason that discrimination in the choice of food is necessary for the attainment of this higher state of mental composition, which cannot be easily obtained otherwise.

Controlling the passions is the next thing to be attended to. To restrain the organs from going towards the objects of the senses, to control them and bring them under the guidance of the will, is the very central virtue in religious culture. Then comes the practice of self-restraint and self-denial. All the immense possibilities of divine realization in the soul cannot get actualized without struggle and without such practice on the part of the aspiring devotee. 'The mind must always think of the Lord.' It is very hard at first to compel the mind to think of the Lord always; but with every new effort the power to do so grows stronger in us.

And then as to sacrificial work, it is understood that the 'five great sacrifices' [worship, study, and several kinds of humanitarian activities] have to be performed as usual.

Purity is absolutely the basic discipline, the bedrock upon which the whole building of bhakti rests. Cleansing the external body and discriminating about food are both easy; but without internal cleanliness and purity these external observances are of no value whatsoever. In the list of the qualities conducive to purity, as given by Ramanuja, there are enumerated truthfulness; sincerity; doing good to others without any gain to one's self; not injuring others by thought, word, or deed; not coveting others' goods; not thinking vain thoughts; and not brooding over injuries received from another.

In this list, the one idea that deserves special notice is *ahimsa*, non-injury to others. This duty of non-injury is, so to speak, obligatory on us in relation to all beings. It does not simply mean, as with some, the non-injuring of human beings and mercilessness towards the lower animals; nor, as with some others, does it mean the protecting of cats and dogs and the feeding of ants with sugar, with liberty to injure brother man in every horrible way. It is remarkable that almost every good idea in this world can be carried to a disgusting extreme. A good practice carried to an extreme and worked out in accordance with the letter of the law becomes a positive evil. The stinking monks of certain religious sects, who do not bathe lest the vermin on their bodies should be killed, never think of the discomfort and disease they bring to their fellow human beings. They do not, however, belong to the religion of the Vedas.

Therefore we must always remember that external practices have value only as helps to develop internal purity. It is better to have internal purity alone, when minute attention to external observances is not practicable. But woe unto the man and woe unto the nation that forgets the real, internal, spiritual essentials of religion and mechanically clutches with death-like grasp at all external forms and never lets them go! The forms have value only so far as they are expressions of the life within. If they have ceased to express life, crush them out without mercy.

The next means to the attainment of bhakti is strength. 'This Atman is not to be attained by the weak.' Both physical weakness and mental weakness are meant here. 'The strong, the hardy', are the only fit students. What can puny little decrepit things do? They will break to pieces whenever the mysterious forces of the body and mind are even slightly awakened by the practice of any of the yogas. It is 'the young, the healthy, the strong', that can score success. Physical strength, therefore, is absolutely necessary. It is the strong body alone that can bear the shock of reaction resulting from the attempt to control the organs. He who wants to become a bhakta must be strong, must be healthy. When the miserably weak attempt any of the yogas, they are likely to get some incurable malady or weaken their minds. Voluntarily weakening the body is really no prescription for spiritual enlightenment.

The mentally weak also cannot succeed in attaining the Atman. The person who aspires to be a bhakta must be cheerful. In the western world the idea of a religious man is that he never smiles, that a dark cloud must always hang over his face, which, again, must be long-drawn, with the jaws almost collapsed. People with emaciated bodies and long faces are fit subjects for the physician; they are not yogis. It is the cheerful mind that is persevering. It is the strong mind that hews its way through a thousand difficulties. And this, the hardest task of all, the cutting of our way out of the net of maya, is the work reserved only for giant wills.

Yet at the same time excessive mirth should be avoided. Excessive mirth makes us unfit for serious thought. It also fritters away the energies of the mind in vain. The stronger the will, the less the yielding to the sway of the emotions. Excessive hilarity is quite as objectionable as too much of sad seriousness, and all religious realization is possible only when the mind is in a steady, peaceful condition of harmonious equilibrium.

It is thus that one may begin to learn how to love the Lord.

Section 3

In bhakti yoga the central secret is to know that the various passions and feelings and emotions in the human heart are not wrong in themselves; only they have to be carefully controlled and given a higher condition of excellence. The highest direction is that which takes us to God; every other direction is lower.

We have finished the consideration of what may be called the preparatory bhakti and shall now enter on the study of the supreme devotion. All such preparations are intended only for the purification of the soul. The repetition of names, the rituals, the forms, and the symbols—all these various things are for the purification of the soul.

The greatest purifier among all such things, a purifier without which no one can enter the regions of this higher devotion, is renunciation. This frightens many; yet, without it there cannot be any spiritual growth. In all the yogas renunciation is necessary. This is the stepping-stone and the real centre, the real heart, of all spiritual culture—renunciation. This is religion—renunciation. When the human soul draws back from the things of the world and tries to go into deeper things; when man, the Spirit, which has here somehow become concretized and materialized, understands that he is going to be destroyed and reduced almost into mere matter, and turns his face away from matter—then begins renunciation, then begins real spiritual growth.

The karma-yogi's renunciation takes the shape of giving up all the fruits of his actions. He is not attached to the results of his labours; he does not care for any reward here or hereafter.

The raja-yogi knows that the whole of nature is intended as a means for the soul to acquire experience, and that the result of all the experiences of the soul is for it to become aware of its eternal separateness from nature. The human soul has to understand and realize that it has been Spirit, and not matter, through eternity, and that this conjunction of it with matter is and can be only for a time. The raja-yogi learns the lesson of renunciation through his own experience of nature.

The jnana-yogi has the harshest of all renunciations to go through, as he has to realize from the very first that the whole of this solid-looking nature is all an illusion. He has to understand that all that is any kind of manifestation of power in nature belongs to the soul and not to nature. He has to know, from the very start, that all knowledge and all experience are in the soul and not in nature; so he has at once and by the sheer force of rational conviction to tear himself away from all bondage to nature. He lets nature and all that belongs to it go; he lets them vanish and tries to stand alone.

Of all renunciations, the most natural, so to say, is that of the bhakti-yogi. Here there is no violence, nothing to give up, nothing to tear off, as it were, from ourselves, nothing from which we have violently to separate ourselves. The bhakta's renunciation is easy, smooth-flowing, and as natural as the things around us. We see the manifestation of this sort of renunciation, although more or less in the form of caricatures, every day around us. A man begins to love a woman; after a while he loves another, and the first woman he lets go. She drops out of his mind smoothly, gently, without his feeling the want of her at all. A woman loves a man; she then begins to love another man, and the first one drops off from her mind quite naturally. A man loves his own city; then he begins to love his country, and the intense love for his little city drops off smoothly, naturally. Again, a man learns to love the whole world; his love for his country, his intense, fanatical patriotism drops off without hurting him, without any manifestation of violence. An uncultured man loves the pleasures of the senses intensely; as he becomes cultured, he begins to love intellectual pleasures, and his sense-enjoyments become less and less. No man can enjoy a meal with the same gusto or pleasure as a dog or a wolf; but those pleasures which a man gets from intellectual experiences and achievements, the dog can never enjoy.

When a man gets even higher than the plane of the intellect, higher than that of mere thought, when he gets to the plane of spirituality and of divine inspiration, he finds there a state of bliss compared with which all the pleasures of the senses, or even of the intellect, are as nothing. When the moon shines brightly all the stars become dim, and when the sun shines the moon herself becomes dim. The renunciation necessary for the attainment of bhakti is not obtained by killing anything, but just comes in as naturally as, in the presence of an increasingly stronger light, the less intense lights become dimmer and dimmer until they vanish away, completely. So this love of the pleasures of the senses and of the intellect is all made dim, and thrown aside and cast into the shade by the love of God himself.

That love of God grows and assumes a form which is called supreme devotion. Forms vanish, rituals fly away, books are superseded; images, temples, churches, religions and sects, countries and nationalities—all these little limitations and bondages fall off by their own nature from him who knows this love of God. Nothing remains to bind him or fetter his freedom. So in this renunciation auxiliary to devotion there is no harshness, no dryness, no struggle, no repression, no suppression. The bhakta has not to suppress any single one of his emotions; he only strives to intensify them and direct them to God.

We see love everywhere in nature. Whatever in society is good and great and sublime is the working out of that love; whatever in society is very bad, nay, diabolical, is also the ill-directed working out of the same emotion of love. It is this same emotion that gives us the pure and holy conjugal love between husband and wife, as well as the sort of love which goes to satisfy the lowest forms of animal passion. The emotion is the same, but its manifestation is different in different cases.

Bhakti yoga is the science of higher love. It shows us how to direct it; it shows us how to control it, how to manage it, how to use it, how to give it a new aim, as it were, and from it obtain the highest and most glorious results, that is, how to make it lead us to spiritual blessedness. Bhakti yoga does not say, 'Give up'; it only says, 'Love—love the Highest!' And everything low naturally falls off from him, the object of whose love is this Highest.

'I cannot tell anything about Thee, except that Thou art my love. Thou art beautiful! Thou art beauty itself.' What is really required of us in this yoga is that our thirst after the beautiful should be directed to God. What is the beauty in the human face, in the sky, in the stars, and in the moon? It is only the partial apprehension of the real, all-embracing divine beauty. 'He shining, everything shines. It is through His light that all things shine.' Take this high position of bhakti, which makes you forget at once all your little personalities. Take yourself away from all the world's little selfish clingings. Do not look upon humanity as the centre of all your human and higher interests. Stand as a witness, as a student, and observe the phenomena of nature. Have the feeling of personal non-attachment with regard to man, and see how this mighty feeling of love is working itself out in the world. Sometimes a little friction is produced, but that is only in the course of the struggle to attain the higher, real love. Sometimes there is a little fight, or a little fall; but it is all only by the way. Stand aside and freely let these frictions come. You feel the frictions only when you are in the current of the world, but when you are outside of it, simply as a witness and as a student, you will be able to see that there are millions and millions of channels in which God is manifesting himself as love.

'Wherever there is any bliss, even though in the most sensual of things, there is a spark of that eternal bliss which is the Lord himself.' Even in the lowest kinds of attraction there is the germ of divine love. One of the names of the Lord in Sanskrit is *Hari*, and this means that he attracts all things to himself. His is in fact the only attraction worthy of human hearts. Who can attract a soul really? Only he! Do you think dead matter can truly attract the soul? It never did and never will. When you see a man going after a beautiful face, do you think it is the handful of arranged material molecules which really attracts the man? Not at all. Behind those material particles there must be and is the play of divine influence and divine love. The ignorant man does not know it; but yet, consciously or unconsciously, he is attracted by it, and it alone. So even the lowest forms of attraction derive their power from God himself. The Lord is the great magnet, and we are all like iron filings; we are being constantly attracted by him, and all of us are struggling to reach him. All this struggling of ours in this world is surely not intended for selfish ends. Fools do not know what they are doing; the work of their life is, after all, to approach the great magnet. All the tremendous struggling and fighting in life is intended to make us go to him ultimately and be one with him.

The bhakti-yogi, however, knows the meaning of life's

struggles; he understands it. He has passed through a long series of these struggles, and knows what they mean, and earnestly desires to be free from the friction thereof. He wants to avoid the clash and go direct to the centre of all attraction, the great Hari. This is the renunciation of the bhakta. This mighty attraction in the direction of God makes all other attractions vanish for him. This mighty infinite love of God which enters his heart leaves no place for any other love to live there. How can it be otherwise? Bhakti fills his heart with the divine waters of the ocean of love, which is God himself; there is no place there for little loves. That is to say, the bhakta's renunciation is that non-attachment for all things that are not God, which results from great attachment to God.

This is the ideal preparation for the attainment of the supreme bhakti. When this renunciation comes, the gate opens for the soul to pass through and reach the lofty regions of supreme devotion. He alone has attained that supreme state of love commonly called the brotherhood of man. The rest only talk. He sees no distinctions; the mighty ocean of love has entered into him, and he sees not man in man, but beholds his Beloved everywhere. Through every face shines to him his Hari. The light in the sun or the moon is all His manifestation. Wherever there is beauty or sublimity, to him it is all His. Such bhaktas are still living; the world is never without them. Though bitten by a serpent, they only say that a messenger came to them from their Beloved. Such men alone have the right to talk of universal brotherhood. They feel no resentment; their minds never react in the form of hatred or jealousy. The external, the sensuous, has vanished from them for ever. How can they be angry, when, through their love, they are always able to see the Reality behind the scenes?

In bhakti yoga the central secret is to know that the various passions and feelings and emotions in the human heart are not wrong in themselves; only they have to be carefully controlled and given a higher and higher direction, until they attain the very highest condition of excellence. The highest direction is that which takes us to God; every other direction is lower.

The conclusion to which the bhakta comes is that if you go on merely loving one person after another, you may go on loving them so for an infinite length of time without being in the least able to love the world as a whole. When at last, however, the central idea is arrived at, that the sum total of all love is God, that the sum total of the aspirations of all the souls in the universe, whether they be free or bound or struggling towards liberation, is God, then alone does it become possible for one to put forth universal love. If we love this sum total, we love everything. Loving the world and doing it good will all come easily then. We have to obtain this power only by loving God first; otherwise it is no joke to do good to the world.

'Everything is His and He is my Lover; I love Him', says the bhakta. In this way everything becomes sacred to the bhakta, because all things are Him. All are His children, His body, His manifestation. How then may we hurt anyone? How then may we not love anyone? With the love of God will come, as sure effect, the love of everyone in the universe. The nearer we approach God, the more do we begin to see that all things are in Him. When the soul succeeds in appropriating the bliss

of this supreme love, it also begins to see him in everything. Our heart thus becomes an eternal fountain of
love. And when we reach even higher states of this love,
all the little differences between the things of the world
are entirely lost. Man is seen no more as man, but only
as God; the animal is seen no more as animal, but as
God; even the tiger is no more a tiger, but a manifestation of God. Thus, in this intense state of bhakti, worship
is offered to everyone—to every life and to every being.

As a result of this kind of intense, all-absorbing love
comes the feeling of perfect self-surrender, the conviction
that nothing that happens is against us. Then the loving
soul is able to say, if pain comes, 'Welcome pain!' If
misery comes, it will say, 'Welcome misery! You are
also from the Beloved.' If a serpent comes, it will say,
'Welcome serpent!' If death comes, such a bhakta will
welcome it with a smile. 'Blessed am I that they all come
to me; they are all welcome.' The bhakta in this state of
perfect resignation, arising out of intense love to God
and to all that are his, ceases to distinguish between
pleasure and pain in as far as they affect him. He does
not know what it is to complain of pain or misery; and
this kind of uncomplaining resignation to the will of
God, who is all love, is indeed a worthier acquisition than
all the glory of grand and heroic performances.

To the vast majority of mankind, the body is everything; the body is all the universe to them; bodily enjoyment is their all in all. We may all manage to maintain
our bodies more or less satisfactorily and for longer or
shorter intervals of time. Nevertheless our bodies have to
go; there is no permanence about them. Blessed are they
whose bodies get destroyed in the service of others.
'Wealth, and even life itself, the sage always holds ready

for the service of others. In this world, there being one thing certain, namely, death, it is far better that this body die in a good cause than in a bad one.' We may drag our life on for fifty years or a hundred years, but after that, what is it that happens? Everything that is the result of combination must get dissolved and die. There must and will come a time for it to be decomposed. Jesus and Buddha and Mohammed are all dead; all the great prophets and teachers of the world are dead. 'In this evanescent world, where everything is falling to pieces, we have to make the highest use of what time we have', says the bhakta; and really the highest use of life is to hold it at the service of all beings.

It is the horrible body-idea that breeds all the selfishness in the world—just this one delusion that we are wholly the body we own, and that we must by all possible means try our very best to preserve and to please it. If you know that you are positively other than your body, you have then none to fight with or struggle against; you are dead to all ideas of selfishness. So the bhakta declares that we have to hold ourselves as if we are altogether dead to all things of the world; and that is indeed self-surrender. Let things come as they may. This is the meaning of 'Thy will be done.' In this state of sublime resignation everything in the shape of attachment goes away completely, except that one all-absorbing love to Him in whom all things live and move and have their being. This attachment of love to God is, indeed, one that does not bind the soul but effectively breaks all its bondages.

Section 4

Object after object is taken up, and the inner ideal is successively projected on them all; and all such external objects are found inadequate as exponents of the ever-expanding inner ideal and are naturally rejected one after another. At last the aspirant begins to think that it is vain to try to realize the ideal in external objects—that all external objects are as nothing when compared to the ideal itself. And in course of time he acquires the power of realizing the highest and the most generalized abstract ideal entirely as an abstraction that is to him quite alive and real.

We may represent love as a triangle, each of the angles of which corresponds to one of its inseparable characteristics. There can be no triangle, without all its three angles; and there can be no true love without its three following characteristics.

The first angle of our triangle of love is that love knows no bargaining. Wherever there is any seeking for something in return, there can be no real love; it becomes a mere matter of shopkeeping. As long as there is in us any idea of deriving this or that favour from God in return for our respect and allegiance to him, so long there can be no true love growing in our hearts. Those who worship God because they wish him to bestow favours on them are sure not to worship him if those favours are not forthcoming. The bhakta loves the Lord because he is lovable; there is no other motive originating or directing this divine emotion of the true devotee.

We have heard it said that a great king once went into

a forest and there met a sage. He talked with the sage a little and was very much pleased with his purity and wisdom. The king then wanted the sage to oblige him by receiving a present from him. The sage refused, to do so, saying, 'The fruits of the forest are enough food for me; the pure streams of water flowing down from the mountains give enough of drink for me; the bark of the trees supplies me with enough of covering; and the caves of the mountains form my home. Why should I take any present from you or from anybody?'

The king said, 'Just to benefit me, sir, please take something from my hands, and please come with me to the city and to my palace.'

After much persuasion the sage at last consented to do as the king desired, and went with him to his palace.

Before offering the gift to the sage the king repeated his prayers, saying, 'Lord, give me more children. Lord, give me more wealth. Lord, give me more territory. Lord, keep my body in better health'—and so on.

Before the king finished saying his prayer, the sage had got up and walked away from the room quietly. At this the king became perplexed and began to follow him, crying aloud, 'Sir, you are going away! You have not received my gifts.'

The sage turned round to him and said, 'I do not beg of beggars. You are yourself nothing but a beggar; and how can you give me anything? I am no fool to think of taking anything from a beggar like you. Go away. Do not follow me.'

There is well brought out the distinction between mere beggars and the real lovers of God. Begging is not the language of love. To worship God even for the sake of salvation or any other reward is equally degenerate. Love knows no reward. Love is always for love's sake. The bhakta loves because he cannot help loving. When you see beautiful scenery and fall in love with it, you do not demand anything in the way of favour from the scenery; nor does the scenery demand anything from you. Yet the vision thereof brings you to a blissful state of the mind; it tones down all the friction in your soul; it makes you calm, almost raises you, for the time being, beyond your mortal nature, and places you in a condition of quite divine ecstasy. This nature of real love is the first angle of our triangle. Ask not anything in return for your love; let your position be always that of the giver. Give your love unto God, but do not ask anything in return even from him.

The second angle of the triangle of love is that love knows no fear. Those who love God through fear are the lowest of human beings, quite undeveloped as men. They worship God from fear of punishment. He is a great being to them, with a whip in one hand and the sceptre in the other. If they do not obey him they are afraid they will be whipped. It is a degradation to worship God through fear of punishment; such worship is, if worship at all, the crudest form of the worship through love. So long as there is any fear in the heart, how can there be love also? Love conquers naturally all fear. Think of a young mother in the street, and a dog barking at her; she is frightened, and flies into the nearest house. But suppose the next day she is in the street with her child, and a lion springs upon the child. Where will be her position now? Of course, in the very mouth of the lion, protecting her child.

Love conquers all fear. Fear comes from the selfish idea of cutting oneself off from the universe. The smaller

and the more selfish I make myself, the more is my fear.
If a man thinks he is a little nothing, fear will surely
come upon him. And the less you think of yourself as
an insignificant person, the less fear will there be for
you. So long as there is the least spark of fear in you
there can be no love there. Love and fear are incompat-
ible; God is never to be feared by those who love him.
The commandment, 'Do not take the name of the Lord
thy God in vain', the true lover of God laughs at. How
can there be any blasphemy in the religion of love? The
more you take the name of the Lord, the better for you,
in whatever way you may do it. You are only repeating
his name because you love him.

The third angle of the love-triangle is that love knows
no rival, for in it is always embodied the lover's highest
ideal. True love never comes until the object of our love
becomes to us our highest ideal. It may be that in many
cases human love is misdirected and misplaced, but to
the person who loves, the thing he loves is always his
own highest ideal. One may see his ideal in the vilest of
beings, and another in the highest of beings; nevertheless,
in every case it is the ideal alone that can be truly and
intensely loved. The highest ideal of every man is called
God. Ignorant or wise, saint or sinner, man or woman
educated or uneducated, cultivated or uncultivated—to
every human being the highest ideal is God. The
synthesis of all the highest ideals of beauty, of sublimity,
and of power gives us the completest conception of the
loving and lovable God.

These ideals exist naturally in some shape or other in
every mind; they form a part of all our minds. All the
active manifestations of human nature are struggles of
those ideals to become realized in practical life. All the

various movements that we see around us in society are caused by the various ideals in various souls trying to come out and become concretized; what is inside presses on to come outside. This perennially dominant influence of the ideal is the one force, the one motive power, that may be seen to be constantly working in the midst of mankind. It may be after hundreds of births, after struggling through thousands of years, that a man finds that it is vain to try to make the inner ideal mould completely the external conditions and square well with them. After realizing this he no more tries to project his own ideal on the outside world, but worships the ideal itself as ideal, from the highest standpoint of love.

This ideally perfect ideal embraces all lower ideals. Everyone admits the truth of the saying that a lover sees Helen's beauty on an Ethiop's brow. The man who is standing aside as a looker-on sees that love is here misplaced; but the lover sees his Helen all the same, and does not see the Ethiop at all. Helen or Ethiop, the objects of our love are really the centres round which our ideals become crystallized. What is it that the world commonly worships? Certainly not the all-embracing, ideally perfect ideal of the supreme devotee and lover. That ideal which men and women commonly worship is what is in themselves; every person projects his or her own ideal on the outside world and kneels before it. That is why we find that men who are cruel and bloodthirsty conceive of a bloodthirsty God, because they can only love their own highest ideal. That is why good men have a very high ideal of God, and their ideal is indeed so very different from that of others.

What is the ideal of the lover who has quite passed

beyond the idea of selfishness, of bartering and bargaining, and who knows no fear? Even to the great God such a man will say, 'I will give you my all, and I do not want anything from you; indeed there is nothing that I can call my own.' When a man has acquired this conviction, his ideal becomes one of perfect love, one of perfect fearlessness born of love. The highest ideal of such a person has no narrowness of particularity about it; it is love universal, love without limits and bonds, love itself, absolute love. This grand ideal of the religion of love is worshipped and loved absolutely as such without the aid of any symbols or suggestions. This is the highest form of the supreme bhakti, the worship of such an all-comprehending ideal as the ideal; all the other forms of bhakti are only stages on the way to reach it.

All our failures and all our successes in following the religion of love are on the road to the realization of that one ideal. Object after object is taken up, and the inner ideal is successively projected on them all; and all such external objects are found inadequate as exponents of the ever-expanding inner ideal and are naturally rejected one after another. At last the aspirant begins to think that it is vain to try to realize the ideal in external objects—that all external objects are as nothing when compared to the ideal itself. And in course of time he acquires the power of realizing the highest and the most generalized abstract ideal entirely as an abstraction that is to him quite alive and real.

When the devotee has reached this point, he is no more impelled to ask whether God can be demonstrated or not, whether he is omnipotent and omniscient, or not. To him he is only the God of love. He is the highest ideal of love, and that is sufficient for all his purposes.

He, as love, is self-evident; it requires no proofs to demonstrate the existence of the beloved to the lover. The magistrate-Gods of other forms of religion may require a good deal of proof to prove them; but the bhakta does not and cannot think of such Gods at all. To him God exists entirely as love.

It is said by some that selfishness is the only motive power behind all human activities. That also is love, lowered by being particularized. When I think of myself as comprehending the Universal, there can surely be no selfishness in me; but when by mistake I think that I am something little, my love becomes particularized and narrowed. The mistake consists in making the sphere of love narrow and contracted. All things in the universe are of divine origin and deserve to be loved. It has, however, to be borne in mind that the love of the whole includes the love of the parts.

This whole is the God of the bhaktas, and all the other Gods, Fathers in Heaven, Rulers, or Creators, and all theories and doctrines and books, have no purpose and no meaning for them, seeing that they have through their supreme love and devotion risen above those things altogether. When the heart is purified and cleansed and filled to the brim with the divine nectar of love, all other ideas of God become simply puerile and are rejected as being inadequate or unworthy. Such is indeed the power of supreme love. The perfected bhakta no more goes to see God in temples and churches; he knows no place where he will not find him. He finds him outside the temple as well as in the temple. He finds him in the wicked man's wickedness, as well as in the saint's saintliness, because he has him already seated in glory in his own heart, as the one almighty, inextinguishable light of love, which is ever shining and eternally present.

It is impossible to express the nature of this supreme and absolute ideal of love in human language. Even the highest flight of human imagination is incapable of comprehending it in all its infinite perfection and beauty. Nevertheless, the followers of the religion of love in its higher as well as its lower forms in all countries have all along had to use inadequate human language to comprehend and to define their own ideal of love. Nay more; human love itself, in all its varied forms, has been made to typify this inexpressible divine love. Man can think of divine things only in his own human way; to us the Absolute can be expressed only in our relative language. The whole universe is to us a writing of the Infinite in the language of the finite. Therefore, in relation to God and his worship through love, bhaktas make use of all the common terms associated with the common love of humanity.

Some of the great writers on the supreme bhakti have tried to understand and experience this divine love in many different ways. The lowest form in which this love is apprehended is what they call the peaceful—the *shanta*. When a man worships God without the fire of love in him, without its madness in his brain, when his love is just the calm, commonplace love, a little higher than mere forms and ceremonies and symbols, but not at all characterized by the madness of intensely active love, it is said to be shanta. We see some people in the world who like to move on slowly, and others who come and go like the whirlwind. The shanta-bhakta is calm, peaceful, gentle.

The next higher type is that of *dasya*, servantship. It

comes when a man thinks he is the servant of the Lord. The attachment of the faithful servant unto the master is his ideal.

The next type of love is *sakhya*, friendship—'Thou art our beloved friend.' Just as a man opens his heart to his friend and knows that the friend will never chide him for his faults, but will always try to help him; just as there is the idea of equality between him and his friend —so equal love flows in and out between the worshipper and his friendly God. Thus God becomes our friend, the friend who is near, the friend to whom we may freely tell all the tales of our lives. The innermost secrets of our hearts we may place before him with the great assurance of safety and support. He is the friend whom the devotee accepts as an equal. God is viewed here as our playmate.

We may well say that we are all playing in this universe. Just as children play their games, just as the most glorious kings and emperors play their own games, so is the beloved Lord himself in sport with this universe. He is perfect. He does not want anything. Why should he create? Activity is always with us for the fulfilment of a certain want, and want always presupposes imperfection. God is perfect. He has no wants. Why should he go on with this work of an ever-active creation? What purpose has he in view? The stories about God creating this world, for some end or other that we imagine, are good as stories, but not otherwise. It is all really in sport; the universe is his play going on. The whole universe must after all be a big piece of pleasing fun to him. If you are poor, enjoy that as fun; if you are rich, enjoy the fun of being rich; if dangers come, it is also good fun; if happiness comes, there is more good fun. The world is just a playground, and we are here having good fun, having a game; and God is with us playing all the while, and we are with him playing. God is our eternal playmate. How beautifully he is playing! The play is finished when the cycle comes to an end. There is rest for a shorter or longer time; again all come out and play.

It is only when you forget that it is all play and that you are also helping in the play—it is only then that misery and sorrows come. Then the heart becomes heavy, then the world weighs upon you with tremendous power. But as soon as you give up your serious belief in the reality of the changing incidents of the three minutes of life, and know it to be but a stage on which we are playing, helping him to play, at once misery ceases for you. He plays in every atom. He is playing when he is building up earths and suns and moons. He is playing with the human heart, with animals, with plants. We are his chessmen; he puts the chessmen on the board and shakes them up. He arranges us first in one way and then in another, and we are consciously or unconsciously helping in his play. And oh, bliss! we are his playmates!

The next is what is known as *vatsalya*, loving God not as our father but as our child. This may look peculiar, but it is a discipline to enable us to detach all ideas of power from the concept of God. The idea of power brings with it awe. There should be no awe in love. The ideas of reverence and obedience are necessary for the formation of character; but when character is formed, when the lover has tasted the calm peaceful love and tasted also a little of love's intense madness, then he need talk no more of ethics and discipline. To conceive of God as mighty, majestic, and glorious, as the Lord of the universe, or as the God of Gods—the lover says he does not care. It is to avoid this association with God of the fear-creating sense of power that he worships God as his own child. The mother and the father are not moved by awe in relation to the child. They cannot have any reverence for the child. They cannot think of asking any favour from the child. The child's position is always that of the receiver; and out of love for the child the parents will give up their bodies a hundred times over. A thousand lives they will sacrifice for that one child of theirs. And therefore God is loved as a child.

This idea of loving God as a child comes into existence and grows naturally among those religious sects which believe in the incarnation of God. For the Mohammedans it is impossible to have this idea of God as a child; they will shrink from it with a kind of horror. But the Christian and the Hindu can realize it easily, because they have the baby Jesus and the baby Krishna. The women in India often look upon themselves as Krishna's mother. Christian mothers also may take up the idea that they are Christ's mother; and it will bring to the West the knowledge of God's divine motherhood which they so much need. The superstitions of awe and reverence in relation to God are deeply rooted in the heart of our hearts, and it takes long years to sink entirely in love our ideas of reverence and veneration, of awe and majesty and glory, with regard to God.

There is one more human representation of the divine ideal of love. It is known as *madhura*, the sweetheart relationship, and is the highest of all such representations. It is indeed based on the highest manifestation of love in this world, and this love is also the strongest known to man. What love shakes the whole nature of man, what love runs through every atom of his being, makes him mad, makes him forget his own nature, transforms him, makes him either a God or a demon, as the love between man and woman? In this sweet representation of divine love God is our husband. We are all women; there are no men in this world. There is but one Man, and that is he, our Beloved. All that love which man gives to woman, or woman to man, has here to be given up to the Lord.

All the different kinds of love which we see in the world, and with which we are more or less playing merely, have God as the one goal. But unfortunately man does not know the infinite ocean into which this mighty river of love is constantly flowing, and so, foolishly, he often tries to direct it to little dolls of human beings. The tremendous love for the child that is in human nature is not for the little doll of a child. If you bestow it blindly and exclusively on the child you will suffer in consequence. But through such suffering will come the awakening by which you are sure to find out that the love which is in you, if it is given to any human being, will sooner or later bring pain and sorrow as the result.

Our love must therefore be given to the highest One, who never dies and never changes, to him in the ocean of whose love there is neither ebb nor flow. Love must get to its right destination; it must go unto him who is really the infinite ocean of love. All rivers flow into the ocean. Even the drop of water coming down from the mountainside cannot stop its course after reaching a brook or a river, however big it may be; at last even that drop somehow does find its way to the ocean.

God is the one goal of all our passions and emotions.

If you want to be angry, be angry with him. Chide your Beloved; chide your Friend. Whom else can you safely chide? Mortal man will not patiently put up with your anger; there will be a reaction. If you are angry with me, I am sure quickly to react, because I cannot patiently put up with your anger. Say unto the Beloved: 'Why do you not come to me; why do you leave me thus alone?' Where is there any enjoyment but in him? What enjoyment can there be in little clods of earth? It is the crystallized essence of infinite enjoyment that we have to seek—and that is in God. Let all our passions and emotions go up unto him. They are meant for him, for if they miss their mark and go lower, they become vile. When they go straight to the mark, to the Lord, even the lowest of them becomes transfigured; all the energies of the human body and mind, howsoever they may express themselves, have the Lord as their one goal. All loves and all passions of the human heart must go to God. He is the Beloved. Whom else can this heart love? He is the most beautiful, the most sublime; he is beauty itself, sublimity itself. Who in this universe is more beautiful than he? Who in this universe is more fit to become the husband than he? Who in this universe is fitter to be loved than he? So let him be the husband, let him be the Beloved.

Aye, the true spiritual lover does not rest even there, even the love of husband and wife is not mad enough for him. The bhaktas take up also the idea of illegitimate love, because it is so strong. The impropriety of it is not at all the thing they have in view. The nature of this love is such that the more obstructions there are to its free play, the more passionate it becomes. The love between husband and wife is smooth; there are no obstructions there. So the bhaktas take up the idea of a girl who is in love with her own beloved, and her mother or father or husband objects to such love; and the more anybody obstructs the course of her love, so much the more is her love tending to grow in strength. Human language cannot describe how Krishna in the groves of Brindaban was madly loved, how at the sound of his voice the ever-blessed *gopis* rushed out to meet him, forgetting everything, forgetting this world and its ties, its duties, its joys and its sorrows.

Man, O man! you speak of divine love and at the same time are able to attend to all the vanities of this world. Are you sincere? 'Where Rama is, there is no room for any desire; where desire is, there is no room for Rama! These never co-exist. Like light and darkness they are never together.'

Section 5

This blessed madness of divine love alone can cure forever the disease of the world that is in us.

When this highest ideal of love is reached, philosophy is thrown away. Who will then care for it? Freedom, salvation, nirvana—all are thrown away. Who cares to become free while in the enjoyment of divine love? 'Lord, I do not want wealth, or friends, or beauty, or learning, or even freedom. Let me be born again and again, and be thou ever my love. Be thou ever my love.' 'Who cares to become sugar?' says the bhakta. 'I want to taste sugar.' Who will then desire to become free and one with God? 'I may know that I am He, yet will I take myself away from him and become different, so that I may enjoy the Beloved.' That is what the bhakta says. Love for love's sake is his highest enjoyment. Who will not be bound hand and foot a thousand times over to enjoy the Beloved?

No bhakta cares for anything except love—except to love and to be loved. His unworldly love is like the tide rushing up the river. This lover goes up the river, against the current. The world calls him mad. I know one whom the world used to call mad, and this was his answer: 'My friends, the whole world is a lunatic asylum. Some are mad after worldly love, some after name, some after fame, some after money, some after salvation and going to heaven. In this big lunatic asylum I am also mad, I am mad after God. If you are mad after money, I am mad after God. You are mad; so am I. I think my madness is after all the best.' The true bhakta's love is this burning madness, before which everything else vanishes for him. The whole universe is to him full of love and love alone; that is how it seems to the lover. So when a man has this love in him, he becomes eternally blessed, eternally happy. This blessed madness of divine love alone can cure for ever the disease of the world that is in us. With desire, selfishness has vanished. He has drawn near to God, he has thrown off all those vain desires of which he was full before.

We all have to begin as dualists in the religion of love. God is to us a separate being, and we feel ourselves to be separate beings also. Love then comes in the middle, and man begins to approach God; and God also comes nearer and nearer to man. Man takes up all the various relationships of life—as father, as mother, as son, as friend, as master, as lover—and projects them on his ideal of love, on his God. To him God exists as all these. And the last point of his progress is reached when he feels that he has become absolutely merged in the object of his worship.

We all begin with love for ourselves, and the unfair claims of the little self make even love selfish. At last, however, comes the full blaze of light, in which this little self is seen to have become one with the Infinite. Man himself is transfigured in the presence of this light of love, and he realizes at last the beautiful and inspiring truth that love, the lover, and the beloved are one.

7

GREAT TEACHERS OF
THE WORLD

Jesus Christ was God—the personal God become
man. He has manifested himself many times in different forms and these alone are what you can
worship.

God in his absolute nature is not to be worshipped.
Worshipping such a God would be nonsense.

We have to worship Jesus Christ, the human manifestation, as God. You cannot worship anything
higher than the manifestation of God. The sooner
you give up the worship of God separate from
Christ, the better for you. Think of the Jehovah
you manufacture, and of the beautiful Christ. Any
time you attempt to make a God beyond Christ,
you murder the whole thing. God alone can worship God. Keep close to Christ if you want salvation; he is higher than any God that you can
imagine.

If you think that Christ was a man, do not worship
him; but as soon as you can realize that he is God,

worship him. Those who say he was a man and then worship him commit blasphemy. 'He that hath seen me [the Son]) hath seen the Father.' Without seeing the Son you *cannot* see the Father.

We can grasp an idea only when it comes to us through a materialized ideal person. We can understand the precept only through the example. Naturally the vast majority of mankind have put their souls at the feet of these extraordinary personalities, the Prophets, the Incarnations of God.

THE UNIVERSE, according to the theory of the Hindus, is moving in cycles of wave-forms. It rises, reaches its zenith, then falls and remains in the hollow, as it were, for some time, once more to rise, and so on in wave after wave and fall after fall.

What is true of the universe is true of every part of it. The march of human affairs is like that. The history of nations is like that; they rise and they fall. After the rise comes a fall; again, out of the fall comes a rise, with greater power. This motion is always going on.

In the religious world the same movement exists. In every nation's spiritual life there is a fall as well as a rise. The nation goes down and everything seems to go to pieces. Then again it gains strength and rises. A huge wave comes—sometimes a tidal wave; and always on the topmost crest of the wave is a shining soul, the Messenger. Creator and created by turns, he is the impetus that makes the wave rise, the nation rise: at the same time, he is created by the same forces which make the wave, acting and interacting by turns. He puts forth his tremendous power upon society, and society makes him what he is.

These are the great world thinkers. These are the

Prophets of the world, the Messengers of life, the Incarnations of God.

Man has an idea that there can be only one religion, that there can be only one Prophet, and that there can be only one Incarnation; but that idea is not true. By studying the lives of all these great Messengers, we find that each was destined to play a part, as it were, and a part only; that the harmony consists in the sum total and not in one note. As in the life of races: no race is born alone to enjoy the world. None dare say so. Each race has a part to play in this divine harmony of nations. Each race has its mission to perform, its duty to fulfil. The sum total is the great harmony.

So, not any one of these Prophets is born to rule the world for ever. None has yet succeeded and none is going to be the ruler for ever. Each only contributes a part; and, as to that part, it is true that in the long run every Prophet will govern the world and its destinies.

Most of us are born believers in a personal religion. We talk of principles, we think of theories, and that is all right; but every thought and every movement, every one of our actions, shows that we can only understand the principle when it comes to us through a person. We can grasp an idea only when it comes to us through a materialized ideal person. We can understand the precept only through the example. Would to God that all of us were so developed that we would not require any example, would not require any persons. But that we are not; and naturally the vast majority of mankind have put their souls at the feet of these extraordinary personalities, the Prophets, the Incarnations of God—Incarnations worshipped by the Christians, by the Buddhists, and by the Hindus. The Mohammedans from the beginning stood against any such worship. They would have nothing to do with worshipping the Prophets or the Messengers, or paying homage to them; but practically, instead of one Prophet, thousands upon thousands of saints are being worshipped. We cannot go against facts! We are bound to worship personalities, and it is good. Remember that word from your great Prophet to the query: 'Lord, show us the Father'—'He that hath seen me hath seen the Father.'

Which of us can imagine anything except that He is a man? We can see him only in and through humanity. The vibration of light is everywhere in this room; why cannot we see it everywhere? You have to see it only in the lamp. God is an Omnipresent Principle—everywhere; but we are so constituted at present that we can see him, feel him, only in and through a human God.

And when these great Lights come, then man realizes God. And they come in a different way from the way we come. We come as beggars; they come as emperors. We come here like orphans, as people who have lost their way and do not know it. What are we to do? We do not know what is the meaning of our lives. We cannot realize it. Today we are doing one thing, to-morrow another. We are like little bits of straw rocking to and fro in water, like feathers blown about in a hurricane. But in the history of mankind you will find that there come these Messengers, and that from their very birth their mission is found and formed. The whole plan is there, laid down, and you see them swerving not one inch from it.

Because they come with a mission, they come with a

message. They do not want to reason. Did you ever hear or read of these great Teachers or Prophets reasoning out what they taught? No, not one of them did so. They speak direct. Why should they reason? They see the Truth. And not only do they see it, but they show it! If you ask me, 'Is there any God?' and I say 'Yes', you immediately ask my grounds for saying so, and poor me has to exercise all his powers to provide you with some reason. If you had come to Christ and said: 'Is there any God?' he would have said 'Yes'; and if you had asked, 'Is there any proof?' he would have replied, 'Behold the Lord!' And thus, you see, it is a direct perception and not at all the ratiocination of reason. There is no groping in the dark, but there is the strength of direct vision. I see this table; no amount of reason can take that faith from me. It is a direct perception.

Then again, when they speak the world is bound to listen. When they speak each word is direct; it bursts like a bombshell. What is in the word unless it has the power behind? What matters it what language you speak and how you arrange your language? What matters it whether you speak correct grammar or with fine rhetoric? What matters it whether your language is ornamental or not? Words but convey the gift; it is but one of the many modes.

Sometimes they do not speak at all. There is an old Sanskrit verse which says: 'I saw the teacher sitting under a tree. He was a young man of sixteen and the disciple was an old man of eighty. The preaching of the teacher was in silence, and the doubts of the doubter departed.' Sometimes they do not speak at all, but yet they convey the truth from mind to mind. They come to give. They command—they are the Messengers; you have to receive the command. Do you not remember in your own scriptures the authority with which Jesus speaks? 'Go ye therefore, and teach all nations. . . . Teaching them to observe all things whatsoever I have commanded you.' It runs through all his utterances, that tremendous faith in his own message. That you find in the life of all these great giants whom the world worships as its Prophets.

These great Teachers are the living Gods on this earth. Whom else should we worship? I try to get an idea of God in my mind, and I find what a false little thing I can conceive; it would be a sin to worship that God. I open my eyes and look at the actual life of these great ones of the earth. They are higher than any conception of God that I could ever form. For what conception of mercy could a man like me form, who would go after a man if he steals anything from me and send him to jail? And what can be my highest idea of forgiveness? Nothing beyond myself. Which of you can jump out of your own body? Which of you can jump out of your own mind? Not one of you. What idea of divine love can you form except what you actually live? What we have never experienced we can form no idea of.

So all my best attempts at forming an idea of God would fail in every case. And here are plain facts, and not ideas—actual facts of love, of mercy, of purity, of which I can have no conception even. What wonder that I should fall at the feet of these men and worship them as God? And what else can anyone do? I should like to see the man who can do anything else, however much he may talk. Talking is not actuality. Talking about God, and the Impersonal, and this and that, is all very good; but these man-Gods are the real Gods of all

nations and all races. These divine men have been wor-
shipped and will be worshipped as long as man is man.
Therein is our faith, therein is our hope, of a reality.
Of what avail is a mere mystical principle?

The purpose and intent of what I have to say to you
is this: that I have found it possible in my life to worship
all of them and to be ready for all that are yet to come.
A mother recognizes her son in any dress in which he
may appear before her; and if she does not do so, I am
sure she is not the mother of that man. Now, as regards
those of you that think that you understand Truth and
Divinity and God in only one Prophet in the world,
and not in any other, naturally, the conclusion which I
draw is that you do not understand Divinity in anybody; you have simply swallowed words and identified
yourself with one sect, just as you would in party
politics, as a matter of opinion. But that is no religion
at all. There are some fools in this world who use
brackish water although there is excellent sweet water
near by, because, they say, the brackish water well was
dug by their father.

Now, in my little experience I have collected this
knowledge: that for all the devilry that religion is blamed
for, religion is not at all at fault. No religion ever perse-
cuted men, no religion ever burned witches, no religion
ever did any of these things. What then incited people
to do these things? Politics, but never religion; and if
such politics takes the name of religion, whose fault is
that?

So when any man stands and says, 'My Prophet is the
only true Prophet', he is not correct; he knows not the
alpha of religion. Religion is neither talk nor theory nor
intellectual consent. It is realization in the heart of our

hearts; it is touching God; it is feeling, realizing that I am a spirit in relation with the Universal Spirit and all its great manifestations. If you have really entered the house of the Father, how can you have seen his children and not know them? And if you do not recognize them, you have not entered the house of the Father.

There is a tendency in us to revert to old ideas in religion. Let us think something new, even if it be wrong. It is better to do that. If a man feeds me every day of my life, in the long run I shall lose the use of my hands. Spiritual death is the result of following each other like a flock of sheep. Death is the result of inaction. Be active; and wherever there is activity, there must be difference. Difference is the sauce of life; it is the beauty, it is the art of everything; difference makes all beautiful here. It is variety that is the source of life, the sign of life. Why should we be afraid of it?

If two men quarrel about religion, just ask them the question: 'Have you seen God? Have you seen these things?' One man says that Christ is the only Prophet: well, has he seen Christ? 'Has your father seen him?'

'No, sir.'

'Has your grandfather seen him?'

'No, sir.'

'Have you seen him?'

'No sir.'

'Then what are you quarrelling for? The fruits have fallen into the ditch and you are quarrelling over the basket!' Sensible men and women should be ashamed to go on quarrelling in that way!

These messengers and Prophets were great and true. Why? Because each one has come to preach a great idea.

Take the Prophets of India, for instance. They are the oldest of the founders of religion.

We take, first, Krishna. You who have read the Gita see all through the book that the one idea is non-attachment. Remain unattached. The heart's love is due to only one. To whom? To him who never changeth. Who is that One? It is God. Do not make the mistake of giving the heart to anything that is changing, because that is misery.

Now, this is one phase; and what is the other message of Krishna? 'Whosoever lives in the midst of the world, and works, and gives up all the fruit of his action unto the Lord, he is never touched by the evils of the world. Just as the lotus, born under the water, rises up and blossoms above the water, even so is the man who is engaged in the activities of the world, giving up all the fruit of his activities unto the Lord.'

Krishna strikes another note as a teacher of intense activity. Work, work, work, day and night, says the Gita. You may ask, 'Then, where is peace? If all through life I am to work like a cart horse and die in harness, what am I here for?' Krishna says: 'Yes, you will find peace. Flying from work is never the way to find peace.' Throw off your duties if you can, and go to the top of a mountain; even there, the mind is going—whirling, whirling, whirling.

Someone asked a sannyasin, 'Sir, have you found a nice place? How many years have you been travelling in the Himalayas?'

'For forty years', replied the sannyasin.

'There are many beautiful spots to select from, and to settle down in; why did you not do so?'

'Because for these forty years my mind would not allow me to do so.'

We all say: 'Let us find peace', but the mind will not allow us to do so.

You know the story of the man who caught a Tartar. A soldier was outside the town, and he cried out when he came near the barracks, 'I have caught a Tartar.'

A voice called out, 'Bring him in.'

'He won't come in, sir.'

'Then you come in.'

'He won't let me come in, sir.'

So, in this mind of ours, we have 'caught a Tartar': neither can we tone it down, nor will it let us be toned down. We have all 'caught Tartars'. We all say: Be quiet and peaceful and so forth. But every baby can say that and thinks he can do it. However, that is very difficult. I have tried. I threw overboard all my duties and fled to the tops of the mountains; I lived in caves and deep forests; but all the same, I 'caught a Tartar', because I had my world with me all the time. The Tartar is what I have in my own mind.

Therefore Krishna teaches us not to shirk our duties, but to take them up manfully, and not think of the result. The servant has no right to question. The soldier has no right to reason. Go forward and do not pay too much attention to the nature of the work you have to do. Ask your mind if you are unselfish. If you are, never mind anything; nothing can resist you. Plunge in! Do the duty at hand. And when you have done this, by degrees you will realize the truth: 'Whosoever in the midst of intense activity finds intense peace, whosoever in the midst of the greatest peace finds the greatest activity, he is a yogi, he is a great soul, he has arrived at perfection.'

Now you see that the result of this teaching is that all the duties of the world are sanctified. There is no duty in this world which we have any right to call menial; and each man's work is quite as good as that of the emperor on his throne.

Listen to Buddha's message—a tremendous message. It has a place in our heart. Says Buddha: Root out selfishness and everything that makes you selfish. Have neither wife, child, nor family. Be not of the world; become perfectly unselfish. A worldly man thinks he will be unselfish, but when he looks at the face of his wife it makes him selfish. The mother thinks she will be perfectly unselfish, but she looks at her baby, and immediately selfishness comes. So with everything in this world. As soon as selfish desires arise, as soon as some selfish pursuit is followed, immediately the whole man, the real man, is gone. He is like a brute; he is a slave; he forgets his fellow men. No more does he say, 'You first and I afterwards', but it is 'I first and let everyone else look out for himself.'

We find that Krishna's message has a place for us. Without that message we cannot move at all. We cannot conscientiously, and with peace, joy, and happiness, take up any duty of our lives without listening to the message of Krishna: 'Be not afraid even if there is evil in your work, for there is no work which has no evil.' 'Leave it unto the Lord and do not look for the results.'

On the other hand, there is a corner in the heart for the other message: Time flies. This world is finite and all misery. With your good food, nice clothes, and your comfortable home, O sleeping man and woman, do you ever think of the millions that are starving and dying? Think of the great fact that it is all misery, misery,

misery! Note the first utterance of the child: when it enters into the world, it weeps. That is the fact: the child weeps. This is a place for weeping! If we listen to Buddha, we should not be selfish.

Behold another Messenger, he of Nazareth. He teaches: 'Be ready, for the kingdom of Heaven is at hand.' I have pondered over the message of Krishna, and I am trying to work without attachment; but sometimes I forget. Then, suddenly, comes to me the message of Buddha: 'Take care, for everything in the world is evanescent, and there is always misery in this life.' I listen to that and I am uncertain which to accept. Then again comes, like a thunderbolt, the message: 'Be ready, for the kingdom of heaven is at hand. Do not delay a moment. Leave nothing for tomorrow. Get ready for the final event, which may overtake you immediately, even now.' That message, also, has a place, and we acknowledge it. We salute the Christ; we salute the Lord.

And then comes Mohammed, the Messenger of equality. You ask, 'What good can there be in his religion?' If there were no good, how could it live? The good alone lives; that alone survives. Because the good alone is strong, therefore it survives. How could Mohammedanism have lived had there been nothing good in its teaching? There is much good. Mohammed was the Prophet of equality, of the brotherhood of man, the brotherhood of all Mussulmans.

So we see that each Prophet, each Messenger, has a particular message. When you first listen to that message, and then look at his life, you see his whole life stands explained, radiant.

Now, ignorant fools start twenty thousand theories

and put forward, according to their own mental development, explanations to suit their own ideas, and ascribe them to these great Teachers. They take their teachings and put their misconstruction upon them. With every great Prophet his life is the only commentary. Look at his life: what he did will bear out the texts.

Will other and greater prophets come? Certainly they will come in this world. But do not look forward to that. I should better like that each one of you become a Prophet of this real New Testament, which is made up all the Old Testaments. Take all the old messages, supplement them with your own realizations, and become a Prophet unto others. Each one of these Teachers has been great; each has left something for us. They have been our Gods. We salute them; we are their servants. And all the same we salute ourselves; for if they have been Prophets and children of God, we also are the same. They reached their perfection and we are going to attain ours now.

Remember the words of Jesus: 'The kingdom of heaven is at hand.' This very moment let every one of us make a staunch resolution: 'I will become a Prophet, I will become a Messenger of Light, I will become a child of God. Nay, I will become a God!'

Section 2

In the midst of all our weakness there is a moment of pause and the Voice rings: Give up all that thou hast; give it to the poor and follow me. This is the one ideal he preaches, and this has been the ideal of all great Prophets of the world: renunciation.

We are now going to study a little of the life of Christ, the Incarnation of the Jews. When Christ was born, the Jews were in that state which I call a state of fall between two waves: a state of conservatism, a state where the human mind is, as it were, tired for the time being of moving forward and is taking care only of what it has already; a state when the attention is more bent upon particulars, upon details, than upon the great, general, and bigger problems of life; a state of stagnation, rather than a forging ahead; a state of suffering more than of doing. Mark you, I do not blame this state of things; we have no right to criticize it. Because had it not been for this fall, the next rise, which was embodied in Jesus of Nazareth, would have been impossible. The Pharisees and Sadducees might have been insincere, they might have been doing things which they ought not to have done; they might have been even hypocrites; but whatever they were, these factors were the very cause of which the Messenger was the effect. The Pharisees and Sadducees at one end were the very impetus which came out at the other end as the gigantic brain of Jesus of Nazareth.

The attention to forms, to formulas, to the everyday details of religion, and to rituals may sometimes be laughed at, but nevertheless within them is strength. Many times in the rushing forward we lose much strength. As a fact the fanatic is stronger than the liberal man. Even the fanatic, therefore, has one great virtue: he conserves energy, a tremendous amount of it. As with the individual, so with the race, energy is gathered to be conserved. Hemmed in by external enemies, driven to focus in a centre by the Romans, by the Hellenic tendencies in the world of intellect, by waves from Persia, India, and Alexandria—hemmed in physically, mentally, and morally—there stood the Jewish race, with an inherent, conservative, tremendous strength, which their descendants have not lost even today. And the race was forced to concentrate and focus all its energies upon Jerusalem and Judaism. But all power when once gathered cannot remain collected; it must expend and expand itself. There is no power on earth which can be kept long confined within a narrow limit. If it is compressed for very long it will expand.

This concentrated energy amongst the Jewish race found its expression, at the next period, in the rise of Christianity. The gathered streams collected into a body. Gradually all the little streams joined together and became a surging wave, on the top of which we find standing out the character of Jesus of Nazareth. Thus, every Prophet is a creation of his own times; created by the past of his race, he himself is the creator of the future. The cause of today is the effect of the past and the cause for the future. In this position stands the Messenger. In him is embodied all that is the best and greatest in his own race—the meaning, the life, for which that race has struggled for ages; and he himself is the impetus for the future, not only to his own race, but to unnumbered other races of the world.

We must bear another fact in mind: that my view of the great Prophet of Nazareth would be from the standpoint of the Orient. Many times you forget that the Nazarene was an oriental of orientals. With all your attempts to paint him with blue eyes and yellow hair, the Nazarene was still an oriental. All the similes, the imageries, in which the Bible is written—the scenes, the locations, the attitudes, the groups, the poetry and symbols—speak to you of the Orient: of the bright sky, of the heat, of the sun, of the desert, of thirsty men and animals, of women coming with pitchers on their heads to fill them at the wells, of the flocks, of the ploughmen, of the cultivation that is going on around; of the water-mill and the wheel of the mill-pond, of the millstones. All these are to be seen today in Asia.

The voice of Asia has been the voice of religion. The voice of Europe is the voice of politics. Each is great in its own sphere. The voice of Europe is the voice of ancient Greece. To the Greek mind, his immediate society was all in all; beyond that it is barbarian. None but the Greek had the right to live. Whatever the Greek did is right and correct; whatever else might exist in the world is neither right nor correct, nor should be allowed to live. It is intensely human in its sympathies—intensely natural, intensely artistic, therefore. The Greek lived entirely in this world. He did not care to dream. Even his poetry was practical. His gods and goddesses were not only human beings, but intensely human, with all human passions and feelings almost the the same as with any of us. He loved what was beautiful, but mind you, it was always external nature. The beauty of the hills, of the snows, of the flowers; the beauty of forms and of figures, the beauty in the human face, and, more often, in the human form—that is what the Greeks liked. And the Greeks being the teachers of all subsequent Europeans, the voice of Europe is Greek.

There is another type in Asia. Think of that huge continent, whose mountain tops go beyond the clouds, almost touching the canopy of heaven's blue; a rolling desert of miles upon miles, where a drop of water cannot be found, neither will a blade of grass grow; interminable forests and gigantic rivers rushing down into the sea. In the midst of all these surroundings the oriental love of the beautiful and of the sublime developed itself in another direction. It looked inside and not outside. Yet it also expressed the same thirst for nature, the same thirst for power, the same thirst for excellence—the idea which is common to the Greek and the 'barbarian'.

But here it extended over a wider circle. In Asia, even today, birth or colour or language never makes a race. That which makes a race is its religion: we are all Christians; we are all Mohammedans; we are all Hindus or all Buddhists. No matter if a Buddhist is a Chinaman or a man from Persia, they think that they are brothers, because of their professing the same religion. Religion is the tie, the unity of humanity. And then again, the oriental, for the same reason, is a visionary, is a born dreamer. The ripples of the waterfalls, the songs of the birds, the beauties of the sun and moon and stars and the whole earth, are pleasant enough; but they are not sufficient for the oriental. He wants to dream a dream beyond. He wants to go beyond the present. The present, as it were, is nothing to him.

The Orient has been the cradle of the human race for ages, and all the vicissitudes of fortune are there: kingdoms succeeding kingdoms; empires succeeding empires; human power, glory, and wealth, all rolling down there —a Golgotha of power and learning. No wonder the Oriental looks with contempt upon the things of this world and naturally wants to see something that changeth not, something which dieth not, something which in the midst of this world of misery and death is eternal, blissful, undying. An oriental Prophet never tires of insisting upon these ideals; and, as for Prophets, you may also remember that without one exception, all the Messengers were Orientals.

We see, therefore, in the life of this great Messenger of light, the first watchword: 'Not this life, but something higher.' And like the true son of the Orient, he is practical in that. You people of the West are practical in your own department—in military affairs, and in managing politics and other things. Perhaps the oriental is not practical in those ways, but he is practical in his own field; he is practical in religion. If one preaches a philosophy, tomorrow there are hundreds who will struggle their best to make it practical in their lives. If a man preaches that standing on one foot will lead to salvation, he will immediately get five hundred to stand on one foot. You may call it ludicrous, but mark you, beneath that is their philosophy—that intense practicality. In the West plans of salvation mean intellectual gymnastics, plans which are never worked out, never brought into practical life. In the West, the preacher who talks the best is the greatest preacher.

So we find Jesus of Nazareth, in the first place, the true son of the Orient, intensely practical. He has no faith in this evanescent world and all its belongings. No need of text-torturing, as is the fashion in the West in modern times; no need of stretching out texts until they will not stretch any more. Texts are not India rubber, and even that has its limits. Now, no making of religion to pander to the sense vanity of the present day! Mark you, let us all be honest. If we cannot follow the ideal, let us confess our weakness, but not degrade it; let not any try to pull it down. One gets sick at heart at the different accounts of the life of the Christ that western people give. I do not know what he was or what he was not! One would make him a great politician; another, perhaps, would make him a great military general; another, a great patriotic Jew, and so on. Is there any warrant in the Bible for all such assumptions? The best commentary on the life of a great Teacher is his own life: 'The foxes have holes, and the birds of the air have nests, but the Son of man hath not where to lay his head.' That is what Christ says is the only way to salvation. He lays down no other way.

Let us confess in sackcloth and ashes that we cannot do that. We still have a fondness for 'me' and 'mine'. We want property, money, wealth. Woe unto us! Let us confess and not put to shame that great Teacher of humanity! He had no family ties. Do you think that that Man had any physical ideas in him? Do you think that this mass of light, this God and not man, came down to earth to be the brother of animals? And yet people make him preach all sorts of things. He had no sex ideas. He was a soul—nothing but a soul, just working a body for the good of humanity; and that was all his relation to the body. In the soul there is no sex. The disembodied soul has no relationship to the animal, no relationship to the body. The ideal may be far away beyond us; but never mind, keep to the ideal. Let us confess that it is our ideal, but we cannot approach it yet.

He had no other occupation in life; no other thought except that one, that he was Spirit. He was a disembodied, unfettered, unbound Spirit. And not only so, but he, with his marvellous vision, had found that every

man and woman, whether Jew or Gentile, whether rich
or poor, whether saint or sinner, was the embodiment of
the same undying Spirit as himself. Therefore the one
work of his whole life was calling upon them to realize
their own spiritual nature. Give up, he says, these superstitious dreams that you are low and that you are poor.
Think not that you are trampled upon and tyrannized
over as if you were slaves; for within you is something
that can never be tyrannized over, never be trampled
upon, never be troubled, never be killed. You are all
sons of God, immortal Spirit.

We have read the different stories that have been
written about him; we know the scholars and their
writings, and the higher criticism; and we know all
that has been done by study. We are not here to discuss how much of the New Testament is true; we are
not here to discuss how much of that life is historical.
It does not matter at all whether the New Testament
was written within five hundred years of his birth; nor
does it matter, even, how much of that life is true. But
there is something behind it, something we want to
imitate. To tell a lie, you have to imitate a truth, and
that truth is a fact. You cannot imitate that which never
existed. You cannot imitate that which you never perceived. There must have been a nucleus, a tremendous
power that came down, a marvellous manifestation of
spiritual power, and of that we are speaking. It stands
there. Therefore we are not afraid of all the criticisms
of the scholars. If I, as an oriental, am to worship Jesus of
Nazareth, there is only one way left to me; that is, to
worship him as God and nothing else. Have we no right
to worship him in that way, do you mean to say? If we
bring him down to our own level and simply pay him a

little respect as a great man, why should we worship at all? Our scriptures say, 'These great Children of Light, who manifest the Light themselves, who are Light themselves, they being worshipped, become, as it were, one with us and we become one with them.'

For, you see, in three ways man perceives God. At first the undeveloped intellect of the uneducated man sees God as far away, up in the heavens somewhere, sitting on a throne as a great Judge. He looks upon him as a fire, as a terror. Now, that is good; there is nothing bad in it. You must remember that humanity travels not from error to truth, but from truth to truth; it may be, if you like it better, from lower truth to higher truth, but never from error to truth. The religions of the unthinking masses all over the world must be, and have always been, of a God who is outside of the universe, who lives in heaven, who governs from that place, who is a punisher of the bad and a rewarder of the good, and so on.

As man advances spiritually, he begins to feel that God is omnipresent, that he must be in him, that he must be everywhere, that he is not a distant God, but clearly the Soul of all souls. As my soul moves my body, even so is God the mover of my soul. Soul within soul.

And a few individuals who have developed enough and are pure enough, go still further, and at last find God. As the New Testament says: 'Blessed are the pure in heart, for they shall see God.' And they find at last that they and the Father are one.

You will find that all these three stages are taught by the great Teacher in the New Testament. Note the common prayer he taught: 'Our Father which art in Heaven, hallowed be thy name', and so on—a simple prayer, a child's prayer. Mark you, it is the 'common prayer' because it is intended for the uneducated masses. To a higher circle, to those who had advanced a little more, he gave a more elevated teaching: I am in my Father, and ye in me, and I in you. Do you remember that? And then, when the Jews asked him who he was, he declared that he and his Father were one; and the Jews thought that that was blasphemy. What did he mean by that? But the same thing had also been taught by the old Jewish Prophets: 'Ye are gods and all of you are children of the Most High.' Mark the same three stages. You will find that it is easier for you to begin with the first and end with the last.

The Messenger came to show the path: that the Spirit is not in forms, that it is not through all sorts of vexatious and knotty problems of philosophy that you know the Spirit. 'Blessed are the pure in heart, for they shall see God.' 'The kingdom of heaven is within you.' Where goest thou to seek for the kingdom of God? asks Jesus of Nazareth, when it is there within you. Cleanse the Spirit and it is there. It is already yours. How can you get what is not yours? It is yours by right. You are the heirs of immortality, sons of the eternal Father.

This is the great lesson of the Messenger; another, which is the basis of all religions, is renunciation. How can you make the spirit pure? By renunciation. A rich young man asked Jesus, 'Good Master, what shall I do that I may inherit eternal life?' And Jesus said unto him, 'One thing thou lackest: go thy way, sell whatsoever thou hast, and give to the poor, and thou shalt have treasure in heaven: and come, take up thy cross, and follow me.' And the man was sad at that saying, and went away grieved; for he had great possessions. We are all more or less like that. The Voice is ringing in our ears day and night. In the midst of our pleasures and joys, in the midst of worldly things, we think that we have forgotten everything else. Then comes a moment's pause and the Voice rings in our ears: 'Give up all that thou hast and follow me. Whosoever will save his life shall lose it; and whosoever will lose his life for my sake shall find it.' For whoever gives up this life for his sake finds the life immortal. In the midst of all our weaknesses there is a moment of pause and the Voice rings: Give up all that thou hast; give it to the poor and follow me. This is the one ideal he preaches, and this has been the ideal of all great Prophets of the world: renunciation. What is meant by renunciation? That there is only one ideal in morality: unselfishness. Be selfless. The ideal is perfect unselfishness. When a man is struck on the right cheek, he turns the left also. When a man's coat is carried off, he gives away his cloak also.

We should work in the best way we can, without dragging the ideal down. Here is the ideal: When a man has no more self in him, no possession, nothing to call 'me' or 'mine', has given himself up entirely, destroyed himself, as it were—in that man is God himself; for in him self-will is gone, crushed out, annihilated. That is the ideal man. We cannot reach that state yet; yet, let us worship the ideal and slowly struggle to reach the ideal, though it may be with faltering steps. It may be tomorrow, or it may be a thousand years hence, but that ideal has to be reached. For it is not only the end, but also the means. To be unselfish, perfectly selfless, is salvation itself; for the man within dies, and God alone remains.

One more point. All the Teachers of humanity are

unselfish. Suppose Jesus of Nazareth was teaching, and a man came and told him: 'What you teach is beautiful. I believe that it is the way to perfection and I am ready to follow it; but I do not care to worship you as the only-begotten Son of God.' What would be the answer of Jesus of Nazareth? 'Very well, brother, follow the ideal and advance in your own way. I do not care whether you give me the credit for the teaching or not. I am not a shopkeeper; I do not trade in religion. I only teach truth and truth is nobody's property. Nobody can patent truth. Truth is God himself. Go forward.'

Quiet, unknown, silent, would he work, just as the Lord works. Now, what will the disciple say? He will tell you that you may be a perfect man, perfectly unselfish, but unless you give the credit to our Teacher, to our Saint, it is of no avail. Why? What is the origin of this superstition, this ignorance? The disciple thinks that the Lord can manifest himself only once. There lies the whole mistake. God manifests himself to you in man. But throughout nature, what happens once must have happened before and must happen in the future. There is nothing in nature which is not bound by law, and that means that whatever happens once must go on and must have been going on.

Let us, therefore, find God not only in Jesus of Nazareth but in all the great Ones who preceded him, in all who have come after him, and all who are yet to come. Our worship is unbounded and free. They are all manifestations of the same infinite God. They are all pure and unselfish; they struggle and give up their lives for us poor human beings. They each and all suffer vicarious

atonement for every one of us, and also for all that are
to come hereafter.

In a sense, you are all Prophets; every one of you is a
Prophet, bearing the burden of the world on your own
shoulders. Have you ever seen a man, have you ever
seen a woman, who is not quietly, patiently, bearing his
or her little burden of life? The great Prophets were
giants; they bore a gigantic world on their shoulders.
Compared with them we are pigmies, no doubt; yet we
are doing the same task. In our little circles, in our little
homes, we are bearing our little crosses. There is no
one so evil, no one so worthless, but he has to bear his
own cross. But with all our mistakes, with all our evil
thoughts and evil deeds, there is a bright spot somewhere, there is still somewhere the golden thread through
which we are always in touch with the Divine. For,
know for certain that the moment the touch of the
Divine was lost there would be annihilation; and because
none can be annihilated, there is always somewhere in
our heart of hearts, however low and degraded we may
be, a little circle of light which is in constant touch with
the Divine.

Section 3

My Master's message to mankind is, 'Be spiritual and
realize Truth for yourself.' He would have you give
up for the sake of your fellow beings. He would
have you cease talking about love for your brother
and set to work to prove your words. The time
has come for renunciation, for realization, and then
you will see the harmony in all the religions of the

world. To proclaim and make clear the fundamental unity underlying all religions was the mission of my Master.

Many of you, perhaps, have read the article by Professor Max Müller in a recent issue of the *Nineteenth Century*, headed 'A Real Mahatman'. The life of Sri Ramakrishna is interesting, as it was a living illustration of the ideas that he preached. Perhaps it will be a little romantic for you who live in the West, in an atmosphere entirely different from that of India; for the methods and manners in the busy rush of life in the West vary entirely from those of India. Yet perhaps it will be of all the more interest for that, because it will bring into a newer light things about which many have already heard.

It was while reforms of various kinds were being inaugurated in India that a child was born of poor brahmin parents on the 18th February 1836, in one of the remote villages of Bengal. The father and mother were very orthodox people. The life of a really orthodox brahmin is one of continuous renunciation. Very few things can he do, and over and beyond them the orthodox brahmin must not occupy himself with any secular business. At the same time he must not receive gifts from everybody. You may imagine how rigorous that life becomes. You have heard of the brahmins and their priestcraft many times, but very few of you have ever stopped to ask what makes this wonderful band of men the rulers of their fellows. They are the poorest of all the classes in the country, and the secret of their power lies in their renunciation. They never covet wealth. Theirs is the poorest priesthood in the world, and therefore the most powerful. The higher the caste, the greater the restrictions. The lowest caste people can eat and drink anything they like, but as men rise in the social scale, more and more restrictions come, and when they reach the highest caste, the brahmin, the hereditary priesthood of India, their lives, as I have said, are very much circumscribed. Compared to western manners, their lives are of continuous asceticism.

The character of the father and the mother of my Master was very much like that. Very poor they were, and yet many a time the mother would starve herself a whole day to help a poor man. Of them this child was born, and he was a peculiar child from very babyhood. He remembered his past from his birth, and was conscious for what purpose he came into the world, and every power was devoted to the fulfilment of that purpose.

While he was quite young his father died and the boy was sent to school. A brahmin's boy must go to school; the caste restricts him to a learned profession only. The old system of education in India, still prevalent in many parts of the country, was very different from the modern system. The students had not to pay. It was thought that knowledge is so sacred that no man ought to sell it. Knowledge must be given freely. The teachers used to take students without charge; and not only so, but most of them gave their students food and clothes. To support these teachers the wealthy families on certain occasions, such as a marriage festival or the ceremonies for the dead, made gifts to them. This boy went to one of these gatherings of professors, and the professors were discussing various topics, such as logic or astronomy—subjects much beyond his age. The boy was peculiar, as I have said, and he gathered this moral out of it—that this is the outcome of all their knowledge. Why are they fighting so hard? It is simply for money; the man who can show the highest learning here will get the highest reward, and that is all these people are struggling for. I will not go to school any more. And he did not: that was the end of his going to school.

This boy had an elder brother, a learned professor, who took him to Calcutta to study with him. After a short time the boy became fully convinced that the aim of all secular learning was mere material advancement, and nothing more, and he resolved to devote himself solely to the pursuit of spiritual knowledge. The father being dead, the family was very poor, and this boy had to make his own living. He went to a place near Calcutta and became a temple priest.

In the temple was an image of the 'Blissful Mother'. This boy had to conduct the worship morning and evening, and by degrees this one idea filled his mind: 'Is there anything behind this image? Is it true that there is a Mother of Bliss in the universe? Is it true that she lives and guides this universe, or is it all a dream? Is there any reality in religion?'

This scepticism comes to the Hindu child. It is the scepticism of our country—is this that we are doing real? And theories will not satisfy us, although there are ready at hand almost all the theories that have ever been made with regard to God and soul. Neither books nor theories can satisfy us; the one idea that gets hold of thousands of our people is this idea of realization. Is it true that there is a God? If it be true, can I see him? Can I realize the Truth?

This idea took possession of the boy, and his whole life became concentrated upon that. Day after day he would weep and say: 'Mother, is it true that thou exist-eth, or is it all poetry? Is the Blissful Mother an imagina-tion of poets and misguided people, or is there such a Reality?' We have seen that of education in our sense of the word he had none, and so much the more natural, so much the more healthy, was his mind, so much the purer his thoughts, undiluted by drinking in the thoughts of others. Well as Professor Max Müller said in the article I have just referred to, this was a clean, original man, and the secret of that originality was that he was not brought up within the precincts of a university. This thought—whether God can be seen—which was uppermost in his mind gained in strength every day until he could think of nothing else. He could no more conduct the worship properly, could no more attend to the various details in all their minuteness. Often he would forget to place the food offering before the image, some-times he would forget to wave the light, at other times he would wave it for hours and forget everything else.

At last it became impossible for the boy to serve in the temple. He left it and entered into a little wood that was near and lived there. About this part of his life he told me many times that he could not tell when the sun rose or set, or how he lived. He lost all thought of himself and forgot to eat. During this period he was lovingly watched over by a relative who put into his mouth food which he mechanically swallowed.

Days and nights thus passed with the boy. When a whole day would pass, towards the evening, when the peal of bells in the temples, and the voices singing, would reach the wood, it would make the boy very sad, and he would cry: 'Another day is gone in vain, Mother, and thou hast not come. Another day of this short life has gone and I have not known the Truth.' In the agony of his soul, sometimes he would rub his face against the ground and weep, and this one prayer burst forth: 'Do thou manifest thyself in me, thou Mother of the Universe! See that I need thee, and nothing else!'

Verily, he wanted to be true to his own ideal. He had heard that the Mother never came until everything had been given up for her. So he began to break himself into that idea; he wanted to be exact, even on the plane of matter. He threw away all the little property he had and took a vow that he would never touch money, and this one idea, 'I will not touch money', became a part of him. It may appear to be something occult, but even in later life, when he was sleeping, if I touched him with a piece of money his hand would become bent and his whole body would become, as it were, paralysed.

The other idea that came into his mind was that lust was the other enemy. Man is a soul, and soul is sexless, neither man nor woman. The idea of sex and the idea of money were the two things, he thought, that prevented him from seeing the Mother. This whole universe is the manifestation of the Mother, and she lives in every woman's body. 'Every woman represents the Mother'; he must bring himself to the state when he would see nothing but Mother in every woman; and he carried it out in his life.

This is the tremendous thirst that seizes the human heart. Later on, this very man said to me: 'My child, suppose there is a bag of gold in one room, and a robber is in the next room; do you think that robber can sleep? He cannot. His mind will be always thinking how to get into that room and obtain possession of that gold. Do you think, then, that a man firmly persuaded that there is a Reality behind all these appearances, that there is a God, and that there is One who never dies, One who is infinite bliss, a bliss compared to which these pleasures of the senses are simply playthings—can rest contented without struggling to attain him? Can he cease his efforts for a moment? No. He will become mad with longing.' This divine madness seized the boy. At that time he had no teacher, nobody to tell him anything, and everyone thought that he was out of his mind. This is the ordinary condition of things: If a man throws aside the vanities of the world, we hear him called mad. But such men are the salt of the earth. Out of such madness have come the powers that have moved this world of ours, and out of such madness alone will come the powers of the future that are going to move the world.

So days, weeks, months passed in the continuous struggle of the soul to arrive at Truth. The boy began to see visions, to see wonderful things; the secrets of his nature were beginning to open up to him. Veil after veil was, as it were, being taken off. Mother herself became the teacher, and initiated the boy into the truths he sought.

At this time there came to this place a woman, of beautiful appearance, learned beyond compare. Later on this saint used to say about her that she was not learned, but was the embodiment of learning; she was learning itself in human form. There too you find the peculiarity of the Indian nation. In the midst of the ignorance in which the average Hindu woman lives, in the midst of what is called in western countries her lack of freedom, there could arise a woman of supreme spirituality. She was a sannyasini; for women also give up the world, throw away their property, do not marry, and devote themselves to the worship of the Lord. She came, and when she heard of this boy she offered to go and see him; and hers was the first help he received. At once she recognized what his trouble was, and she said to him: 'My son, blessed is the man upon whom such madness comes. The whole of this universe is mad: some for wealth, some for pleasure, some for fame, some for a hundred other things. They are mad for gold, or husbands, or wives; for little trifles, mad to tyrannize over somebody, mad to become rich, mad for every foolish thing except God. And they can understand only their own madness. When another man is mad after gold they have fellow-feeling and sympathy for him, and they say he is the right man, as lunatics think that lunatics alone are sane. But if a man is mad after the Beloved, after the Lord, how can they understand? They think he has gone crazy, and they say, "Have nothing to do with him." That is why they call you mad, but yours is the right kind of madness. Blessed is the man who is mad after God. Such men are very few.' This woman remained near the boy for years, taught him the forms of the religions of India, initiated him into the different practices of yoga, and, as it were, guided and brought into harmony this tremendous river of spirituality.

Later, there came to the same grove a sannyasin, one of the begging friars of India, a learned man, a philosopher. He was an idealist. He did not believe that this world existed in reality, and to demonstrate that, he would never go under a roof; he would always live out of doors, in storm and sunshine alike. This man began to teach the boy the philosophy of the Vedas, and he found very soon, to his astonishment, that the pupil was in some respects wiser than the master. He spent several months with the boy, after which he initiated him into the order of sannyasins, and took his departure.

When as a temple priest his extraordinary worship had made people think him deranged, his relatives had taken the boy home and married him to a little girl, thinking that that would turn his thoughts and restore the balance of his mind. But he had come back and as we have seen, merged deeper in his madness. Sometimes, in our country, boys are married as children and have no voice in the matter; their parents marry them. Of course such a marriage is little more than a betrothal. When they are married they still continue to live with their parents, and the real marriage takes place when the wife grows older, when it is customary for the husband to bring his bride to his own home. In this case, however, the husband had entirely forgotten that he had a wife. In her far-off home the girl had heard that her husband had become a religious enthusiast and that he was even considered insane by many. She resolved to learn the truth for herself; so she set out and walked to the place where her husband was. When at last she stood in her husband's presence, he at once admitted her right to his life— although in India any person, man or woman, who embraces a religious life is thereby freed from all other obligations. The young man fell at the feet of his wife and said: 'As for me, the Mother has shown me that she resides in every woman, and so I have learned to look upon every woman as Mother. That is the one idea I can have about you. But if you wish to draw me into the world, as I have been married to you, I am at your service.'

The maiden was a pure and noble soul and was able to

understand her husband's aspirations and sympathize with them. She quickly told him that she had no wish to drag him down to a life of wordliness, but that all she desired was to remain near him, to serve him, and to learn of him. She became one of his most devoted disciples, always revering him as a divine being. Thus through his wife's consent the last barrier was removed and he was free to lead the life he had chosen.

The next desire that seized upon the soul of this man was to know the truth about the various religions. Up to that time he had not known any religion but his own. He wanted to understand what other religions were like. So he sought teachers of other religions. By teachers you must always remember what we mean in India: not a bookworm, but a man of realization, one who knows truth at first hand and not through an intermediary. He found a Mohammedan saint and went to live with him; he underwent the disciplines prescribed by him. To his astonishment he found that when faithfully carried out, these devotional methods led him to the same goal he had already attained. He gathered a similar experience from following the true religion of Jesus the Christ. He went to all the sects he could find, and whatever he took up he went into with his whole heart. He did exactly as he was told, and in every instance he arrived at the same result. Thus from actual experience he came to know that the goal of every religion is the same, that each is trying to teach the same thing, the difference being largely in method and still more in language. At the core, all sects and all religions have the same aim; they only quarrel for their own selfish purposes.

That is what my Master found, and he then set about

to learn humility, because he had found that the one idea in all religions is 'Not I, but Thou', and he who says, 'Not I', the Lord fills his heart. The less of this little 'I' the more of God there is in him. That he found to be the truth in every religion in the world, and he set himself to accomplish this. Now, there was a family of pariahs living near the place. The pariahs number several millions in the whole of India, and are so low in society that some of our books say that if a brahmin, coming out from his house, sees the face of a pariah, he has to fast that day and recite certain prayers before he becomes holy again. Now, my Master would go to a pariah and ask to be allowed to clean his house. The pariah would not permit it; so in the dead of night, when all were sleeping, Ramakrishna would enter the house. He had long hair, and with his hair he would cleanse the dirty places, saying, 'O, my Mother, make me the servant of the pariah; make me feel that I am even lower than the pariah.'

For years he thus educated himself. One of the *sadhanas* [disciplines] was to root out the sex idea. The soul has no sex; it is neither male nor female. It is only in the body that sex exists, and the man who desires to reach the Spirit cannot at the same time hold to sex distinctions. Having been born in a masculine body, this man wanted to bring the feminine idea into everything. He began to think that he was a woman; he dressed like a woman, spoke like a woman, gave up the occupations of men, and lived in the household among the women of a good family, until, after years of this discipline, his mind became changed, and he entirely forgot the idea of sex; thus the whole view of life became changed to him.

We hear in the West about worshipping woman, but this is usually for her youth and beauty. This man meant by worshipping woman, that to him every woman's face was that of the Blissful Mother, and nothing but that. I myself have seen this man standing before those women whom society would not touch, and falling at their feet bathed in tears, saying: 'Mother, in one form thou art in the street, and in another form thou art the universe. I salute thee, Mother, I salute thee.' Think of the blessedness of that life from which all carnality has vanished, which can look upon every woman with that love and reverence, when every woman's face becomes transfigured, and only the face of the Divine Mother, the Blissful One, the Protectress of the human race, shines upon it!

This rigorous, unsullied purity came into the life of that man. All the struggles which we have in our lives were past for him. His hard-earned jewels of spirituality, for which he had given three-quarters of his life, were now ready to be given to humanity; and then began his mission. All Hindus come to pay respect to an extraordinary teacher; they crowd around him. And here was such a teacher. But the teacher had no thought whether he was to be respected or not; he had not the least idea that he was a great teacher; he thought that it was the Mother who was doing everything, and not he. He always said: 'If any good comes from my lips, it is the Mother who speaks; what have I to do with it?' That was his one idea about his work, and to the day of his death he never gave it up. This man sought no one. His principle was: first form character, first earn spirituality, and results will come of themselves. His favourite illustration was: 'When the lotus opens, the bees come of their own accord to seek the honey. So let the lotus of your character be full-blown, and the results will follow.' This is a great lesson to learn. My Master taught me this lesson hundreds of times, yet I often forget it.

Few understand the power of thought. If a man goes into a cave, shuts himself in, and thinks one really great thought and dies, that thought will penetrate the walls of that cave, vibrate through space, and at last permeate the whole human race. Such is the power of thought. Be in no hurry, therefore, to give your thoughts to others. First have something to give. He alone teaches who has something to give. For teaching is not talking, teaching is not imparting doctrines, it is communicating. Spirituality can be communicated just as really as I can give you a flower. This is true in the most literal sense. This idea is very old in India and finds illustration in the West in the theory of apostolic succession. Therefore, first make character—that is the highest duty you can perform. Know truth for yourself, and there will be many to whom you can teach it afterwards; they will all come.

This was the attitude of my Master. He criticized no one. For years I lived with that man, but never did I hear those lips utter one word of condemnation for any sect. He had the same sympathy for all sects; he had found the harmony between them. A man may be intellectual or devotional or mystic or active; the various religions represent one or the other of these types. Yet it is possible to combine all the four in one man, and this is what future humanity is going to do. That was his idea. He condemned no one, but saw the good in all.

This man lived near Calcutta, the capital of India, the most important university town in our country, which was sending out sceptics and materialists by the hundreds every year; yet many of these university men—sceptics and agnostics—used to come and listen to him. I heard of this man, and I went to hear him. He looked just like an ordinary man, with nothing remarkable about him. He used the most simple language, and I thought, 'Can this man be a great teacher?' I crept near him and asked him the question which I had been asking others all my life: 'Do you believe in God, sir?'

'Yes', he replied.

'Can you prove it, sir?'

'Yes.'

'How?'

'Because I see him just as I see you here, only in a much intenser sense.'

That impressed me at once. For the first time I found a man who dared to say that he saw God, that religion was a reality—to be felt, to be sensed in an infinitely more intense way than we can sense the world. I began to go to that man day after day, and I actually saw that religion could be given. One touch, one glance, can change a whole life. I have read about Buddha and Christ and Mohammed, about all those different luminaries of ancient times, how they would stand up and say, 'Be thou whole', and the man became whole. I now found it to be true; and when I myself saw this man, all scepticism was brushed aside. It could be done. My Master used to say: 'Religion can be given and taken more tangibly, more really, than anything else in the world.'

Religion is not talk or doctrines or theories, nor is it sectarianism. Religion cannot live in sects and societies. It is the relation between the soul and God; how can it be made into a society? It would then degenerate into business, and wherever there are business and business principles in religion, spirituality dies. Religion does not consist in erecting temples or building churches or attending public worship. It is not to be found in books or in words or in lectures or in organizations. Religion consists in realization.

The first idea in this attempt to realize religion is that of renunciation. As far as we can, we must give up. Darkness and light, enjoyment of the world and enjoyment of God, will never go together. 'Ye cannot serve God and mammon.' Let people try if they will, and I have seen millions in every country who have tried; but after all it comes to nothing. If one word remains true in the saying, it is: Give up everything for the sake of the Lord. This is a hard and long task, but you can begin it here and now. Bit by bit we must go towards it.

The second idea that I learned from my Master, which is perhaps the most vital, is the wonderful truth that the religions of the world are not contradictory or antagonistic. They are but various phases of one Eternal Religion. There never was my religion or yours, my national religion or your national religion. There never existed many religions; there is only the one. One infinite Religion existed through all eternity and will ever exist, and this Religion is expressing itself in various countries in various ways. Therefore we must respect all religions and we must try to accept them all as far as we can.

Religions manifest themselves not only according to race and geographical position, but according to individual powers. To learn this central secret that the Truth may be one and yet many at the same time, that we may have different visions of the same Truth from different standpoints, is exactly what must be done. Then, instead of antagonism to anyone, we shall have infinite sympathy with all. Knowing that as long as there are different natures born in this world, the same religious truth will require different adaptations, we shall understand that we are bound to have forbearance with each other. Just as nature is unity in variety—an infinite variation in the phenomenal, that in and through all these variations of the phenomenal runs the Infinite, the Unchangeable, the absolute Unity—so it is with every man. The microcosm is but a miniature repetition of the macrocosm. In spite of all these variations, in and through them all runs this eternal harmony, and we have to recognize this. This idea, above all other ideas, I find to be the crying necessity of the day.

The third idea of his life was intense love for others. The first part of my Master's life was spent in acquiring spirituality, and the remaining years in distributing it.

So men came in crowds to hear him, and he would talk twenty hours in the twenty-four, and that not for one day, but for months and months, until at last the body broke down under the pressure of this tremendous strain. His intense love for mankind would not let him refuse to help even the humblest of the thousands who sought his aid. Gradually there developed a vital throat disorder, and yet he could not be persuaded to refrain from these exertions. As soon as he heard that people were asking to see him, he would insist upon having them admitted and would answer all their questions. When expostulated with, he replied, 'I do not care. I will give up twenty thousand such bodies to help one man. It is glorious to help even one man.' There was no rest for him. Once a man asked him: 'Sir, you are a great yogi; why do you not put your mind a little on your body and cure your disease?' At first he did not answer, but when the question had been repeated, he gently said: 'My friend, I thought you were a sage, but you talk like other men of the world. This mind has been given to the Lord. Do you mean to say that I should take it back and put it upon the body, which is but a mere cage of the soul?'

So he went on preaching to people. The news spread that his body was about to pass away, and people began to flock to him in greater crowds than ever. One day he told us that he would lay down the body that day, and repeating the most sacred word of the Vedas he entered into samadhi and passed away.

His thoughts and his message were known to very few capable of giving them out. Among others, he left a few young boys who had renounced the world and were ready to carry on his work. Attempts were made to crush them; but they stood firm, having the inspiration of that great life before them. Having had the contact of that blessed life for years, they stood their ground. These young men, living as sannyasins, begged through the streets of the city where they were born, although some of them came from high families. At first they met with great antagonism, but they persevered and went on from day to day spreading all over India the message of that great man, until the whole country was filled with the ideas he had preached. This man, from a remote village of Bengal, without education, by the sheer force of his own determination, realized the Truth and gave it to others, leaving only a few young boys to keep it alive.

Today the name of Sri Ramakrishna Paramahamsa is

known all over India. Nay, the power of that man has spread beyond India, and if there has ever been a word of truth, a word of spirituality, that I have spoken anywhere in the world, I owe it to my Master; only the mistakes are mine.

This is the message of Sri Ramakrishna to the modern world: 'Do not care for doctrines, do not care for dogmas or sects or churches or temples. They count for little compared with the essence of existence in each man, which is spirituality, and the more this is developed in a man, the more powerful is he for good. Earn that first, acquire that, and criticize no one; for all doctrines and creeds have some good in them. Show by your lives that religion does not mean words or names or sects, but that it means spiritual realization. Only those can understand who have felt. Only those who have attained to spirituality can communicate it to others, can be great teachers of mankind. They alone are the powers of light.'

The more such men are produced in a country, the more that country will be raised; and that country where such men absolutely do not exist is simply doomed; nothing can save it. Therefore my Master's message to mankind is, 'Be spiritual and realize Truth for yourself.' He would have you give up for the sake of your fellow beings. He would have you cease talking about love for your brother and set to work to prove your words. The time has come for renunciation, for realization, and then you will see the harmony in all the religions of the world. You will know that there is no need of any quarrel; and then only will you be ready to help humanity. To proclaim and make clear the fundamental unity underlying all religions was the mission of my Master. Other teachers have taught special religions which bear their names, but this great teacher of the nineteenth century made no claim for himself. He left every religion undisturbed because he had realized that, in reality, they are all part and parcel of the one Eternal Religion.

THE SOURCES OF THE TEXT

What Religion Is: In the Words of Swami Vivekananda was designed originally as a book for a western audience generally not having access to the Complete Works of the Swami—as a seamless presentation of the Swami's doctrine—to be read straight through unburdened by bibliographical references to the Works. Recently (1998) the Editor was asked to state the sources in Swamiji's Works of the texts which were used to make up the book. They are listed—generally condensed—as follows. Since page numbers in successive editions of the Works vary, the texts have been identified by "Vol." (Volume number in the works) and title of the text.

Chapter One: The Ideal of a Universal Religion

Introductory quotation: Vol. I: Chapter II, verse 25, of Patanjali's
    Yoga Aphorisms: "Concentration: Its Practice"

    Section 1:   I: "Soul, God and Religion"
    Section 2:   VI: "The Methods and Purpose of Religion"
    Section 3:   II: "The Way to the Realization of a Universal
                         Religion"
    Section 4:   II: "The Ideal of a Universal Religion"

Throughout the book the quotation introducing each section has been taken from the text condensed to make up that section.

Chapter Two: Principles and Practices of Vedanta

Introductory quotation: II: "Maya and Freedom"
    Section 1:   I: "The Spirit and Influence of Vedanta"

Chapter Three: Self-Realization through Knowledge

Chapter Four: Self-Realization through Control of Mind

Chapter Five: Self-Realization through Selfless Work

Chapter Six: Self-Realization through Love of God

Chapter Seven: Great Teachers of the World